Global Hospitality Industry and Service Quality Management

Global Hospitality Industry and Service Quality Management

Vineet Taing

RANDOM PUBLICATIONS

NEW DELHI - 110 002 (INDIA)

Global Hospitality Industry and Service Quality Management

ISBN 978-93-5111-310-2

Published in 2014 in India by
RANDOM PUBLICATIONS
Reprint : 2016
4376-A/4B, Gali Murari Lal, Ansari Road
New Delhi-110 002
Phone: +9111-43580356, 23289044
E-mail: randomexports@gmail.com; sales@randompublications.com; info@randompublications.com

Type Setting by: Friends Media, Delhi-110089
Digitally Printed at: Replika Press Pvt. Ltd.

Preface

Hospitality is the relationship between the guest and the host, or the act or practice of being hospitable. This includes the reception and entertainment of guests, visitors, or strangers. The word *hospitality* derives from the Latin *hospes*, meaning "host", "guest", or "stranger". *Hospes* is formed from *hostis*, which means "stranger" or "enemy" (the latter being where terms like "hostile" derive). In the West today hospitality is rarely a matter of protection and survival, and is more associated with etiquette and entertainment. However, it still involves showing respect for one's guests, providing for their needs, and treating them as equals. Cultures and subcultures vary in the extent to which one is expected to show hospitality to strangers, as opposed to personal friends or members of one's in-group.

Hospitality ethics is a discipline that studies this usage of hospitality. In India hospitality is based on the principle *Atithi Devo Bhava*, meaning "the guest is God". This principle is shown in a number of stories where a guest is literally a god who rewards the provider of hospitality. From this stems the Indian approach of graciousness towards guests at home, and in all social situations. The hospitality industry is a broad category of fields within the service industry that includes lodging, restaurants, event planning, theme parks, transportation, cruise line, and additional fields within the tourism industry. The hospitality industry is a several billion dollar industry that mostly depends on the availability of leisure time and disposable income. A hospitality unit such as a restaurant, hotel, or even an amusement park consists of multiple groups such as facility maintenance, direct operations (servers, housekeepers, porters, kitchen workers, bartenders, etc.), management, marketing, and human resources. Usage rate or its inverse "vacancy rate" is an important variable for the hospitality industry. Just as a factory owner would wish a productive asset to be in use as much as possible (as opposed to having to pay fixed costs while the factory isn't producing), so do restaurants, hotels, and theme parks seek to maximize the number of customers they "process" in all sectors. This led to formation of services with the aim to increase usage rate provided by hotel consolidators. Information about required or offered products are brokered on business networks used by vendors as well as purchasers. In looking various industries, "barriers to entry" by newcomers and competitive advantages between current players are very important.

Generally, after registering, members have the option of providing very detailed information and pictures of themselves and of the sleeping accommodation being offered, if any. The more information provided by a member improves the chances that someone will find the member trustworthy enough to be their host or guest. Names and addresses may be verified by volunteers. Members looking for accommodation can search for hosts using several parameters such as age, location, sex, and activity level. Home stays are entirely consensual between the host and guest, and the duration, nature, and terms of the guest's stay are generally worked out in advance to the convenience of both parties. No monetary exchange takes place except under certain circumstances (e.g., the guest may compensate the host for food). After using the service, members can leave a noticeable reference about their host or guest. Instead of or in addition to accommodation, members also offer to provide guide services or travel-related advice. The websites of the networks also provide editable travel guides and forums where members may seek travel partners or advice. Many such organizations are also focused on "social networking" and members organize activities such as camping trips, bar crawls, meetings, and sporting events. Some networks cater to specific niche markets such as students, activists, religious pilgrims, and even occupational groups like police officers. Quality in the tourism and hospitality industry involves consistent delivery of products and guest services according to expected standards.

This book titled, "Global Hospitality Industry and Service Quality Management", provides readers with an introductory overview of hospitality management. An introduction to major concepts and issues of hospitality business management is given. An overview of tools and techniques of hospitality management is discussed in detail. Focus lies on global hospitality industry customers and service quality; training technology and vocational work; and other issues in hospitality management and service organizations. Efforts have been made to know more about hospitality warehouse management and logistics solutions. In addition, this book is helpful in discussing the steps towards business development and service improvement in hospitality industry. Efforts are made towards better understanding of quality management and services management in hospitality sector. A detailed bibliography and elaborate index make this publication user-friendly, besides related appendix.

—Editor

Contents

Preface (v)

1. **Hospitality Management: An Introductory Overview** 1
Practices of Hospitality; Hospitality Paradigms; Understanding Hospitality; Innovations in Hospitality Firms; Stakeholder Roles in Service Quality.

2. **Hospitality Business Management Concepts and Issues** 24
Business of Tourism and Hospitality; Investment, Planning and Development in the Accommodation Sector; Psychology of Management and Hospitality Industry; Management of Small Hospitality Firms; Role Travel Industry and Tour Operators ; Case Study: EICs and the Hospitality Industry; Case Study: Hotel Operations and Development in North America.

3. **Hospitality Management: Tools and Techniques** 49
Understanding Student and Graduate Attitudes; Understanding Stakeholders Outside Academia; Totwards Making Graduates as Hospitality Managers; Scenarios for Graduations to Hospitality Managers; Understanding Multi-unit Managers and Hospitality Industry; Towards Having an Alternative Source of Labor for Hospitality Industry; Case Study: Flexibility in NSW Registered Clubs; Results in Hospitality Occupation Preferences; "Experience Rules" in Hospitality Industry; Placement Process in Hospitality Industry; Counter-Arguments to the Need for Deregulation in Hospitality Industry.

4. **Focus on Global Hospitality Industry Customers and Service Quality** 78
Understanding Consumer Behaviour and Customer Service; Understanding Service Research and Customer Orientation; Understanding Service Concept in Hospitality Industry; Understanding Finance and Performance in Hospitality Industry; Understanding Hospitality Education and Training Literature; Understanding between Service Quality and Customers in Hospitality Industry; Understanding between Education and Training in Hospitality Industry

5. **Towards Hospitality Warehouse Management and Logistics Solutions** **90**
Approach to Warehouse Management; Finance, Strategies and Performance in Hospitality Industry; Integrated Logistics Solutions Enterprise Agreements in Hospitality Sector; Enterprise Agreements in Hospitality Sector

6. **Training Technology and Vocational Work** **99**
Industry Perspectives and Vocational Work in Hospitality Sector; Case Study: Results of Career Profession Study on Iris Graduates in Hospitality Sector; Methodology for Analysis: Job of Controller in Hospitality Industry.

7. **Other Issues in Hospitality Management and Service Organizations** **123**
Guidelines for Inter-Vendor Cooperation and Systems Integration; Case Study Examples of International Hospitality Management; Service Innovation and Customer Choices in the Hospitality Industry.

8. **Towards Business Development and Service Improvement in Hospitality Industry** **144**
Customers and Service Improvement in Hospitality Industry; Research Methodology.

9. **Quality Management and Services Management in Hospitality Sector** **159**
Explaining Service Quality and Customers in Hospitality Industry; Understanding Brand Loyalty in Hospitality Industry; CRM in Business; The Framing of the Regulations in Hospitality Industry; Teaching Order or Chaos in HRM with Refernce to Hospitality Industry; An Assessment of the Human Resource Demands of the Hospitality Industries; Methodology of Measuring Quality in Hospitality Industry; Staffing and Hospitality Service Delivery; A Conceptual Quality Assurance Framework in Hospitality Delivery; Factors Contributing to the Success of Quality Assurance Systems and Necessary Steps; Segmentation, Branding, and Service Customization in Hospitality Industry; Background; Innovations in Hospitality Firms.

Appendix **211**

Glossary **226**

Bibliography **240**

Index **254**

1

Hospitality Management: An Introductory Overview

> "Hospitality means primarily the creation of free space where the stranger can enter and become a friend instead of an enemy. Hospitality is not to change people, but to offer them space where change can take place. It is not to bring men and women over to our side, but to offer freedom not disturbed by dividing lines."
>
> —*Henri J.M. Nouwen*

Hospitality Management is the study of the hospitality industry. A degree in the subject may be awarded either by a university college dedicated to the studies of hospitality management or a business school with a relevant department. Degrees in hospitality management may also be referred to as hotel management, hotel and tourism management, or hotel administration. Degrees conferred in this academic field include BA, Bachelor of Business Administration, BS, MS, MBA, and PhD. Hospitality management covers hotels, restaurants, cruise ships, amusement parks, destination marketing organizations, convention centers, and country clubs.

Hospitality management is that subject which prepares students for careers in the management of hotel and catering organizations. In the UK, the term "hotel and catering" was widely preferred until the 1990s when the term "hospitality", imported from the USA, began to replace it. The teaching of hospitality management, or in much of Europe "hotellerie", has a long history. The School at Lausanne, Switzerland was established at the end of the nineteenth century doing much to establish that country's reputation as the "home" of the best quality hospitality management education. In the USA, Cornell University's School of Hotel and Restaurant Administration was established in the first quarter of the century and by the end of the century there were around 175 four-year degree programmes in hospitality studies in the USA and many more two-year, associate degree courses (Barrows, 1999). In the UK the story is slightly different.

There were two advanced schools of hotel management before the 1960s: London's Battersea College of Technology, that became the new University of Surrey in the 1960s; and The Scottish Hotel School, formed in Glasgow in 1944 on the Swiss model, that became part of the new University of Strathclyde, in 1964 (Mennell, 1985; Gee, 1994). Neither offered degrees until they acquired university membership. The growth of polytechnics (alternatives to universities focusing primarily on vocational skills) from the late 1960s onwards saw a growth in the number of hotel schools offering hospitality degrees at undergraduate and, later, in some cases, postgraduate level. These polytechnics themselves became "new" universities from 1992 on. Elsewhere in Europe, hospitality management has resolutely remained a non-degree subject – in Germany, France, Italy and the Nordic countries confined for the most part to diploma-equivalent qualifications in institutions of further rather than higher education. There have been a small number of exceptions to this rule in some countries, especially within the last decade or so, but for the most part the availability of conventional degrees or degree equivalents is a function of private rather than public educational enterprise, with many such commercial operations relying on degree franchises from the UK.

Until the mid-1980s, few of those providing hospitality education had any doubt about what they were doing – preparing students for careers in the hotel and catering sector. During the 1990s, however, a variety of pressures created tension as to the mission and role of this form of specialized education. In the UK, of particular interest to government funding agencies for higher education and internal allocators of funds within universities was how separate course provision could be justified for hospitality management. Hitherto, such justification had been on grounds of the "uniqueness" of hospitality management courses (a view strongly supported by industry opinion) and their distinctive focus on accommodation management and food service systems, often marked by the presence in hotel schools of high-cost training restaurants and related specialist equipment.

Nevertheless, changing economic circumstances led many institutions to realize that the "additional cost" element of higher hospitality management education could be eliminated or reduced. The growth of general business education in most universities meant that students studying for hospitality management degrees could take general classes in management while specialized training was provided by means other than expensive in-house facilities. For example, in some cases, food and beverage and accommodation management training was outsourced to further education colleges with "craft" facilities. This approach in fact allowed for some growth in the number of hospitality courses in the early part of the 1990s, a trend that now seems endangered by falling applications.

However, it also obviated a need for separate hotel schools and in several universities during this period, many were indeed absorbed by other departments, often general business schools. Few voices have been raised in concern or protest at the small rationalization of degree level hospitality education that has taken place in the UK since the early 1990s. As a line of defence, the supposed "uniqueness" of hospitality management education seems to have lost a little of its persuasiveness. Defence of the subject area at higher education has been made more difficult by the nature of its knowledge base. Until the 1980s, and outside the USA, hospitality management had little research scholarship to fall back on in justification of its distinctiveness. Rather than having a developed knowledge base, hospitality instead had a skills base and close industry orientation. For institutions concerned with diminishing resources and more precise reward mechanisms, notably the funding made available as part of periodic research assessment exercises, this has further allowed for ease in the rationalization of provision. Recently, the attention of academics in the hospitality field, notably in the UK, has started to turn to the intrinsic nature of the subject, and in particular how "hospitality" and "hospitality management" might be defined (e.g. Wood, 1994; Lashley and Morrison, 2000). Whether it is a coincidence that this has occurred at a time when hospitality management provision within UK higher education has enjoyed fluctuating fortunes remains to be established.

It would be wrong to pretend that such developments presage unanimity of view or purpose. Nevertheless, a process of self-inspection without introspection has begun.

In contrast to arguments marshalled in the past to defend hospitality education within the higher education system, the emphasis now appears, in the UK at least, to be shifting from arguments based on exception (the supposed "uniqueness" of hospitality management) to one based on intrinsic intellectual characteristics. These developments to some extent mirror a similar and earlier, if subtly different, process in the USA where, from early considerations of the nature of "hospitality", the emphasis has shifted to the nature of pedagogy in hospitality education. Perhaps from the perspective of the discussion here, the most significant observations to be made about revived interest in the nature of hospitality and hospitality management are that:

(i) Such interest explicitly addresses questions about the operationalization of meaning – that is, it seeks to address the question "What are we talking about?", and therefore attempts to circumscribe both subject area and subject practice.

(ii) Without the widespread adoption of the term "hospitality management" it is questionable as to whether such considerations would have emerged at all.

To talk about "hotels and catering" is to simultaneously identify subject, locus and practice. The term "hospitality" permits of a much wider range of considerations, for "hospitality" can be found in a variety of locations: hotels, restaurants and places where the provision of hospitality and hospitality services is but one facet of a social institution, as, for example, in hospitals and prisons. Interest in clarifying the meaning of "hospitality" is now regarded by many as a legitimate and necessary intellectual enquiry in its own right and a prerequisite to advancing the subject, for a related discussion in this respect).

Practices of Hospitality

Jones (1996) suggests that the term "hospitality" in recent years has emerged from the way that hoteliers and caterers would like their image to be perceived.

Hotels

The essence of hospitality is the provision of food, refreshments and accommodation for those who are away from home. This activity in Europe was formalised in the Middle Ages by monasteries, which operated "guest houses" for Christian pilgrims, which later developed to roadside inns for travelling. The proliferation of inns and hotels is, therefore, linked with developments in travelling and journeys. Medlik (1994) suggests that travel may be distinguished in three main chronological phases, from stagecoach to railway and steamships in the 1840s to motor cars and aircraft today. Transport technology has opened up travel for business and pleasure to a mass market and has increased the need for accommodation and food away from home. Hotels can, therefore, be described according to the criteria of location (city centre, resort, roadside), trade (commercial, leisure, holiday) or standard (luxury, budget, downscale).

Catering

In the UK, the growth of catering provision mirrored not only greater travelling, but also the progress of industrialisation. Travelling for business purposes or commuting to work became possible through the growth of the rail network and this was reflected after the First World War by the emergence of popular catering, as exemplified by ABC and Lyons "tea shops" (Jones, 1996). Another major developmental factor was the large-scale communal feeding (Medlik, 1994) when nutrition, efficiency and hygiene were brought to the fore. The catering industry of the 1990s is a competitive, multicultural one which continues to increase in size and diversity.

Case Study: UK Hospitality Industry

Because of the connection with travel and leisure, the tourism and hospitality industries are often linked together. Tourism for business or pleasure requires accommodation and food for travellers who are away from home. The image of the hospitality industry is difficult to characterise. A report commissioned by the Hotel and Catering Industry Training Board found that the industry image as an employer was favourable, but that it represented mostly cooking and waiting (Ellis, 1981). Low wages were criticised, but high pay did not appear a priority for most people, providing other work requirements were satisfied. The hospitality industry is often referred to a "people" industry in that it is characterised by labour intensity and because of its reliance on service rather than product differentiation for competitive advantage (Adam and Maxwell, 1995).

The hospitality industry is fragmented and heterogeneous, being largely made up of small firms: 81 per cent of hotels and 94 per cent of restaurants and bars have fewer than 25 employees (Department of National Heritage, 1996). The industry in the UK has grown rapidly since the Second World War, largely in line with economic growth and there is evidence of a greater standardisation of facilities and service, particularly of branding (Teare, 1996).

The industry is increasingly coming under the influence of a few key players and is becoming more internationalised. Brander-Brown and Harris (1995) suggest that the "hospitality industry has experienced significant paradigm shifts over the past decades". In the earlier two-thirds of this century it was described as an entrepreneurial industry that was highly individualistic and fragmentary. The latter third of this century has witnessed a shift to the dominance of complex, multinational and multidivisional hospitality firms. Knowles (1994) suggests that the scope of the hospitality industry is difficult to define, perhaps because of the lack of a conclusive definition of hospitality operators. For example the guest house and bed and breakfast sector is a dynamic one in which operators may choose to sell spare rooms according to season and personal convenience. There are a number of classificatory systems, both official and academic, including those from the Standard Industrial Classification

(SIC) and the Hotel & Catering Industry Training Board (HCITB) who group activities according to the type of operation or the level of commerciality. Despite this lack of clarity, the service sector is growing and the UK hospitality industry is a major employer, employing 2.5 million people or 10 per cent of the working population (Hotel and Catering Training Company, 1994).

The absence of a clear classification framework is reflected in the nature of the hospitality product, which is a complex amalgam of components, some of which are difficult to identify and specify. Mullins (1992) contends that hospitality operations combine a productive and service element and that it is the service element which causes most problems. Problems seem to arise in the interpersonal relationships that characterise service which affects perceptions of quality and value. Further, the immediacy of service demands can make it difficult to provide consistent cover in busy periods. Buttle (1986) defines the hospitality product as a set of those satisfactions and dissatisfactions which make up the hospitality "experience". One major problem is that the customer judges satisfaction by means of a subjective frame of reference, which, because it is inconsistently and individually applied, presents hospitality operators with a problem. For example, dealing with unjustified customer complaints can be a source of frustration for operational staff and is often due to the consumer's view of quality.

Although facilities may be specified according to established star rating criteria, customer satisfaction is a function of the match between perceived expectations and actual provision. All of this reinforces the view that, as the hospitality product is imperfectly understood, the vision cannot always be effectively translated by service staff into consistent customer satisfaction. One answer is greater research through partnership between industry and academia.

Management and Operations

Management plays a central role in co-ordinating organizational tasks, structure, people and technology. Some writers observe that hospitality managers differ from their counterparts in other non-service industries. Venison (1983), for example, remarks that hotel managers need to be at the "front of house" in order to communicate with staff and customers, to check standards of service and to take corrective action to remedy problems as they occur. Shaner (1978) acknowledges the unique demands of hospitality and his study concludes that its managers value honesty and capability above all others. Worsfold's (1989) research found hotel managers to be more assertive, more venturesome and imaginative than other managers. This is reinforced by Stone (1988) who adds that they tend to be more calm, realistic, assertive, competitive, cheerful, bolder, independent, cynical, practical and have a lower scholastic and mental capacity. These studies suggest that hospitality management is a unique activity which requires a special set of attributes and specific training.

There is a move to ensure consistency by branding and pre-planning product and service. An example of this phenomenon is McDonald's, who have routinized work and tightened control by operating with a small administrative core and a large predominantly unskilled workforce. In contrast, managers of smaller hospitality units need to encourage functional flexibility and participation in order to reconcile erratic work demands with the need for higher standards.

Operations

Operations concern the way that organizations deliver their product/ service to the consumer (Jones, 1996) and this is a key concern for the effective practice hospitality. Johnston (1987) divides operations into three activities; customer processing operations, information processing operations and product processing operations. Thus, the accommodation function is a customer processing operation while foodservice combines product processing with customer processing.

Many hospitality firms make their operations more complex in the attempt to try to please as many customers as possible, but often their quality standards may suffer as a result. Thompson (1967) suggests that an ideal operation is one in which "a single product is produced at a continuous rate and as if inputs flowed continuously at a steady rate and with specified quality". This ideal has been reflected in the trend towards specialisms in food concepts (fast food, ethnic) which cater for specific market segments and offer a standard service delivery system. It is suggested that the operational characteristics of hospitality include:

- *service* – inter-personal, immediate and a major satisfier/ dissatisfier;
- *processes* – planned and controlled by management, implemented by employees, sometimes erratically;
- *information* about customers, competitors and trends is very important, but many hospitality firms have not worked out effective ways of information storage, retrieval and manipulation;
- *work* – long operational hours involve shifts and variable trade patterns can cause periodic pressures; and
- *functional* – tasks are predominantly organized into departments, which typically conflict with each other.

Effective hospitality operations must incorporate planning with technology and people management. There is a need to reconcile the tension between management's need to control activities and yet permit employees to participate and to be empowered.

Major Operations

Hospitality operations are not a homogeneous group, but they share a number of common characteristics (Mullins, 1992):

- skills: a wide range of skills are required but there are also high numbers of unskilled staff;
- staff may live on the premises;
- many employees are poorly paid;
- staff often expect to work long and "unsocial" hours;
- there is a large proportion of female, part-time, casual, and foreign staff; and
- labour mobility and turnover are high.

The Department of National Heritage (DNH) report of 1996 describes a vicious circle in the hospitality labour market in which staff turnover discourages training and makes it difficult to attract staff in an industry where pay levels are low.

The DNH calls for a number of measures including the dissemination of good practice, improving the image of the industry and the co-ordination of effort through teamwork. Fascinating insights into hospitality operations are afforded through the research of such ethnographic writers as Gabriel, Whyte, Goffman and Mars and Nicod. These authors spent time observing what went on in hospitality units and paint a picture of conflict which causes dissatisfaction but camaraderie among groups of workers. Ervin Goffman's (1959) study, for example, observed how waitresses "managed" the service interaction by controlling the behaviour of customers. He views such interactions as "dramaturgical performances" by individuals or teams who act as a kind of exclusive "secret society".

This bonding can provide social rewards and can provide an occupational environment that allows relationships to be carried over to non-work domains (Mars and Nicod, 1984).

In summary, the hospitality industry may be said to be:

- important but insufficiently researched;
- fragmented but increasingly dominated by larger players;
- operationally-centred but needing a more strategic focus;

- unable to accurately define its product offering;
- traditionally managed by managers with specific competences;
- known for low productivity but needing higher performance;
- generally unwilling to train staff; and
- unable to use the talents of its employees fully.

These are, of course, generalisations, but they seek to characterise the worst problems of the hospitality industry so as to generate some possible solutions. The second part of this paper gives a view of the knowledge base of the industry and the ways that it might develop in the future.

Hospitality Paradigms

As the practice of hospitality became more widespread and professional after the World War II, so it sought to acquire a knowledge base through which it could improve its operations and develop the managers of the future. Inevitably, it drew from existing disciplines and established philosophical sources as the incremental process of research began to establish hospitality management as a discipline in its own right.

In the early days, the debate arose as to whether hospitality activities could be differentiated from other services. Levitt famously argued that the "production line" approach could be applied to any business operation and that there was no such notion as services. Other writers such as Dann (1990) and Wood (1983) contend that the hospitality industry could not be pigeonholed with other service-oriented activities as it displays sectoral and specific characteristics that differentiate its organizations and operations. The search for a unique hospitality paradigm may be described under the following headings:

- General management and business strategy
- Operations management
- Marketing
- Services and performance measurement
- People
- Hospitality research.

Understanding Hospitality

Perhaps a reasonable starting point in the "search for hospitality" would be one of a back to basics nature, i.e. the dictionary definition/s of hospitality. In tracing the contemporary evolution of the term "hospitality" during this century, dictionary definitions from the 1930s to the present tend to stress a central theme which is summed up in the recent Collins Concise English Dictionary Plus definition of hospitality as "kindness in welcoming strangers or guests" (Hanks, 1989, p. 604). Unfortunately this theme of kindness and generosity in making guests or strangers feel welcome or at ease suggests that hospitality is a rather narrow and one-way process without any clear parameters.

Thus, the dictionary definitions of hospitality tend to be relatively loose and unstructured in nature, and consequently too imprecise for the purpose at hand. By contrast the view of hospitality commonly portrayed in the contemporary, hospitality-related literature tends to have a greater degree of specificity and structure and be more instrumental in nature. Cassee (1983, p. xiv) proffered a relatively holistic definition of hospitality as; "a harmonious mixture of tangible and intangible components – food, beverages, beds, ambience and environment, and behaviour of staff"; and contended that the hospitality "concept comprises much more than the classical ideas of preparing good food and providing a comfortable bed". This definition was then subsequently modified slightly by Cassee and Reuland (1983, p. 144) to; "a harmonious mixture of food, beverage, and/or shelter, a physical environment, and the behaviour and attitude of people".

In a related, but slightly different vein, Burgess (1982) explored the relationship between gift exchanges and hospitable behaviour. In this he relied on a dictionary definition of hospitality, but suggested that hospitality may be subdivided into private, public and institutional contexts and that these are likely to embrace a wide spectrum of different forms of hospitality. Both the focus Burgess (1982) places on the issue of "exchange" in relation to hospitality and the widening of the concept to include private as well as public contexts for the incidence of hospitality are, as will be argued later, valuable contributions to improving the definition of hospitality. Similarly, Reuland *et al.* (1985) reflect the exchange issue raised by Burgess. Their model essentially contends that hospitality is an exchange process within which the exchange transaction comprises three elements; products, employee behaviour, and the physical environment.

More recently, as King (1995, p. 220) identifies, Hepple *et al.* (1990) concluded from their review of the literature that the "modern" view of hospitality embraces four distinct characteristics.

Main Features

- It is conferred by a host on a guest who is away from home.

- It is interactive, involving the coming together of a provider and receiver.
- It is comprised of a blend of tangible and intangible factors.
- The host provides for the guest's security, psychological and physiological comfort.

However, what Burgess (1982), Cassee and Reuland (1983) and Hepple *et al.* (1990) have in common is their failure to adequately define hospitality *per se*. In common with others, for example King (1995), they confuse hospitable behaviour, or hospitableness, with hospitality and fall into the trap of suggesting that one of the important features of hospitality is making the guest "feel at home". The nature and importance of the distinction between hospitableness and hospitality will be addressed later in this paper but the "feel at home" issue deserves further comment at this point. This purported characteristic is so historically and socially value laden, and imbued with totally unwarranted assumptions, that even a cursory examination will find it to be patently nonsensical.

In many hospitality situations, both private and public, the last thing which guests or receivers wish to feel is "at home". The whole "feel at home" issue is predicated on the assumption that an individual's home life is akin to some kind of stereotypical middle-class idyll, but if an individual has a miserable home life the last thing they would wish to be made to feel is as though they were at home!Even if an individual's home life is comfortable, safe and rewarding, a major motive for, and benefit from, staying in a hotel, eating out at a restaurant or someone else's home is that the individual feels different from being at home.

There is a novelty value, a chance to do and experience something different, a freedom from everyday home-based routines and obligations, involved in receiving hospitality away from home. Hence, hospitality is invariably designed to make guests feel as though they were not at home, and is desired for this very aspect. This said, the more general, social scientific, approach taken by these authors to define hospitality has some merit as it seeks to reflect the holistic nature of the concept. Where it falls down is that the definitional forms used in these approaches are too vague and imprecise. Other commentators in the early 1980s, and many since, have tended to take a narrower, commercial or economic perspective to defining hospitality. For example, Tideman's (1983, p. 1) definition of hospitality as; "the method of production by which the needs of the proposed guest are satisfied to the utmost and that means a supply of goods and services in a quantity and quality desired by the guest and at a price that is acceptable to him so that he feels the product is worth the price"; is clearly rooted in this perspective, and frankly could be a definition of almost any economic activity. There is nothing in Tideman's definition to indicate anything different or distinctive about hospitality, perhaps save the reference to a "guest", compared to other forms of economic activity.

In a similar vein Pfeifer (1983, p. 191) also puts forward a definition of hospitality from a strongly supply-side economic perspective; "Hospitality consists of offering food, beverage and lodging, or, in other words, of offering the basic needs for the person away from home". This type of product-oriented, commercial, supply-side economic perspective tends to dominate in the literature and is more recently typified by Jones (1996b, p. 1) who comments that; "The term 'hospitality' has emerged as the way hoteliers and caterers would like their industry to be perceived ... In essence hospitality is made up of two distinct services – the provision of overnight accommodation for people staying away from home, and the provision of sustenance for people eating away from home". The main problems with this type of hospitality definition are first that it concentrates exclusively on one side of the hospitality exchange, and second that it also tends to be one designed to simultaneously define both the concept of hospitality and the nature/parameters of the commercial hospitality industry. As many authors contend (Muhlmann, 1932; White, 1970; Gray and Ligouri, 1980; Heal, 1990; Wood, 1994; King, 1995) the idea and practice of hospitality are not a new phenomenon.

The nature of, and motives for, providing hospitality have changed over time and broadly reflect the evolution of different societies and their particular imperatives. Thus the form of, and motives for providing, hospitality have been subject to a variety of religious, political, social and economic influences across both time and space. Such influences have tended to root and bound hospitality within the particular politico-legal and socio-economic conditions, and priorities, (contemporary norms) of the time and/or location concerned. As King (1995) points out these influences tend to become embedded as "obligations", "rituals", and "rules" which, over time, coalesce into generally accepted societal customs, norms, and taboos relating to the form and function of hospitality within a particular spatio-temporal context. This would tend to imply that any attempt to define hospitality *per se* is doomed to failure. If hospitality is subject to such apparent spatio-temporal variation, how can a valid universal definition be achieved? The answer to this lies in making a distinction between the particular configurations that hospitality provision may take, the motive/s for providing it, and its essential nature.

Clearly hospitality provision may exist on a large or small scale, take a number of different forms depending on whether it occurs within private/

domestic or public/commercial contexts, and be provided for primarily social or economic motives. However, regardless of the scale, form, motives for, and particular context of hospitality provision it is possible to identify its generic essence which, by definition, is not contingent.

The literature suggests that the concept of hospitality is closely associated with human interactions (King, 1995), the provision/consumption of certain types of products (Tideman, 1983; Pfeifer, 1983; Jones, 1996b), and constitutes a type of exchange process designed to generate mutual benefits for the parties involved (Burgess, 1982; Reuland *et al.*, 1985; King, 1995), or is a "harmonious" combination of all of these (Cassee, 1983; Cassee and Reuland, 1983). Hospitality therefore includes hospitable behaviour and motives but is something more than this. This is a distinction the *Collins Concise English Dictionary Plus* fails to recognise as it defines hospitableness as being "welcoming to guests or strangers" (Hanks, 1989, p. 604), a definition which is barely distinguishable from its definition of hospitality referred to above. To claim that the existence of hospitable behaviour is synonymous with the provision of hospitality would be patent nonsense.

Hospitable behaviour may be displayed in many different circumstances, for many different reasons, none of which have anything to do with providing hospitality. For example, receptionists, salespeople, and secretaries in manufacturing and service companies alike would be expected to welcome and deal with visitors in a hospitable manner but invariably would not be expected to provide hospitality. Of course this begs the obvious question; what distinguishes hospitality from hospitableness? A contemporaneous human exchange, which is voluntarily entered into, and designed to enhance the mutual wellbeing of the parties concerned through the provision of accommodation and food or drink.

This definition transcends the issues of form, motives, scale, and context and focuses attention on the essential elements of the hospitality concept. The inclusion, and purposive ordering, of the product parameters (accommodation, food, drink) serves to differentiate hospitality from hospitable behaviour. Thus, for hospitality to exist something more than hospitable behaviour must be evident. It is this "holy trinity" of accommodation, food and drink which facilitates such a differentiation between the two. Without these the definition could be seen to refer to a wide variety of mutually beneficial exchange situations. Hence the product component is an integral foundation of the hospitality concept. Attentive readers will note that the order in which these three product components are presented here is different from that commonly found in the literature; namely food, drink and accommodation.

The term "accommodation" is used to mean something slightly different in this definition from its common usage in other definitions of hospitality. In the latter it is frequently used to refer to hotel guest accommodation of one kind or another. Here it is used to denote any type of accommodation where hospitality is provided. This naturally includes hotel accommodation but also embraces the other types of accommodation, such as public restaurants, cafes, public houses, employee and institutional restaurants, event catering marquees etc., normally associated with the provision of hospitality in commercial contexts and used extensively in Standard Industrial Classification (SIC) definitions of the hospitality industry (Medlik and Airey, 1978; Ryan, 1980; Odgers, 1988; Jones, 1996b). However, in addition to these, the term accommodation is also used here to refer to any domestic accommodation used to provide hospitality because the intention is to define hospitality not the hospitality industry. The narrower use of the term betrays its origins; namely an attempt to define the hospitality industry rather than the essence of hospitality *per se*.

It is this distinction which appears to cause so much confusion for commentators seeking to define hospitality as they are effectively conflating the two separate issues of the nature of hospitality on the one hand, and the parameters of the commercial hospitality industry on the other. Indeed, this latter aspect is often further confused by authors taking SIC based definitions of the hotel and catering industry and automatically transposing these into a definition of the hospitality industry; a venture doomed to failure from the outset.

The use of this wider view of accommodation and its placement in the definition at the beginning of the "holy trinity" also assists in delimiting the scope of hospitality contexts. The alternative order of food and/or drink and/or accommodation prevalent in many definitions potentially creates untold problems for anyone seeking to define hospitality and/or the hospitality industry. Food and/or drink is provided for customers by a wide range of retail establishments, most notably supermarkets, which have nothing to do with the provision of hospitality and would not normally be regarded as hospitality organizations or contexts, or to constitute a part of the hospitality industry.

Conversely, many operations based on the provision of take-away food, home delivery, and/or food and beverage vending would be regarded as hospitality operations by many commentators and thus be included within the scope of conventional definitions of the hospitality industry. However, it could be argued that these are essentially retailing operations having little or no difference from supermarkets or shops which sell hot or cold pre-prepared food for their customers to take away and consume elsewhere. Similarly to consider vending provision, with no element of human additionality, such as food and/or drinks machines in leisure centres or cinemas as constituting the provision of hospitality would appear to be ludicrous. In this sense those definitions of hospitality which both put the provision of food and/or drink in a pre-eminent place within their wording and suggest that accommodation may be an optional feature are misleading and potentially problematic. Therefore, not only do the different usage and placement of the term "accommodation" in the definition of hospitality advocated here offer a more inclusive and useful view of the hospitality concept *per se*, they also hold significantly greater promise for developing a more robust definition of the hospitality industry. Having established the importance of the accommodation issue to the definition of hospitality advanced here, attention now needs to be turned to an explanation of the significance of its other elements. The view that hospitality involves an "exchange" is indisputable, be this of a tangible or intangible nature, or both. However, it is equally indisputable that many other, non-hospitality, activities involve an exchange.

The particular nature of the hospitality exchange, which differentiates it from other types of exchange, is partly delimited by the specific product focus associated with the provision of accommodation/food/drink but also by this particular type of exchange being "contemporaneous" in nature. Much is made in the literature of the simultaneity of production and consumption in relation to hospitality, and this is reflected through the incorporation of the term "contemporaneous" in the definition. As contemporaneity refers to something which exists or occurs at the same time it therefore indicates the existence of the type of close temporal relationship between the production and consumption aspects of the hospitality exchange subscribed to by most commentators.

This is also a feature which further supports the contention made earlier that operations based purely on take-away, home delivery, vending etc. formats should be excluded from a definition of hospitality, and the hospitality industry. In addition, the reference to this being a "human" exchange is also designed to challenge the view that the mere provision of food or drink for consumption constitutes the incidence of hospitality. This not only reflects the concern of many commentators to ensure that relevant aspects of service are included in any definition of hospitality, but again strengthens the claim that situations or contexts based on the inert retailing of food and drink should be excluded. The view expressed in the definition that hospitality is an exchange "voluntarily entered into and designed to enhance the mutual wellbeing of the parties concerned" is also an important feature of hospitality.

There are situations, currently included in definitions of the hotel and catering industry, which often purport to constitute incidences of hospitality, but which are essentially non-voluntary in nature. The most striking example of this is to be found in prisons, and to a lesser extent hospitals and residential care establishments.

In these environments accommodation, food and drink are invariably provided for the inmates, patients or residents but this is an exchange not always voluntarily entered into by the participants, nor is it necessarily designed to enhance mutual wellbeing in the hospitality sense. Catering is certainly provided in such situations but, as has been argued earlier, hospitality is more than the provision of food and drink and/or accommodation alone, and is something greater than the incidence of hospitable behaviour. Again this should mean that situations/contexts which are currently, and uncritically, regarded by many to be a part of the hospitality industry be re-examined. It is significant to mention that as we travel and communicate in ever-increasing numbers, we are discovering that most people, regardless of their political or religious orientation, race, or socio-economic status, want peaceful world in which all are fed, sheltered, productive and fulfilled. The story is told about a Senator approaching Abraham Lincoln amids the passions of the Civil War and saying, "Mr. President I believe that enemies should be destroyed". Lincoln replied, "I agree with you sir, and the best way to destroy an enemy is to make him a friend".

Through travel, people are finding friends in every corner of the earth: finding common bonds with the rest of humanity and spreading messages of hope for a peaceful world. Tourism properly designed and developed, has the potential to help bridge the psychological and cultural distances that separate people of diverse races, colours, religions and stages of social and economic development.

Through tourism we can come rather to an appreciation of the rich human, cultural and ecological diversity that our world mosaic offers: to evolve a mutual trust and respect for one another and the dignity of all life on earth. "The world is becoming a global village in which people from different continents are made to feel like next door neighbours. In facilitating more authentic social relationships between individuals, tourism can help overcome many real prejudices, and foster new bonds of fraternity. In this sense tourism has become a real force for world peace." Pope John Paul II The tourism industry, combined with our world parks systems, can make a contribution to living in harmony with our environment as well. The tourism industry makes possible the setting aside and preservation of vast tracts of land as national parks and wilderness areas. More than 3,000 protected areas in 120 countries and covering more than 4 million square miles are now preserved in their natural state. Visitors to these areas experience the beauty and majesty of the world's finest natural features and come away with a heightened appreciation of environmental values.

In national parks town sites such as Banff and Jasper, we have the opportunity for "Man" to be co-creators with nature, bringing the best of human design in juxtaposition with the best of nature. Tourism contributes to both preservation and development of the world's cultural heritage. It provides governments with the rationale for the preservation of historical sites and monuments and the motivation for indigenous groups to preserve unique dimensions of heritage in the form of dance, music and artifacts. Tourism also provides both the audience and the economic engine for museums, the performing and visual arts and the restoration of historical areas. Severe poverty, stemming from under-development, is not only an active cause of conflict, but is inherently a form of violence. Pope Paul VI once said that "development is the new name for peace". The tourism industry is a human resource immense industry. It has the capacity to generate foreign exchange and a high ratio of government revenues as a proportion of total expenditures.

As well, it has a capacity for both forward and backward linkages with other sectors of the economy. Properly designed, it can contribute to social and cultural enrichment as well as economic development. For those reasoned is increasingly attractive as an industry among developing nations. The 5,000 international conferences held each year increasingly draw on people of all nations to share their concerns, proposo solutions to problems; exchange ideas; and create "opportunity networks". The growth in student exchanges, cultural exchanges, twinning of cities, and international sporting events not only give us an appreciation of our differences, but also show us the commonality of our goals and aspirations as a human family.

The collective outcomes of these travel and tourism experiences help all humankind to appreciate the full meaning of the "Global Village" and the bonds that people everywhere have with one another. Approximately 400 million persons will travel to another country in 1988. This number is growing by 5-7 per cent each year. Millions more will act as "hosts" to these travellers as part of their daily job and/or as interested residents of the host country. These millions of daily person-to-person encounters are potentially a powerful force for improved relations among the people and nations of the world; relations which emphasise a sharing and appreciation of cultures rather than the lack of trust bred by isolation.

"Peace is a daily, a weekly, a monthly process, gradually changing inions, slowly eroding old barriers, quietly building new structures . . . peace does not rest in the charters and covenant alone. It lies in the hearts and minds of all people. And if it is cast out there, then no act, no pact, no treaty, no organization can hope to preserve it without the support and wholehearted commitment of all people. So let us not rest all our hopes on parchments and on paper—let us strive to build peace, a desire for peace, a willingness to work for peace in the hearts and minds of all of our people"—(John F. Kennedy).

The countdown to the 21st century has begun. Less than 15 years remain before the dawning of a new millennium, a period in which the late Buck Minister Fuller believed humankind would-be taking its "final exam." Humankind will pass its "final exam" when we recognise the need to live in harmony with our fellow human beings, as well as with nature when we recognise that we are our brother's keeper.

For the first time in human history, at the problems which the world faces are man-made problems. And so too, humankind has the capacity to solve them. Ninety per cent of the scientists who ever lived are alive today, and our corporate and political will to do so. In the 1960s, President John F. Kennedy had a vision of putting a man on the moon within that decade. The articulation of this vision brought about the marshalling of human, scientific and fiscal resources to make that vision a reality. So too, the year 2000 offers an occasion for visionary thinking.

There are roughly 40-50 million persons engaged in the tourism industry around the world. The value of the global tourism plant is in the trillions of dollars. Just as John Kennedy's vision put a man on the moon within a decade, the vision of tourism leaders around the world cans Marshall immense human and physical resources to help achieve global peace in this century. The tourism industry has achieved its goal of becoming the world's largest industry. It now has the promise of becoming the world's first "Peace Industry"; an industry which recognises, promotes and supports the belief that every traveller is potentially an "Ambassador for Peace"; an industry which will be a model for other industries to follow.

Innovations in Hospitality Firms

Hotel Type

The emergence of "boutique" hotels during recent years is an excellent example of an innovative offering in an otherwise standardized industry. The boutique hotel typically features a contemporary or minimalist décor while also offering many additional lifestyle amenities. Hotel guests tend to perceive boutique hotels as a stylish location for which they are willing to pay premium room rates for (*Binkley*). Recently, the boutique hotel trend has crossed over into the mid-priced hotel market (*Chittium*). Rather than focusing exclusively on the functionality of the hotel product offering, mid-price hotels are beginning to consider the aesthetic appearance of the building's structure and décor (*Chittium*). Hotels' guest rooms as well as lobbies are being redesigned in order to stand out amongst the basic hotel offerings.

For example, Choice Hotels are planning a new chain of hotels, tentatively named the Diplomat that will feature flat-screen TVs and stylish shelving in its guest-rooms (*Chittium*). Another higher-priced hotel chain has adopted amenities that are typically associated with boutique hotels while pricing its rooms to be competitive with the mid-priced market. These innovative changes are expected to boost their occupancy rates beyond their rivals (*Binkley*). Amenities being offered will include platform beds with no box springs, wire storage racks rather than dressers, plasma television screens, and complimentary wireless DSL access (*Binkley*).

The trendy boutique hotel is an innovation to the traditional hotel experience and an attractive option to consider when designing a hotel service concept, especially when it crosses the traditional industry boundaries into co-branded fashion and jewelry concepts.

Another example of innovation in hotel services is the use of information technology. One study determined which of the recent technological innovations were most beneficial, least beneficial, and had future benefits for hotels (*Reid and Sandler*). The technological innovations that were found to be most beneficial included: a wake up system, electronic door locks, in-room pay-per-view, video cassette players, multiple phone lines, video library, personal computers, voice mail, computer modem connections, video check out, electronic in-room safes, and a software library (*Reid and Sandler*). However, it may be impractical for a specific hotel or chain to adopt all available technological amenities due to a lack of operational capabilities or limited resources. Instead, hotels must determine which technological innovations will most benefit their organization. Aside from customer preferences for technology, the addition of new technological features to a hotel's service concept has distinct phases of adoption (Namasivayam et al.).

The technology adoption process includes:

- customer signaling, such as internet booking and in-room modems;

- enabling management, such as management email;
- enabling employees, such as voice mail;
- customer service revenue add-ons, such as ATM and interactive TVs;
- customer service value add-ons, such as internet access and in-room fax machines; and
- wireless technology, such as curbside check-in, voice recognition, and smart cards (Namasivayam *et al.*, 2000).

With the intricacies of implementing technological advances to the service concept, hotel managers need to also take into consideration the adoption process of implementing technology on top of understanding the operational capabilities of the hotel.

Customization of Service

Customizing the service experience for hotel guests is another means of service innovation. Some examples of service customization include: allowing guests to have flexible check in/out times, personalizing room décor, or having child care options available. Customized options adapt the hotel's service offering to each individual guest's preferences. However, customization is not easy to implement due to the operational capabilities of the firm. For example, a flexible check in/out policy could lead to labor scheduling problems. Adding such a policy successfully requires the alignment of hotel's marketing and operational activities. Skinner provides a product-oriented example of the importance of balancing marketing and operational activities. He suggests that while it may seem profitable to add more products/features to the product mix, it may be too difficult operationally to implement (*Skinner*). This dilemma is equally applicable to a service setting, in which adding more services may not operationally be possible. As we discussed earlier, service innovation is a crucial aspect of a firm's ability to differentiate itself from its competitors and can contribute more to a firm's revenues. Yet, service innovation research is lacking in comparison to product innovation.

In this study, we address this discrepancy by presenting an analysis of hotel travelers' preferences for innovative service offerings and the role innovation plays in service development. The next section describes our research methodology in exploring the innovative choice drivers for business and leisure hotel travelers.

Stakeholder Roles in Service Quality

It is significant to mention that in profiling a quality management programme designed for the Australian hospitality industry, Dwan (1994,

p. 55) comments that quality management requires a "market focus to business strategy, an organized approach to planning and managing customers' service experiences, customer-centred and enthusiastic staff and a solid underlying management system". Dwan's comments are instructive as they highlight the involvement of three key stakeholders in effective quality management: customers, management and employees. The importance of these stakeholders is reflected in the various articles reviewed here. The construct of quality has traditionally been viewed from the customer's perspective and is often defined as meeting or exceeding customer expectations (Gronroos, 1984). However, while leading researchers in the field, Parasuraman *et al.*, maintain that there are universally valid and applicable determinants of service quality (1985), criticisms of this assumption (Carman, 1990) have led to methodologies to assess service quality in specific industry settings.

For example, Walker (1996) used focus groups of clients of five accommodation categories in Tasmania, Australia, to generate a set of attributes germane to measuring service quality within the specific industry context. These formed the basis of two survey instruments, the first administered at check-in to assess perceived customer importance of these attributes and the second at check-out to assess customer perceptions of these attributes' standards. Walker concluded that the locus of service quality is individually and contextually grounded, such that service quality is defined in different ways by different people with reference to different contexts and considerations. Kivela (1996) also took a customer perspective in formulating a model of the restaurant choice process. Like Walker (1996), Kivela recognized that attributes important to restaurant patrons are industry specific and determined both by individual factors (such as age, gender, income, education, life cycle and reasons for eating out) and external factors (such as the customer's experience at the restaurant, media and merchandising efforts and communications with others).

The model can also be used to predict return patronage intentions which depend on customer satisfaction with the dining experience. Lyons (1996) also focused on customer satisfaction in restaurants. More specifically, she used qualitative methods to study restaurant complaint behaviour in Queensland, Australia. She concluded that factors influencing complaint behaviour were the intensity of customer dissatisfaction and a host of personal and situational variables. Importantly, complaint behaviour in restaurants differed from that in other industries owing to social factors and the intangible causes of dissatisfaction.

Just as the preceding articles have emphasized that customer expectations, satisfaction and assessment of quality are individually and contextually specific, implicit in other publications is the notion that cultural factors are also important. For example, in their study of Japanese tourists' expectations and perceptions of service provided in Australian hotels, Reisenger and Waryszak (1994) found that the tourists perceived hotel employees to be less professional, friendly, informative, helpful, concerned about customers and able to speak Japanese than they had expected. Provision of more information, more Japanese speaking staff, staff training in Japanese language and culture, and welcome and farewell gifts, were recommended. Also adopting a customer perspective, King (1994a) explored the question of whether international tourists to Australia expect authentically Australian hospitality experiences. He proposed numerous ways in which authentic hospitality product development can be incorporated into physical items (e.g. food and drink), sensual benefits (e.g. service and atmosphere) and psychological benefits (e.g. comfort and status) so that tourist satisfaction levels can be improved.

Two articles in the review period studied service quality from the perspective of employees. Ross (1993) examined the perceptions of hospitality staff regarding management's service quality expectations, concluding that politeness, hard work and efficiency were the major perceived management service quality elements.

Furthermore, being hard working and efficient was associated with higher levels of need for achievement, while politeness was inversely related to need for autonomy. Providing an Asian perspective, Huyton *et al.* (1994) investigated whether the extreme disparity between the perceived wealth of hotel visitors and the personal environment, lifestyle and existence of hotel employees in China would influence the latter's service attitudes and abilities. However, their interviews revealed this assumption to be incorrect and that Western materialism was seen by many employees as something worth striving for. Providing a management perspective, Yourston (1995) emphasised increasing importance of quality management to hospitality managers, and discussed the potential of the Australian quality assurance standard AS 3900 to improve the competitive edge of the Australian hospitality industry in a global market.

Positive elements are that the standard has been developed specifically for service industries and its inclusion of a small business module is appropriate to the structure of the Australian hospitality industry. In their empirical investigation of the relationships between market orientation, organizational innovation and business performance, Wilson and McPhail (1995) also reinforced that success in hospitality firms depends not only on service excellence when providing current services, but also on market intelligence to identify opportunities which add value to existing service offerings. They concluded that within hospitality firms, superior business performance is, to a large extent, dependent on the organization's ability to engender a service culture.

REFERENCES

Aylsworth, K. (1996), "Hotels adopt to please business traveler", *Grand Rapids Business Journal*, pp. B1.

Bond, H. (1995), "Frequent-guest programs build brand loyalty", *Hotel and Motel Management*, Vol. 210 No.3, pp. 23.

Bowen, J.T., Shoemaker, S. (1998), "Loyalty: a strategic commitment", *The Cornell Hotel and Restaurant Administration Quarterly*, pp. 12-25.

Connell, J. (1992), "Branding hotel portfolios", *International Journal of Contemporary Hospitality Management*, Vol. 4 No.1, pp. 26-32.

Coopers & Lybrand (1996), *Hospitality Directions: Forecasts and Analyses for the Hospitality Industry*, Coopers & Lybrand, New York, NY.

Enghagen, L., Hott, D. (1992), "Students' perceptions of ethical issues in the hospitality and tourism industry", *Hospitality Research Journal*, Vol. 15 No.2, pp. 41-50.

Kotler, P., Bowen, J., Makens, J. (1996), *Marketing for Hospitality and Tourism*, Prentice-Hall, Inc., London.

Sarabakhsh, M., Carson, D., Lindgren, E. (1989), "The personal cost of hospitality management", *Cornell HRA Quarterly*, Vol. 30 No.1, pp. 72-6.

2

Hospitality Business Management Concepts and Issues

"There is no hospitality like understanding."

—*Vanna Bonta*

A historical view of the US lodging industry and the environment is presented by Stipanuk (1996) in the above mentioned issue of the *Cornell Quarterly*. Historical records show that from the early part of the twentieth century hoteliers have been concerned with environmental-management initiatives. Although the industry may have lapsed in its environmental responsibilities during the rush to expand in the 1980s, as a whole, the lodging industry has posted many positive environmental accomplishments. In fact, the term "ecoresort" has been coined for lodging properties that have become efficient in preserving their surrounding environment.

In order to meet this and other challenges, hospitality managers must establish programmes and procedures designed to preserve the environment. Khatri (1996) identifies an environmental-improvement programme based on four "Rs": reduce, reuse, recycle, and rethink. For example, the island resorts which enacted this programme dealt with a shortage of potable water by altering their system to use seawater, and they solved their soil erosion problem by mulching the ground with coconut husks. A more structured programme was offered by DeFranco and Weatherspoon (1996) who presented a two-page environmental-procedures inventory for hotel operators. This self-inspection inventory comprised checklists which concentrate on energy, solid waste, and water conservation. The importance of environmental programmes such as these can not be overlooked, and managers at all levels must be concerned with how their operation can potentially effect the environment.

Business of Tourism and Hospitality

As already mentioned the world of travel and tourism has been revolutionised. Tourism is today's fast growing business and expected to be the world's largest industry in the 2001-millenium. The world have become a global community for travellers, opening up places, unimaginable decade earlier—the secrets of Himalayas, the wonders of Antarctica, the rain forests of the Amazon, the beauty of the Tahiti, the Great Wall of China, the dramatic Victoria Falls, the origin of Nile, and the wilds of Scottish Islands.

Tourism has become a global business whose expanding market now leaves no place untouched. Tourism and travel now affect every continent, country, and city. Every one's economy is impacted either by their people travelling elsewhere (import spending in other places) or travel service exports (expenditure by nonresidents in that place). The Himalayan region has to decide how much travel service it want to capture. Due to location, climate, limited resources, size and cultural heritage, this region have no real choice but to engage in tourism to grow, develop and improve its living standards. The areas in the region differ in their dependence on/or interest in, attracting tourists. Areas engage in tourism with mixed emotions, and at times, ambivalence.

There are instances, where places are concerned that tourism is destroying its culture, as farm land becomes resort and new jobs unravel family values. These areas may not formally welcome tourists. Some people and businesses benefit, others may not. The regional economy may be better off from tourism, however, the costs and losses—quality of life, convenience, cultural or social values—are not worth the benefits. Should the region place too much emphasis on tourism and hospitality industries? Are these full of risks? These are the questions need to be debated. The region must decide the *three* broad alternatives:

- Pursue tourism even more aggressively in well-developed areas because its physical and historical beauty provides it with a competitive advantage in this industry.
- Hold tourism in its present level and invest in building other industries more aggressively, and
- Build tourism and other industries in a balanced way.

In fact, the decision is quite tough because of conflicting interest of different voting blocks. Not all regions and people are enthusiastic about tourist generated jobs. This region may think of expanding tourism when its thriving business decline.

Tourism's primary benefit is jobs through hotel, restaurants, retail establishment and transportation. The region must decide on not only how many tourists it wants and how to balance tourism with other industries or strategies but also what kind of tourists it wants. The choice will be constrained by the area's climate, natural topography and resources, history, culture and facilities. Like any other business, tourist marketers must know the actual and potential customers, their needs and wants, determine which markets to serve and decide on appropriate products services and programmes to serve these markets. Not every tourist is interested in a particular destination.

The region will waste its money trying to attract everyone who travels. The region, instead of a short gun approach, should take a rifle approach and sharply define its target market. The region should identify its natural target markets in *two* ways. One is to collect information about its current tourists:

- Where do they come from?
- Why do they come to this place?
- What are their demographic characteristics?
- How satisfied they are?
- How many are repeat tourists?
- How much do they spend?

Examine all these questions and determine which tourists are easiest to attract and which are worth attracting. The *second* approach is to audit the region's attraction and conjecture about the types of tourists who would have an natural interest in them. The aim in this approach is to identify new sources of tourists. Do not assume that the current tourists reflect all the potentially interested groups.

Different tourists are attracted by different place features. The local/area/district/municipal authorities must ask questions keyed to segmentation visually, such as, attractions sought, market areas or locations, customers. After identifying its natural target market, the region has to see research where these tourists are found.

Which areas out side contain a large number of citizen who have the means and motivation to enjoy the particular place? Badrinath area attracts mainly religious tourists. The best source for these tourists are Gujarat, Maharashtra, Uttar Pradesh, Madhya Pradesh and even foreign markets. This analysis can uncover too many or too few natural target market. If you have identified many, next step is to calculate the potential profit from attracting each segment.

The potential profit of a target tourist segment is the difference between the amount that the tourist segment would spend and the cost of attracting and serving this segment. The attraction cost will depend on the master plan. The serving cost depend on the infrastructure requirements. Now rank the potential segments in order of their profitability and concentrate on attracting those segments highest on the list. For example, Haridwar, Rishikesh Badri-Kedar region of Uttarakhand's primary market is religious tourists for sentimental, historical, and religious reasons are drawn to this area. The area should create a deep infrastructure of educational, social, and political groups that are likely to visit this region. Summer work-study vacations for young students, groups for to study artifacts and religions questions, etc., could be arranged.

Some religious minded people visit this area as many as ten or fifteen times during their life time. They receive deep experience rather than a superficial one. Depending on their special interest, they meet leaders, study with scholars, with village residents. So doing, they bond with the region and through word of mouth encourage others to visit their 'Deva Bhumi'. The region can begun marketing to a broader audience by launching a campaign with these tourist generating market, that feature a combined visit. The task is to build these new markets and not allow erosion of its successful primary market. If the analysis identifies too few natural tourist segments in the area, the local government must undertake investment marketing. A natural market is attracted by existing features of the place where as an investment market is attracted by new features that might be added to the region. Investment marketing consists of allocating money toward infrastructure improvements, such as hotels, transportation, etc., and attraction that can potentially attract new types of tourist.

The pay-off from investment marketing comes only some years later but this lag is necessary if the region can not identify a sufficient number of natural tourist segments. The region should better off attract fewer but higher income tourists who stay longer and spend more. Back packers and campers should spend more to enjoy its natural, unspoiled beauty. They should tour not only its mountains, water and ancient building but also its literary treasure and attract high income culture-seeking tourists to visit this area where the speech and wit of old can be experienced today. Hotel and restaurant facilities should be improved as an act of investment marketing.

Whatever tourist segment the region aims at, it needs to be very specific. A ski resort like Auli could attract only skiers; swimming and natural reef would attracts snorkels and divers; arts, and crafts would attract the art crowd; gambling would attracts gaming tourists. Tourist must be segmented by additional characteristics such as the Valley of Flowers, Winter Park; snow slopes, lakes, winter resort, river boating, rafting, mountain trails, etc. to elude the tourists. The area should expand from single season to year-around business. For example, from winter skiing to summer recreational, educational and cultural attractions. Market and attractions of these areas are subjected to change over time. A small area attraction may grow to natural and international attraction and later on the entire region explode in competition for tourists competition, results is hot and cold tourist attractions, ups and downs, or ins and outs.

A region's attractiveness can be minimised by violence, political instability, natural catastrophe, adverse environmental factors, and overcrowding. There are examples, of Greece and Thailand, highly depended on tourism, where infrastructure investment has lagged tourist development. The results are tourist fall off due to high pollution, inadequate sanitation and major traffic congestion. Greece's natural treasure, the formerly white marble Parthenon in Athens, stand as a pollution-stained symbol of environmental neglect.

Similarly, Thailand's beautiful beach resort and temples have been severely damaged by pollution and poor sanitation. Regions that fail to maintain the necessary infrastructure run significant risks. The region should be ready to respond to changing demographics and life-styles. The growing percentage of retired people and vacations may expand the tourist business. Hotel and airlines should accommodate these trends with low-cost excursion packages. Business travel should, include mixed business and leisure. To capture the trend towards shorter vacations, with in driving distance of home, will help in the growth of new local and regional tourist attractions. The whole region should determine its best tourism target. Older citizen and retires drive the regional economy. They have high income, high consumption, and low service demand levels. They take their pension, social security checks securities to the region.

Thus, older citizens are much more than a tourist marketing, their visits lead to permanent residency. The region should market to families, college students, and foreign visitors. Attracting the fixed income elderly, the region could gain the distinction of having the oldest population. Accommodating changing life-styles and need is a dynamic challenge for the tourism in the light of demographic trends. Tourist competition is going to be fierce amidst a growing and constantly changing tourist market. Besides new areas, competition expands when declining area up-grade and make new investment in regional development. A major trend in regional revival is heritage development, i.e., the task of preserving the history of the region, their buildings, their people and customers, the machinery and other artifacts that portray history. Counter examples exists of regions/area rediscovering their past, capitalising on the birth place of famous person; and event, a battle or other hidden gems. A region should rely on various monitors for identification.

The area may bear nickname of its economic heritage. With shorter holidays, and family vacation, many areas have new opportunities to access to the tourist market. The environmental movement has compelled the tourist industry to adopt earth-friendly approaches, and the region should seek to develop 'green' images. Developers and architects should accommodate changing tastes in designs hotels — low rise, more green space, nature architecture, and energy efficient.

We find the tourist places in this region are more sensitive to zoning, density land use, and the problems of over-building. Now government tourist agencies, airlines, hotel chains and tourist organizations are all talking about green issues, and how best to accommodate growth while respecting environmental values. Event based tourism will be a vital component of tourist attraction programmes. Small and rural areas should begin with village festival/melas or to establish their identify. All local newspapers should publish listing of events, festival, and celebration occurring with in 2-3 kilometer. Regional and local/ area tourism offices should do the same.

Travel agencies, restaurants, hotels, airport, train and bus stations should all have even-based calendars for posting. Every area/region should have a listing of forth-coming events and programmes of scheduled events to attract tourists regionally and nationally. Tourism investment ranges from relatively low-cost market entry for festivals or event to multi-million rupee infrastructure, costs of stadiums, transits systems, airport and convention center. To create a strong destination pull, attractions, facilities and services should be in a convenient and accessible location. In a planned economy the government controls, plans and directs tourists development. Tourism is necessary for an area/region to earn currencies for trade and development and serves regional purposes.

Tourist development and expansion in this region is totally dependent on public investment. This is inadequate because of lack of private investment and market mechanism to respond to changing consumer need and wants. The region should promote investment through joint ventures, foreign ownership and time sharing for individual investors. The state investment in infrastructure should work with private investment in tourist amenities such as hotels, restaurants, golf courses, shopping areas, etc. Regional tourism could be build on public-private partnerships, joint development in planning, financing and implementation. Public authority should clear, develop, and write down land costs and make infrastructure investment. The region should provide or subsidise tax incentives for private investment in hotels, convention centers, transit, and parkings.

Non-profit Development Corporation from airlines to hotels should carry out restoration. The tourist industry should provide tax revenues, from fuels, leases, bed taxes and sales taxes to support long-term bond for capital construction of tourist-related infrastructure and other public improvements. Such steps will make it possible for this region to increase its tourist attraction. The region could also require much more finance and investment for tourism promotion.

The area/region must expand public services, public safety, traffic and crowd, emergency health, sanitation and street cleaning. It should promote tourism internally to it's own citizens, and businesses—retailers, travel agencies, restaurant, financial institutions, public and private tourist, lodging, police and public servants. It should invest in recruiting, training, licensing, and monitoring tourist—related business and employees cab drivers should have professional training and service, which should include language exams, safety programmes, and location skills.

The region should respond to the travel-basics of 'cost', 'convenience' and 'timeliness' in order to attract tourists. Every tourists to this region would weigh the costs against the benefits of the destination — and investment of time, effort, and resource against a reasonable return in education, experience, fun, revolution and prospective memories. Convenience includes time involved in travel airport to lodging, language barriers, cleanliness and sanitary concerns, access to interests, (i.e., valleys, attractions, amenities), and special needs (elderly, disabled, children, dietary, medical care, communication, auto rental, etc. Timeliness embraces those factors that introduce risk to travel; wars, terrorism, civil disturbances and political instability, currency fluctuations and convertibility, airlines and transit safety, and sanitary conditions. It is a general rule, that all the areas of the region and tourist business should be competitive in costs, minimise risks, and maximise conveniences and amenities.

Tourist packages should range from total planning of hour-by-hour details to multiple options and choices. To accommodate multiple tourist needs, packages should range from destination to destination, no frills only to site-and event-based full-frills luxury. Travellers also make comparisons about the relative advantages and disadvantages of competing destination, e.g., geography (local, regional, national, international), special interests (hiking, snorkeling, trekking, recreation), and amenities (music, art, entertainment, etc.) All major hotels should provide in-home video packages to assist visitors in planning local tours, booking events, including skiing various sites. Bus companies should prepare half-day, full-day and evening tours to highlight the area's attractions. Concentrating attractions, services and facilities on an area will definitely create excitement, adventure, and crowds. A major strategy for regional tourist attraction is concept integration, i.e., try all diverse elements into one center theme. Associating honeymoon with snow hills, and water-falls, the tourist season could be extended. It would appeal to newly married.

Hotels could offer honeymooners a choice of heart-shaped both tubs, Jacuzzis, Canopy beds and waterbeds. The entire romantic aura of champagne waiting in the room, mirror on the ceilings, and quiet and discreet quarters, will encourage the honeymoon market. The large number of honeymooners could find a complete package of dramatic beauty and business community, resulting in a satisfying tourist experience. The region needs to monitor closely, the relative popularity of its various attractions by determining the number and type of tourists attracted to each location. It should seek to deepen its attractions quality which will transcend the specific attraction and become a platform for building a place's appeal, features, and sites alone will not attract visitors.

The region should seek to deepen the travel experience by holding greater values and making the experience more significant and rewarding. Such appeals should be couched in history, culture, and people. The region should be made foreign friendly' by creating tours that emphasise nationality interest designing vouchers in a variety of languages, and providing hassle-free currency exchanges. Tour packages should try to deepen cultural bond and ties between the region and the visitors and thus provide value-added dimension and friendship.

Competition extends to restaurants, facilities, sports, cultural amenities, and entertainment. The region/area should have best hotels, best culinary fairs, museums and theatres, athletic teams, best wine and drinks, best chefs, and best natives, cultural or ethical flair. Regional campaign should be carried out in special publication. In addition to specific sites and attractions, critical amenities are also of vital importance to tourism and hospitality business. The whole region-at first glance seems to bad set as a tourist attraction.

It suffered from a poor image and a non-existence industrial base. It requires to recognise the problems and allocate one time grant to explore tourist markets. The audit of potential attractions may be promising, which require a crucial decision. The region needs to be reinvented as a short-break holiday market and be promoted as a weekend packages. The message should reach the main stream tourists. The locals will take pride in the new attention. A general confidence could be derived with the cooperation of all. The result could be a sharp pick-up in holiday packages. Tourist competition involves image-making. The regional image will be heavily influenced by pictorial creation of the area, often in movies, and on television and some times by music, and other cases of by popular entertainers, and celebrities.

Decades later, this regional image still persists. The region exploits the pilgrim as a successful image of the Himalayas. The region should take advantages of its news events, sport and entertainment stars, movies, and whatever else it could to stimulate tourist interest and convey a regional image. Television also affects relative regional/area attractiveness. Changing of an image of an area is quite difficult. In selecting a mix of communication messages and channels will help in determining the regional identify. State's media investment in attracting tourist is bound to grow rapidly in the future. It should produce multi-language travel guides, video tapes, radio segments, and selected segments for hikers, trackers golfers, fishers, bicyclists and adventure enthusiasts. Partnership could be formed with travel, recreation and communication business on joint marketing efforts. Advertise in national magazines and travel publications and thus help in vertical marketing with business travel promotions to link the growing business leisure segment of the travelling public. Target its own travel agencies and agent. The region should also target tourism to its own resident, regionalising attractions with brochures, maps and calendars of event targeted for sub-regions. The region should constantly discover hidden assets that have vast tourism potentials, for example, Auli skiing discovered in Uttaranchal/Uttarakhand, needs to be advertised as a tourist product to a particular target. Effective regional image requires congruence between advertising and the region.

Glossy photographs of sunrise, sunset, valleys, streams, wildlife, fountains, springs, houses, and events need to have some relationship to what tourist actually experience, otherwise there is a great risk of the region loosing tourist-goodwill and generating bad word-of-mouth. Travel agents should be extremely responsive to region/area. Feedback from customers and tourist could provide the best or worst privation of a place depending on their experience.

Organization & Management of Regional Tourism

Making an area/region tourist friendly is the task of the central tourist authority, i.e., the Ministry of Tourism. Tourism promotion is the responsibility of the government and promotion hospitality business is entrusted to be travel-tourist business. In smaller area tourist-travel activities could be assigned to local chamber of commerce and private organizations.

Business of Hospitality

- Trade shows
- Conventions
- Assemblies
- Conferences, and
- Consumers shows.

In fact, the key revenue factors are the size of the group, its length of stay and its service demands. The meetings market is growing very fast and there is a need for meeting space requirement. The hospitality business requires attractive exhibition facilities combined with ample meeting space. Convention includes exhibits and displays, and combining exhibitions with meetings. When hotel's occupancy falls below profitability, pressure mounts to expand exhibition and meeting space as a method to increase hotel occupancy rates. Convention and trade show business involves dealing with dedicated specialists such as trade association directors, site selection committees, and convention specialists who make site selection recommendations based on price, facilities, and various amenities.

Space at reasonable rate, discounted hotels, restaurants, theatres, airlines, auto rentals, and other amenities are all part of competitive packaging. Facilities should be upgraded to meet aesthetic and convenience needs—restaurants, shops, rest rooms, cleanliness, security, proximity to shopping areas and recreations, etc. The Himalayan region is not an interesting site for conventioneers. It has outstanding dry weather, and beautiful natural scenery that includes some of the greatest mountain ranges, snow and skiing in the world.

The region is not in a position to attract large conventions and trade shows. The space compares unfavourably. Hospitality locations know their target market and respective niches. It travels a growing universe of new and expanding player whose markets may be local villages, cities, statewide, regional, national and international. When time is tough, organizations outback on travel for professional development, trade shows, and even sales contact. Some travel is being replaced by video conferences, teleconferences, and other media methods.

Investment, Planning and Development in the Accommodation Sector

The articles which are discussed under this theme are notable for their diversity. Some have focused on long-term trends in sector development, some on property investment, and others on more specific managerial and operational concerns in specific properties. Two articles are concerned with historical trends in various sectors of the accommodation industry. McCulloch (1992) traced the origins of the contemporary Youth Hostel Association (YHA) movement, from the wandering scholars and travelling apprentices of earlier centuries, to its development in reaction to harsh conditions of urban life in industrial nineteenth century Europe, to the current liberalisation of YHA policies to accommodate budget and backpacker markets in Australia and other destinations.

However, despite the importance of the backpacker market, this sector has attracted relatively little research. Such a comment could also be made about the caravan park industry, the focus of Kelly's (1994) article. He reviewed historical development of the industry in Australia and drew on a survey of users, as well as park usage data from Britain and the USA, to identify important future issues for the Australian sector. These included the potential for conflict in parks catering for both tourists and long-term residents, the need for the sector to market its product more effectively, and the value of a national rating system. King and Whitelaw (1992) take a somewhat different line in examining the resort sector in Australia.

Their concern lay in defining the term "resort" in view of the characteristics of properties advertised as such. They noted the inconsistent use of the term, displaying a mismatch between consumer understanding and the way the term is used for both classification purposes by motoring associations and marketing purposes by tour operators and the properties themselves. They postulated that this ad hoc use of the term is a "recipe for confusion". Moving to New Zealand, Short (1996) clarified some issues relevant to future growth and development of the hotel sector. He concluded that if current trends continue, visitor arrivals will continue to climb, maintaining high interest in hotel investment and development, particularly from international hotel chains.

However, he warned that, with industry exposure to economic vagaries, hotel managers need to think strategically to encourage customer loyalty and repeat business, to maintain profitability within their captured market share. Daly *et al.* (1996) also focused on hotel investment by investigating the perceptions of financiers towards tourism investment in Australia. In explaining Australia's continued reliance on foreign investors, especially for large projects in luxury markets, they identified lack of expertise in assessing such high risk investments with variable cash flows, reluctance by Australian investors to invest heavily or in the long-term in the tourism industry, the growth in publicly listed companies, which make them more accessible to foreign investment, and the "hands-off" approach to tourism policy and investment taken by the Australian government.

Daly *et al.* likened tourism investment to a gambling game, "being high risk, understood by few and with no referee". Foreign ownership of tourism facilities was also the central topic of Dwyer and Forsyth's (1994) article. They argued that the size of leakages overseas from tourist expenditure depends on how foreign owned facilities source their inputs compared to domestic owned facilities. They analysed the disbursement of prepaid and optional expenditure on a package tour to Australia to reveal that additional outflows owing to foreign ownership are quite low. A framework is provided whereby the income generating effects of foreign and domestic owned tourism facilities, in both their development and operational stages, can be determined in any country. In addition to the effects of hotel ownership structure, two articles have focused on the role of local government in hotel development. Stanton and Aislabie (1992) discussed the functions of local government regulation in encouraging resort development.

They pointed to a potential conflict, as local government is responsible not only for ensuring development is consistent with land use guidelines and does not burden the local community, but also for encouraging and promoting local economic development. Similarly, Saville (1994) identified the town planning role of local authorities in specifying land use, height, size, site cover, parking and vehicular access of developments as important influences on hotel design. Saville also examined the engineer's role in ensuring hotel operators' design standards are achieved and in offering valuable advice for the maintenance and serviceability of systems, particularly those which promote efficient energy use. Weenink (1994) argued that improperly managed energy use in the hotel sector is both unacceptable and costly and that there are many sources of helpful information and direction.

Government agencies provide professional advice and energy logging, advising on energy per room compared with similar hotels, providing more friendly and accessible electrical demand metering, and ways of reducing this demand. Hotel associations provide a centralised databank of practical information for use by hotel designers, builders, operators and owners.

Burton's (1995) article is also instructive in providing many practical ideas that can be implemented to reduce energy usage in tourist and recreational facilities. Energy conservation was also addressed by A'Vard (1996) in her case study of environmental policies at an Australian island resort. The resort was designed to be self-sufficient and to minimise impacts on one of the most delicate ecosystems on earth. A'Vard's account of environmentally friendly practices in all resort areas, including landscaping, power and water usage, noise pollution, housekeeping, front office, guest relations, concierge, marina and administration, may have practical applications for resorts generally.

Psychology of Management and Hospitality Industry

The practice of management is constantly developing, altering the nature of the demands placed on managers and skills which may be needed by them. This section considers some articles which address psychological trends, particularly the mental qualities and behaviour of managers in the hospitality industry. In 1989, Worsfold investigated the personality profile of the hospitality manager with a view to developing selection techniques that could effectively predict management performance. His study suggests that personality is considered less important than other necessary attributes such as "assertiveness, independence, mental stamina and low levels of anxiety". In addition, he found that hotel managers were more venturesome, uninhibited and imaginative than managers in other industries. Interestingly, he found that female managers had higher scores for independence and tough poise than their male counterparts. Goal-oriented management behaviour is also studied by Whitney who considers the conflicts caused by the business realities of the 1990s.

He identifies "ethical dissonance" as a source of stress; that is, mental discord in managers that arises from conflict in "what they believe" and "what they practice". Managers particularly at risk from "ethical burnout" are those with strong traditional orientation and relatively weaker career orientation. Whitney suggests that excellent managers are marked by the maturity to "hold high ethical ground under fire" as they have the internal qualities to deal with confusing external phenomena. Solutions to this increasingly common and complex problem require holistic and long-term responses and are philosophical as well as operational in nature. Managerial job stress was also studied in 1991 by Brymer *et al.* who attempt to link the relationships between perceived job stressors and experienced strain. The study contends that "managers in the hotel industry not only perceived their jobs to be stressful, but experienced numerous strains as a result of perceived stressors". Some suggestions were made for strain reduction based mostly on greater employee control over their work.

These articles infer that, although managers in the hospitality industry may possess positive psychological attributes, they perceive that their jobs are becoming more stressful. This increased stress may be caused by mental conflicts between perceptions and reality, all of which reinforce the view that the practice of management is becoming more difficult in the 1990s. This review has identified seven themes which exemplify some emerging issues of importance to the hospitality and tourism industries in recent years. The first three themes address issues facing organizations and governments in international locations. They show the wealth of new opportunities that exist for the tertiary sector in many parts of the world, but emphasize that these opportunities need to be carefully managed if they are to be sustained over the long term.

The last four themes addressed generic issues concerning planning, service, finance and management. A common message is that organizations should adopt a more planned and professional approach to managing operations in the 1990s if they are to achieve and maintain long-term success.

Management of Small Hospitality Firms

It is important to recognise that a distinct and significant range of management issues confronts small hospitality firms. Specifically, the following section considers: the role of marketing; quality management; the value and application of information technology; the relationship of business planning and small firm success; strategic management and growth; and entrepreneurship. Of necessity, the discussion of each issue is circumscribed by available space; readers are referred to Thomas (1998b) for a more comprehensive assessment.

Role Travel Industry and Tour Operators

The hotel classification systems devised and run by national hotel associations and/or government authorities are not necessarily used by travel professionals, particularly when they are dealing with clients from outside the market where the accommodation is provided. It is well known that the major Tour Operators assess prospective hotels according to their own criteria and then provide their own description in their promotional material. Reproduced below are very general descriptions given by some of the major tour operators in the UK as to what their classifications mean. In this case, *First Choice* is the most specific.

First Choice

Our universal ratings system is based on the views (at the time of Travel Industry – Hotel Guides The Official Hotel Guide (OHG) – USA This Guide is widely recognised by travel agents as a comprehensive and reliable source of information on hotels around the world.

Basic, comfortable, budget ranged

Standard popular accommodation. These hotels normally feature a selection of public areas including a restaurant

Large, modern or well-established accommodation with a wide range of facilities

High standards of comfort & service The company points out that "Accommodation of similar ratings, but in different countries, cannot always be meaningfully compared."

Thomson Holidays

Thomson T ratings are based on our annual appraisals and customers' views taken from the end of-season Customer Satisfaction Questionnaires. Hotels and apartments are rated from "2T" for no-frills, good value accommodation to "5T" for more comfort and a wider range of facilities. To a very few of our best hotels, we award a Blue Ribbon classification. These are internationally renowned luxury hotels which offer an exceptional standard of comfort. There may be some differences between accommodation that shares the same T rating category. This is where our T-plus rating can be a useful extra guide

Airtours

Our "A" ratings are awarded by specially trained Airtours staff, based on such criteria as the public area furnishings, food & drink outlets, room & leisure facilities & service. They range from AA for simple accommodation to AAAAA offering the highest quality & level of service Thomas Cook publication) of senior managers both in the UK & overseas.

As can be seen, none of these are particularly objective, but this information at least provides some insight into how the tour operators go about rating accommodation.

The Official Hotel Guide

(OHG) provides comprehensive, in depth profiles of 29 000 hotels and resorts worldwide. For over 38 years, travel professionals have relied on its unique classification system and unbiased profiles to help them successfully match their clients to the right hotel. Its rich content has made it the hotel directory that travel professionals pay hundreds of dollars to subscribe to year after year.

NorthStar, parent company of OHG, has now incorporated OHG into its Hotel & Travel Index which it claims is the industry's leading print and online hotel information source for travel professionals with 79 000 hotels online.

Views of Main Stakeholders

National Tourism Administrations (NTAs) and the World Tourism Organization (WTO): Since 1988 WTO ceased to be engaged in harmonising hotel classification standards region-wise and worldwide, partly due to the lack of coordinated and clear approach in favour of hotel classification by its Government Members and partly in response to the negative view on government intervention in this area by its Affiliate (private sector) Members representing the hotel industry. On an individual basis, however, both governments and private consultants have never ceased to approach the Organization and its Secretariat to ask for "WTO hotel classification", fielding sectoral support missions and technical cooperation to establish classification in respective countries and regions (at the time of preparing this report, a WTO-sponsored mission is taking place in Maldives), or at least for recommending WTO-trusted experts to do this job.

The Secretariat has also taken note of such projects taking place without WTO having been consulted as an intermediary. As a result, WTO has never "freed itself" from hotel classification and over the years has sent dozens of missions and consultants to interested countries and regions to do hotel and related classification, but without defining common "WTO standards" for such missions and consultants. It has been seen through this experience that, certainly, States are sovereign and that it is legitimate for their governments represented by NTAs to seek classification and that they need international referents and support in this effort. Their objectives appear to be similar to those sought by the private sector, first of all to ensure fair competition in the hotel industry, also to provide for "transparency at first sight" for the consumer.

Trade related aspects of classification have also become important for the national hotel industry, especially in developing countries where private and government investors have made important investments and great sacrifices to upgrade their hotel facilities and now expect to be fairly remunerated for this effort while observing that differences in their favour with the attributes of the same category establishments in the tourism sending countries appear to be widening. Reference to unequivocal internationally recognised standards can therefore help them defend their economic interests when it comes to negotiating contracts with wholesale tour operators.

From the WTO perspective, the lack of common understanding of hotel classification standards has also led to confusing quality aspects of the supply of hotel services (largely responding to the general question of HOW they are supplied) with physical and quantitative aspects of hotel establishments (required to respond to the question of WHAT) which normally intervene in classifications, while both aspects are important for competition. This converging approach can be seen, for example, in CEN (European Committee for Standardisation) standard EN ISO 18513-2000 followed by ISO, while WTO experience, also expressed in the WTO definition of quality in tourism, as well as national experience, such as Spanish ICTE, shows that attribution of a hotel establishment to a given category level does not imply an automatic attainment of quality criteria, although the higher the category, the higher the quality potential of the establishment. These considerations suggest that an international agreement on the meaning and guidance on hotel classification could satisfy the various demands and constitute a service to Governments, the private sector, consumers and the international community at large.

Hotel Industry-National Hotel Association involvement in classification: Within the hotel industry, views can diverge diametrically on the need (or not) for a national classification scheme. Two classic examples are provided by the national hotel associations of Israel and Denmark, the former having abandoned classification, while the latter has adopted it after operating without classification for a number of years.

The Hotel Industry in Israel-12 years without classification or grading: (Information provided by Abraham Rosental, Director-General, Israel Hotel Association-IHA)

> In April 1992, the system of grading hotels according to stars was cancelled and no other official system has taken its place.
>
> Today, twelve years later, IHA can evaluate if the decision to cancel the grading system proved itself correct or not, if the "great damage to tourism to Israel", which many in the tourism industry predicted, came true, or if perhaps the goals of cancellation were realized.
>
> In order to determine what happened since then, it is necessary to take into consideration the situation of hotels before the government cancelled the regulations for grading hotels, the situation today and expectations for the future.
>
> *Background*
>
> *(i) Government involvement:* The rationale behind the government grading system was to give official information on the standard of hotels in the country and to control the criteria for grading according to the star system. But in reality, from the 300 or so hotels in Israel, some 60 of them did not have star grading at all. They were published under the classification as 'not yet graded", "not recommended", holiday villages, camping grounds, apartment hotels, and so on.

The official information concerning their level did not exist at all. The rest of the hotels were grouped into 6 grades mainly in the 3-4 and 5 star categories. Therefore, most if the hotels were concentrated in total, into three standards of grading. For instance, there were about 80 hotels in the 4 star category and it was obvious to all that there were great differences among them and it was not possible to ascertain much about a specific hotel in a similar large group. The grading of part of the hotels did not reflect the reality.

There were hotels which, having received their high grade, lowered their standards during the years and it was difficult, if not downright impossible to change their grade. Additional difficulties in grading were discovered also in comparisons between city hotels and holiday hotels, new hotels and old hotels, small and large hotels and between regular hotels and apartment hotels and suite hotels. The grading of a hotel created certain expectations from the client. A great part of the complaints received about hotels were in the style of "this is not the service of a hotel graded X stars.... Who gave the hotel the stars..."etc....

(ii) Travel agent reaction: The situation was worsened by travel agents who published tour packages to Israel in the old and known manner of "overnight in a 4 star hotel in Jerusalem...". These travel agents did not promise a specific hotel, or certain level of services – they only promised to give the client a hotel of a certain grade and nothing more.

(iii) Hotel reaction: When there are many hotels with the same grade, it is clear that there is a very good 4 star hotel whose rates are expensive and there is a bad 4 star hotel whose rates are cheap. In fact, there have been many cases in which travel agents ordered the cheaper hotels for their clients ... however, they stood by their promise to supply a 4 star hotel, but the ones who suffered where the clients themselves who thought that this was the level of hotels in Israel.

A situation was created whereby hotels used to sell their grading and not their diverse and various services. The grade influenced the rates and it was acceptable, of course, that a higher graded hotel would receive a higher rate. As a result of this, there was a fear that lower graded hotels would not make any special effort—because in any case they would not get anything for their efforts, while hotels of higher grades also will not try improve themselves since their grades are solid and go on forever.

Healthy Competition

With the cancellation of the grading, the new name of the game is competition. Each hotel must establish itself from the aspect of the product, the service, publicity and marketing.

The Name of the Game is the Name

That is to say, that which determines now is the name of the hotel – what does it supply, what services does it give and what is its real level.

In short, does it have a good name or a bad name in the market? Indeed, with the cancellation of grading, we have witnessed a wave of renovations by hotels. Hotels began to publicise themselves more and in particular to publicise their services and their amenities which they offer their clients. They started to be concerned about their good name and understood that this would bring clients.

This healthy competition became a regular method of operation. Moreover, wholesalers abroad began to sell hotels and not grades. Israeli agents "were forced" to become better acquainted with hotels in the country and to know what they were selling – no longer to be satisfied with knowledge of the grade of the hotel alone.

Hotels entered into intensive competition, the power of the market did its work and stabilised the hotels in the country according to actual levels.

Hotels aspire to improve themselves diligently in order to put themselves in better standing in the hotel market. The Hotel Industry is no longer frozen and conservative.

Case Study: EICs and the Hospitality Industry

It is interesting that in spite of the low figures for usage only half of the EICs surveyed felt that they were under-utilized by the sector. One reason given to explain the low level of usage was that trade associations met the industry's information needs. It is important to consider this point in the light of recent research. One study which looked at the perceptions of trade and professional associations in the run-up to the single market found considerable variation in their perceptions and practices; some were extremely proactive in pointing out the implications of the European dimension while others adopted a passive role.

Robinson and Mogendorff's work seems to indicate that the main hospitality trade association in the UK adopts a more casual approach to European integration than some of its continental counterparts. This, coupled with a general shortage of sector-specific information provision, suggests that EIC inaction is inappropriate.

Perceived Needs, Costs and Publicity

EIC managers seem uncertain as to any specific information requirements which may support hospitality firms, with 38 per cent of respondents not answering this question. Of those that did, all but three felt that the information needs would differ from other sectors but few gave details. Where the answer was developed, respondents tended to emphasize sector-specific legislation such as food law and elements of health and safety. Only one centre pointed to possible value of tendering information and one mentioned support in the areas of sales and marketing.

The questionnaire survey points to some variation in the formal charging policies of EICs. Of more interest, however, is the apparent divergence between written policy and practice.

The case studies revealed clearly a desire on the part of EICs to provide a supportive and, in many respects, non-commercial service. The objective, both in principle and practice, was certainly not to maximize revenue. This generally implied a free service for straightforward requests for information and basic advice with one of the centres also providing extensive free consultancy for firms, including the preparation of business plans. Moreover, the case studies also suggested the existence of a variable tariff, articulated informally, which operated on an ability to pay basis. The main methods used to publicize EIC services are presentations, exhibitions and seminars (75 per cent), issuing press releases (42 per cent) and placing promotional leaflets in public places (38 per cent).

While these methods might reach a wide audience, it is far from certain that it would include hospitality firms. Indeed, a review of the available promotional literature suggests that, even if hospitality operators do come into contact with the material, they may not consider it appropriate for them.

Tenders Electronic Daily and Eurokom

The information yielded as a result of the two-month TED search was interesting and contrary to the perceptions of the EIC personnel interviewed who, generally, expected little from this service as far as hospitality tenders were concerned. Clearly there are logistical problems which would limit the number of firms in the UK responding to invitations to tender for services in other European countries. Nevertheless, for some operators these are not insurmountable, given adequate information and support. Since the rhetoric of EU policy on public procurement emphasizes the importance of participation from firms in different member states, informing them of the opportunities which do exist is essential.

The findings of this study suggest that few hospitality firms would currently be aware of those for their industry. For many services TED will become much more important now that the services directive is operational (July 1993). Briefly, public bodies (including private sector utilities) are required to publish all notices relating to contracts above an ECU 200 (£141,431) threshold. The impact on the hospitality industry is not yet clear (though initial indicators are discussed below) because these services are considered "residual" (Annex 1B) and are therefore subject to more limited reporting requirements. It is interesting that one of the case study centres noted that a local hotel company had used the system to promote its services abroad. Unfortunately, at this stage, the effectiveness of the initiative is not known because respondents to the Eurokom message were invited to deal directly with the firm.

The Potential Value of EICs

There are new opportunities currently emerging, particularly for contract caterers, as a result of EU moves to liberalize public procurement. By way of illustration, similar research carried out before the services directive became operational revealed a significantly lower incidence of invitations to tender for hospitality, services than those shown (16 in total for a comparable two-month period between December 1992 and January 1993). It is noteworthy that the tendering opportunities publicized through TED apply to the UK as well as continental Europe. Thus even smaller or medium-sized organizations with no European aspirations may well be missing opportunities for contracts in their domestic markets. Moreover, the expertise of EICs in terms of preparation of tenders and in identification of potential partners for consortia activity is clearly under-utilized.

The inherent advantages that larger operators enjoy are not, therefore, being challenged in spite of the availability of information and support. Prima facie, the EIC access to the Eurokom network offers further potential benefits to hospitality businesses. The example cited earlier of an hotel company informing regular EU visitors to its area of the services available at their establishment highlights how the mechanism might be used creatively as part of a marketing strategy, even by one unit operators. Equally, organizations seeking to recruit foreign nationals, perhaps on a seasonal basis, could usefully consider the network. Eurokom is currently being used for this purpose by at least some companies in other member states. It is clear that in the UK a central plank of EU policy is not, contrary to the inference from the Commission's sectoral usage statistics, achieving its goal of supporting the business development of a sector composed mainly of small firms. It may be argued that this is almost inevitable in the context of the way the network is currently organized, with each centre expected to meet the needs of all industries in its locality.

There may, therefore, be a case for specialization, with individual EICs concentrating their activity on particular groups of industries which share common features. Such an organizational change should also encourage personnel within these centres to become familiar with the needs of hospitality firms and to design more conducive promotional strategies. For many companies, such a shift in policy would, inevitably, make the appropriate EIC geographically remote. In many instances, however, EIC services such as details of directives, grant availability, industry-specific publications, Eurokom messages and TED searches, may be accessed easily by telephone.

It would appear appropriate for trade associations, as representatives of the industry, to lobby for a reconsideration of policy. Even within existing structures, there can be little doubt that the synergy created by closer collaboration between trade associations and EICs would benefit hospitality firms. Current trends within the industry point to increasing concentration which, by some accounts, has negative implications for small and medium-sized operators. Although EU policy attempts to militate against the excesses of such trends by offering support for SMEs, as far as this sector is concerned the central instrument of that policy is currently ineffective. A possible explanation for this is that firms obtain their European business information from elsewhere.

The evidence in terms of easily available sector-specific information and the lead provided by the industry's main trade association suggests otherwise. A more plausible interpretation is that firms remain inactive; neither exploiting new opportunities nor preparing for challenges. This points to greater scope for EIC involvement in supporting business development in this industry. It is argued that current organizational arrangements and lack of collaboration with representative associations is not conducive to improvement in the short term. The findings of the project also highlight lamentable omissions in current hospitality research. Prerequisites to enhancing the impact of business development strategies are, *inter alia*, a greater understanding of how small and medium-sized hospitality businesses search and process information, more detailed analysis of the effectiveness of other agencies in informing firms within the sector and an examination of alternative methods of developing information networks to communicate business opportunities. Failure to address these issues does not augur well for businesses which face an increasingly competitive environment.

Case Study: Hotel Operations and Development in North America

Marketing Strategy and Segmentation

Hotels use many different kinds of segmentation strategy. Mehta and Vera describe a five-star hotel in Singapore that has divided its market into eight segments, including individual, corporate, airline crews, and group tours. Comparing this segmentation strategy to other commonly used schemes, the authors found that the hotel's segmentation strategy method worked effectively to separate the segments on the basis of how they choose and evaluate hotels before and after their stay.

Furthermore, the study indicates that such segmentation strategies based on income and nationality are weak, while purpose of travel is an effective basis for segmentation. Hanks *et al*. report on a new pricing strategy used by firms such as Marriott that help hotels maximize revenue by offering different room products to different market segments. The author states that the key to this approach is to segment the markets and keep them segmented. For example, Marriott has set up “fenced rates” discounts for its leisure travellers, that tie them to certain restrictions such as advanced purchase and no refund.

The author suggests that this pricing strategy discourages high-rate segments from attempting to trade down because of the restrictions. A study done by Toh and Rivers suggests that frequent-guest programmes (FGP) have little effect on most travellers’ hotel choice. For those who are aware of such programmes, reasons cited for lack of use include loss of flexibility in selecting hotels, too few trips to earn anything, and unattractive rewards.

However, frequent guest programmes may be important to a select group of travellers. McCleary and Weaver note that business travellers may be willing to pay more to earn FGP benefits. The authors recommend that, because of the possible size of the segment which may be influenced by FGP programmes, it is risky for hotel chains to drop their FGP programmes unless the entire industry does so.

Customer Service and Satisfaction

Lewis and Nightingale argue that focusing on service is different from focusing on the customer. They suggest that service be defined relative to customers’ needs, and the price of a room reflect the guests’ expectations as to the desired level of service. In another study, Barsky and Labagh describe how Western hotels can emulate the service standards of Asian hotels with some additional employee training and some changes in operating procedures.

Technological Innovations

Emmer *et al*. report on a trend involving travel agents booking hotel rooms electronically via global distribution systems (GDS). The authors state that the key for travel agents to rely on GDS listings is to make sure that the rates offered electronically are complete, accurate, and the lowest available. Reid and Sandler describe other lodging trends involving technology including electronic door locks, computer modems, in-room VCRs, and in-room fax machines. The authors report that offering such innovations to save money or for the guests’ benefit tends to improve the general level of service within the lodging industry as a whole.

Another technological trend is noted by Warren and Ostergren who report that with the advent of computer technology, hotel marketers can engage in micro-marketing, where you can use databases to capture vast information on customers and market directly to their needs. Operations are in general regarded as possessing the broad characteristics of centrality and importance. They are also seen as system-led, time-constrained yet immediate entities. The principle of centrality is that operations are the central function and focus of most organizations and the means by which the consumer is provided with the product. Within the hospitality industry, this product and service delivery takes the form of a physical interaction between employee and customer. Human interaction is crucial to consumer satisfaction and its corollary, dissatisfaction, and therefore is of major concern to operations managers. The concept of importance reflects the fact that operations are an important core activity which have responsibilities for most of the organization's resources. Most management time is spent in reviewing operational changes and allocating human and financial resources to those potential changes. Operations are regarded as system-led, because operations managers are concerned with satisfying customers by ensuring that the production and service system operates efficiently. They are time-constrained because consumer satisfaction depends on delivery of the product within time parameters. Fast-food, for example, is expected to be produced quickly and efficiently. Finally, operations are regarded as immediate because they represent a pervasive system of activities affecting every area of the organization. Without operations, no product would be produced or served and no profit would be made. The immediate, all-pervasive and crucial nature of operations encourages the view that this activity should be studied as an integrated practice within hospitality management. Erection of barriers between the component activities of catering and accommodation is therefore spurious and unnecessary. However, the hospitality industry, being a service industry, must take account of the particular nature of the products and services offered, namely:

- they are perishable and cannot always be inventoried;
- they cannot usually be stored or kept for later use or consumption;
- they are often diverse and personalized in nature;
- demand can be difficult to determine and may fluctuate quite considerably, e.g. there may be a heavy demand at meal-times and none at other times of the day;
- most services cannot be transported and must be provided or utilized on site;
- most services have a high labour input.

One of the main perceived differentiators of hospitality is that its main activity is operations, to the extent that its managers are primarily concerned with operational matters. Hospitality management has, therefore, drawn heavily on the burgeoning literature on service operations management by authors such as Harris and Wild. These authors recognise that the move away from pure "production operations" (such as design and distribution) should incorporate service such as hospitals, offices and supermarkets as well as the service component of manufacturing. Harris (1989) defines operations management as "the management of a system which provides goods or services to or for a customer, and involves the design, planning and control of the system".

A central sub-theme within this discipline has been the debate in reconciling the tension between product and service standardisation and customisation. Because actual service delivery fluctuates, some argue that only accurate product specification can deliver consistent quality, especially when skilled workers (such as chefs) are in short supply. This leads to a deskilled workforce and others (such as McLaughlin, 1995) argue that standardisation and variety reduction do not offer what customers want, and deserve. These authors call for greater understanding of the requirements of mass customisation and the deterministic tools of forecasting and modelling these systems.

3

Hospitality Management: Tools and Techniques

> "True hospitality is marked by an open response to the dignity of each and every person. Henri Nouwen has described it as receiving the stranger on his own terms, and asserts that it can be offered only by those who 'have found the center of their lives in their own hearts'."
>
> —*Kathleen Norris*

Views advanced in the round table discussion are summarised under three main headings.

Course design and the skills base:

- There was general agreement that soft skills (e.g. IT skills, communication, team working, problem solving, numeracy, motivational skills, literacy) should be provided as a priority. HE should find innovative means of giving students opportunities to acquire these soft skills especially in relation to people care and management skills.
- Courses should consider the inclusion of foreign languages as a compulsory element of the curriculum.
- Language competences would greatly supported if students were given the opportunity to undertake full year placements in hotels and other tourism businesses abroad (e.g. Continental Europe).
- Universities and colleges should use semester/term-time work experience of students as an educational opportunity and bring work-based experiences to enrich student learning.
- Teaching should embrace work-related contexts where possible,

e.g. high quality case studies which apply general business skills within hospitality and tourism

- Greater clarity is required in HE and industry in relation to the balance between vocational/sector needs and academic requirements. It is important that all stakeholders appreciate that both are critical to produce high value, successful tourism.
- Greater emphasis could be given on training for a graduate's first job destination. Employers report that they need to top-up graduate skills, mainly in practical skills.
- It may be valuable for HE to undertake selection interviews as part of the recruitment process for programmes in hospitality and tourism. Interviews should aim to find the applicants who demonstrate the capacity to develop people skills.
- With an ageing population it is important to recognise that older tourists have special needs. Perhaps the sector can learn from the approaches of other service industries to address the needs of the "grey market".
- Universities could focus on producing the top-level management staff for tourism and hospitality. Students with a less academic orientation could focus on training for front-line and operational jobs.

Understanding Student and Graduate Attitudes

- It is critical that students appreciate that there is a strong practical element to their studies and future careers.
- Attitudes can be as important as the knowledge gained in studies. People management and customer care attitudes are particularly important.
- Students and new graduates should approach the industry with a positive image of its opportunities and working conditions. Currently some work experience (casual or formal requirements) gained during studies colours student views negatively through a combination of various factors including extensive work demands, low wages and relatively poor working conditions. This does little to encourage the best graduates to work in the sector.
- Graduates should understand that they will enter a sector dominated by small businesses and owner-businesses. These often possess a culture of long hours and hard physical and mental work.

Understanding Stakeholders Outside Academia

- It is important that public sector initiatives are monitored, relative to their role in management education and development. Taking over from the Hospitality Training Foundation in 2004 will be the Sector Skills Council for Hospitality, Leisure, Travel and Tourism (now established as People First) both as an agency to support the industry but also to work with to ensure positive change in attitudes and measures to increase the quality of management and management education
- Staff investment is important for sectors to demonstrate its appreciation of staff as its key resource. This means investing in staff rewards, incentives, development and working conditions to create a culture where the workforce values high quality customer care.

Most of the round table discussion centred on how HE could prepare individuals for future management. While views were diverse there was a noteworthy emphasis from many discussants on the importance of providing individuals with appropriate attitudes and aspirations to guide their career trajectories and industry vision. Thus the role of HE must be more than just to provide a skills base. The role of industry at undergraduate level was less clear and a number of initiatives for co-operation were suggested, while it was recognised that employers could help reverse negative public images of the sector by addressing issues of rewards and incentives.

Totwards Making Graduates as Hospitality Managers

There have been a number of investigations of hospitality graduate skills and the needs of the hospitality industry over a period of 20 years and it seems the same themes and concerns continue to be evident. Whilst it is to be expected there will be changes in curriculum content and industry needs over time, for example in respect of information technology, there continues to be a distinction between industry and student perceptions of what skills and roles are appropriate for graduates entering the industry.

Students have been criticised for having unrealistic expectations of the types of responsibilities they may be given and consequently the types of skills they will be expected to exercise on entering the industry (Purcell and Quinn, 1996). At the same time industry tend to discount student's formal qualifications on the grounds of lack of experience and frequently we hear the complaint that students are "over qualified but under experienced" for even entry level management positions. The analysis of the specific skill descriptions that managers ranked skills related to the interpersonal, problem solving and self-management domains as most important.

However, they tended to discount, both relevant to the other skill descriptions and compared to student perceptions, those skills associated with the conceptual and analytical domain. This is an important finding since it is these skills that are emphasised in most bachelor degree level programs and it seems judicious to consider the causes of this dichotomy. In developing this discussion three themes emerge – those of expectations, experience and education. This discussion identifies only two or three key issues relevant to each theme and does not attempt a comprehensive discourse.

Expectations

On completion of their university studies graduates have well-developed academic skills and the results of this study indicate that they have an expectation that industry will allow them to apply the conceptual and analytical skills that have been emphasised in their courses. Yet industry focuses on graduates' lack of practical experience, and perhaps youth, and insists that they commence employment in operational roles. Even high achieving students are recruited into management training schemes that consist essentially of operational experiences for the first 12 or 18 months.

This problem may be exacerbated by the fact that relatively few managers in the hospitality industry have first hand experience of tertiary education and may consequently have a poor understanding of graduate's strengths. Only about one third of the respondents to this survey had a university degree and these were concentrated in the specialist areas of human resources and marketing. The result is that graduates become frustrated that the higher order skills learned at university are not utilised by industry and anecdotal evidence at least suggests that many of them seek more challenging opportunities in other industry sectors or through further education. This represents a significant loss of investment and potential talent for the industry.

Experience

Industry justifies the need for this operational grounding on graduates' lack of experience yet many graduates claim extensive part-time work experience and have often, in addition, completed a period of internship. It is hardly surprising that some graduates perceive themselves to have already served an "apprenticeship" for management through three or four years of university study combined with the associated practical and work experience requirements of most hospitality degree programs. However, the work experience components that are common to many hospitality degrees are primarily, or even exclusively, comprised of operational experiences and rarely do students get any exposure to management activities and this would also apply to the other work experiences gained by students during the course of their studies. Thus, while graduates may have operational work experience, for access to the ranks of lower management industry is seeking higher level supervisory or specialist experience.

In part this deficiency is unavoidable because of undergraduates' youth and lack of life experience but poor curriculum design and deficient management of the educational process must also share the blame. Many undergraduate students perceive they are trapped between the need to study full-time to "get the degree out of the way" and the need to build up the kinds of industry experience they would not be allowed to experience until they have moved into full-time employment. A more co-operative and patient approach to the learning experience by universities, industry and the students themselves may be more fruitful.

Work experience of all types and particularly exposure to management decision making assists students to make sense of the theoretical material that forms the bulk of their university course. It is common to see mature age students with work and life experience and the self-management skills that come with maturity excel in university study (Hoskins *et al.*, 1997). So the quality of the university learning experience appears to be enhanced by prior and concurrent work experience.

There are potential benefits to all stakeholders in designing management development programs that include periods of academic study and practical experience that are flexible enough to enable students to benefit from both forms of knowledge development. Thus, there may be strong arguments for encouraging mature age entry to university hospitality management programs and also the increased use of part-time study options. Increased access to tertiary education in many western countries over the last decade has made it easier for mature age students to return to university study but universities can play a more active role in selling the benefits of building formal management qualifications on a solid foundation of practical experience.

Universities need to work more closely with industry and be more proactive in managing the quality, not just the quantity, of the industry experiences undertaken by students and so provide the types of experience that will be valued in graduate recruitment.

Education

The results of this study seem to suggest that the emphasis academics place on development of conceptual and analytical skills in students is, at least to some extent, unappreciated by potential employers of graduates. But, university departments delivering these programs are often involved in an internal struggle for academic respectability and must demonstrate a focus on traditional academic skills that is equivalent to other bachelor of business related programs. Thus, a substantial move away from the focus on conceptual and analytical skills, particularly in the final stages of the degree program, is not an acceptable option for the educational stakeholders in this partnership of teachers, students and employers. A partial solution is not to change the broad skill development objectives but to ensure that the learning experiences are as relevant as possible by using more case study learning approaches, more applied projects, and more mentoring and shadowing activities. None of these learning strategies are new but effective implementation of them requires more active involvement of industry.

The use of case studies has long been advocated as a means of replicating reality but they tend to either replicate the complexity of the real world, through the use of extended and detailed information, or the urgency of decision making in practice, through the imposition of time and other constraints. Rarely are they able to combine both elements. A solution may be to use more “live” case studies based on actual businesses that are willing to reveal a substantial amount of information about their strategies and operations thereby enabling students to develop a depth of understanding about the business and to observe, or even participate in, “real” business decisions.

For example, students nearing the end of their degree, when provided with sufficient information, may be able to observe or even be involved in business decisions about whether to accept a particular conference booking or how to remodel a restaurant. Students can make a positive contribution to these decisions, particularly in smaller businesses, by providing research and modelling services using university resources. The focus in this paper has been on the skills needed by graduates to get into graduate traineeships with major hospitality employers. But structured graduate programs are offered almost exclusively through the major international hotel chains in the Asia Pacific region and only a small proportion of graduates will get this opportunity.

This highlights two related issues of concern for educators – over supply of graduates and lack of transitional career opportunities. Hospitality and tourism courses have become very popular in Australian universities and recent growth in the number of graduates with a major study area in hospitality must raise concerns that the supply of graduates will outstrip demand by industry for their services. Hospitality educators can counter this problem of over supply by encouraging the establishment of more traineeships and increasing curriculum emphasis on business entrepreneurship.

In Australia there is still significant potential for university departments to work with employers who are not affiliated with major chains to create additional graduate traineeships thereby increasing the number of transitional opportunities available to the growing pool of graduates. Although traineeships with regional independent operators may not offer the glamor of the major international chains, the quality of the experience may actually be better in a small business that encourages multi-skilling and gives graduates more scope to assume responsibility.

However, not all graduates aspire to work for an employer. Many undergraduates express a desire to manage their own small hospitality business. Educators can assist them to do this by developing curriculum that encourages development of the skills needed to successfully start and manage small businesses – perhaps offering majors in hospitality entrepreneurship. Universities must change their focus from producing graduates to fill existing jobs to producing graduates who can create new jobs in a dynamic growth sector of the economy. It is a great concern that many of the strongest graduates of tertiary hospitality management programs leave the industry because of unfulfilled expectations. These results suggest that students and academics are investing time and effort in developing conceptual and analytical skills that will not, at least immediately, be valued by employers of hospitality graduates. In response, the paper has suggested a number of strategies for re-focusing hospitality curriculum, ensuring better learning outcomes for students of hospitality management, and maximising retention of graduates once they are in industry.

Most of these strategies rely on greater co-operation between education providers and industry to design educational curriculum, undergraduate industry experience programs, and graduate internships that challenge participants and maximise the learning that can be gained through the synergies of a collaborative industry-education approach.

Scenarios for Graduations to Hospitality Managers

No one way forward was agreed on the best HE approach to develop graduates for hospitality and tourism. There was consensus on the provision of management expertise and on developing positive industry employment attitudes (generally and during the students' undergraduate learning). There was further agreement that HE and industry should act as partners and recognition by employers that learning is continuous and requires their investment. These issues provided a baseline for the three scenarios which were developed post the event and which are presented below.

The authors do not claim they were articulated in the manner presented, though every attempt is made to remain true to the spirit of the contributions. However, the authors' views are likely to influence the scenarios to an extent. The intention of producing three scenarios is not to provide a definitive statement on graduateness. Scenarios are value free (i.e. none is preferable to another) and are not intended to be mutually exclusive. Each scenario gathers characteristics under three headings: individual graduate characteristics; the role of HE; and industry roles. Thus their focus is on the inputs and outcomes of the undergraduate experience. Three main scenarios are presented. The professional developer scenario emphasises an operations specialist with contemporary expertise and a strong customer focus. HE concentrates on operations management with high levels of contemporary relevance and technological expertise.

Employers invest to ensure that HE has the knowledge (and, where appropriate resources) to provide relevance to the current environment. Undergraduates are highly sensitised to industry conditions. Their operational direction requires little immediate on-the-job training. However, the need to develop generic management skills will be important to ensure career development (unless industry wishes to keep graduates in essentially technical-type positions). The management platform for a portfolio strategist is a stronger orientation in generic management. HE concentrates on developing people management skills and customer focus orientations. Graduates see hospitality and tourism management as sharing much with other sectors. They are mentally flexible across functions and hierarchies. Industry needs to invest in quality work-based learning opportunities for students and induction into operations and industry-specific technologies at the first employment stage.

These graduates aim to develop a range of expertise which suits their preferences as well as employer/industry needs. While industry leaning, and likely to join hospitality and tourism on graduation, these individuals are happy to work wherever their skills are valued. Pragmatic mavericks form the third scenario. They have a grounding in hospitality and/or tourism, but their academic education is mainly led by entrepreneurial and value-added business approaches. Operations "how to" expertise receives little formal attention, most of this being obtained in vacation employment or industry placements.

The pragmatic maverick has a highly developed set of personal skills as well as business development expertise. She or he follows a CDP agenda which reflects their personal perceptions of the benefits obtained. Their desire for a career in hospitality responds to employment packages that suit their preferred lifestyles: they may wish to work in large or small organizations, inside or outside hospitality and tourism. A variant to this profile of a pragmatist with industry leanings was also suggested. This is a non-hospitality/tourism graduate who enters employment, initially on a short-term basis. Because they enjoy working in the industry they decide to explore these career opportunities.

However, it was suggested, poor work conditions or career prospects usually mean that they (pragmatic "tourists") enjoy only a short visit before exiting the industry. That the development of managers is a key human resources concern to the future health of hospitality and tourism sectors, increasingly affected by globalisation and competitiveness, is hardly a novel conclusion. Neither astounding is the view that appropriate skills sets should be appropriate for future needs. What the review did reveal was the perception that generic management skills were very important, though there was a strong feeling that these should be applied sensitively to the vocational settings.

The desirability of close liaison between industry and HE was emphasised. This was expressed in broader terms than the reiterating requirements of high quality work experience and career advice. Graduate attitudes and skills are factors which should be nurtured from the initial career decision and throughout professional life. Given the bonds between major stakeholders and potential synergies arising from joint initiatives, there is a clear message for greater co-operation and partnerships amongst all players. A call for collaboration is, once again, nothing new, though difficult to enact in a fragmented industry. It could be argued that some public sector initiatives (e.g. Tourism Training Scotland), whilst designed to bring players together, have lacked the strategic power to concentrate on long-term issues of management development. If the current public sector focus on lifelong learning enables long-term and fundamental issues which affect both attitudes and skills development, graduates as a group and HR for the sector are likely be better placed to make a contribution to the health of this important part of society.

Understanding Multi-unit Managers and Hospitality Industry

Whilst there have a been a number of studies of what hospitality managers do at unit level (for a review of this literature see Lockwood and Guerrier, 1990), there is little or nothing known about what operations managers above unit level do. For instance, Muller and Campbell (1995) state the literature regarding multiunit (*sic*) restaurant management is surprisingly sparse given the segment's economic magnitude. Of those studies that are known, most focus on the lowest level of multi-unit management, area management. In the late 1980s Terry Umbreit and colleagues conducted a series of studies in the USA considering the responsibilities of area managers and the extent to which they were adequately prepared for their strategic role (Umbreit and Tomlin, 1986; Umbreit, 1989; Mone and Umbreit, 1989; Umbreit and Smith, 1991). This research suggested that:

- there were five dimensions of restaurant area management – financial management, restaurant operations, marketing and promotions, facilities and safety, and human resource management;
- job tasks and managerial emphasis were very different at area manager level from unit management;
- human resource management skills were a major problem for area managers;
- area managers were inadequately prepared for their multi-unit position; and
- there was a range of perceptions as to the role of multi-unit managers.

Remarkably, Muller and Campbell (1995) report a study of three levels of multi-unit management within a single, US-wide quick service restaurant chain. Their findings confirmed ambiguity as to the role of multi-unit managers. Once again human resource management skills are a major issue for this level of manager. They also confirm that the five proposed dimensions of multi-unit management indicate a moderate degree of reliability ... are useful and adequate for (further) exploratory research.

More recently, and probably for the first time in this country, Goss-Turner and Jones (1998) investigate the role of area managers in the UK hospitality industry through case studies of eight chain operations. They show that the area manager's span of control varies widely, from just three units up to 20. Likewise the organization structure of firms, notably the levels of management from unit management up to CEO may vary.

They suggest the influences on this variance in organizational form appear to be:

- strategic vision – either cost leadership or market growth through differentiation;
- branding – single brand firms organize geographically, but multi-brand firms may organize by brand or geography or both;
- age of firm – older, mature companies tend to have traditional hierarchies;
- rate of growth – some firms adding new units, and consequently adding new areas or redesignating existing ones, do not modify the span of control, but others are increasing span;
- geographical location of business units;
- size of business unit – vary in a number of different ways – sales volume, sales revenue, operating capacity, number of employees and so on. There tends to be a close correlation between these factors, i.e. the larger the physical capacity of the unit the larger its sales revenue;
- type of business unit – hotels, restaurants and pubs – have some distinctive differences;
- industry norms – most sectors have a tradition of area management and a convention as to how many units should be assigned to an area; for instance the pub sector has wider spans of control than the restaurant sector;
- uniformity of business units – units within firms may vary in size either because there is more than one brand or because of local market conditions.

Goss-Turner and Jones (1998) go on to propose that area manager behaviour is affected by:

- *span of control* – varies widely (for reasons discussed above), so behaviour with respect to the frequency and duration of their visits to units will vary as a consequence;
- *levels of management* – often only one level of manager between the area management and operations director, notionally at regional level or operations director level, and never more than two intervening levels;
- *relationship to other functional areas* – human resources, sales and marketing, and accounts interfaces varied widely in terms of the size and within the firm, and in terms of reporting relationships;

- *organizational policies* – branding tends to increase the level of centralised policy-making with the adoption of standards of performance manuals, operating manuals, rigid training programmes, and quality audits;
- *organizational culture* – younger firms, tending also to be smaller, exhibited a culture based around the strong influence of the firms' founder, whereas older and larger firms tended to be more bureaucratic, although increasingly trying to adopt a more task-based cultural orientation;
- *geographical location of business units*, which affects the frequency and duration of visits to units.

These studies, whilst interesting and valuable, do little to investigate or support the model of strategic operations management proposed above. This is because area managers are at the interface between strategic and operational management. Their role is almost exclusively concerned with implementation. However, we know almost nothing about the role and activities of more senior managers with operational responsibilities within the industry – operations directors, regional directors, brand managers, and so on. Moreover, there is anecdotal evidence to suggest that there are specialists within multi-unit firms with specific expertise in some of the strategic functions identified above, notably site selection, hotel/restaurant design, management information systems, and new product/service development. We also know nothing about their role, nor more especially their integration into a team for the achievement of strategic goals.

Towards Having an Alternative Source of Labor for Hospitality Industry

In 1994, there were more than 5 billion people in the world; these people were very unevenly distributed (de Souza and Stutz, 1994). Recent statistics show that Europe (511 million) and Russia (149 million), along with the other republics of the Soviet Union (135 million), were home to about 16 per cent; Africa (654 million) to 12 per cent; Latin America (453 million) to 8 per cent; North America (283 million) to 5 per cent; and Oceania (28 million) to less than 1 per cent of the world's population (WTTC, 1995). Given such large variations among continents, it is not surprising that national population figures show even more variability. Ten out of the world's nearly 200 countries account for two-thirds of the world's people. The ten most populous countries.

Five countries – China, India, the USA, Indonesia, and Brazil – contain half of the world's population. Approximately 21 per cent of all people live in China, 16 per cent in India, 5 per cent in the USA, and 3 per cent each in Indonesia and Brazil. Six of the top ten countries in population size – China, India, Indonesia, Japan, Bangladesh, and Pakistan – are in Asia. Only three of the ten most populous nations are considered to be developed (the USA, Russia, and Japan). If we look into the population distribution by region, it becomes apparent that most people are concentrated in a few parts of the world. Four major areas of dense settlement are East Asia, South Asia, Europe, and the eastern USA and Canada.

In addition, there are minor clusters in Southeast Asia, Africa, Latin America, and along the US Pacific coast. The United Nations projects world population at 6.1 billion in 2000 and 8.5 billion in 2050. Almost all of this increase will occur in the developing countries. The largest absolute increase is projected for Asia, reflecting its huge population base. Future population growth will further accentuate the uneven distribution of the world's population.

Unemployed Highly Skilled and Educated Labor in the World

It is pertinent to note that education and training are often the keys to employment, but in developing countries many remain unemployed despite, or because of, their high level of education. In Asian countries, the least educated often have the lowest recorded unemployment rates, since a majority are involved in subsistence activities such as farming. Unemployment in the selected countries by educational level. In India, while the unemployment rate in 1989 for people with no education was 2 per cent, that for those with secondary education was 9 per cent, and for university graduates 12 per cent. In Bangladesh, about 40 per cent of people with a master's degree are either unemployed or underemployed. In Thailand during 1973-1983, unemployment rates among university graduates ranged from 20 per cent to 35 per cent. In Africa, too, secondary school graduates are more likely to be unemployed than those with less education. Graduate unemployment, not yet as high as in some Asian countries, is expected to rise in the years ahead with cuts in recruitment to government service, where many graduates would previously have expected automatic employment.

The current worry regarding the labor shortage can be solved by using these unevenly distributed labor forces throughout the world. The labor shortage in the international market, and in the hospitality industry particularly, means that there is a shortage of skilled labor, not unskilled labor forces. There are plenty of unskilled workers who want to have a job in the world.

Case Study: Flexibility in NSW Registered Clubs

Methodology

The results presented in this paper were obtained from a survey of registered clubs in NSW undertaken in June 1996. The sample comprised 1,381 member clubs of the NSW Registered Clubs Association of NSW (RCA). This Association has, as members, over 90 per cent of all registered clubs operating in NSW and the ACT. Very small clubs constitute the majority of clubs which do not belong to the RCA. The manager of each registered club in the sample was sent a copy of the questionnaire, a freepost reply envelope, and an explanatory letter from the researcher. A reminder letter was sent to all registered clubs two weeks after the initial posting. There were 435 usable responses from the survey, representing a response rate of approximately 32 per cent.

The survey collected demographic details and information about employment relations in registered clubs, including the level of unionisation, the determination of wages, the extent of industrial disputes and the type of employment in the sector. SPSS was used to calculate frequencies, percentages, means and standard deviation for the data collected from the survey. To gain an insight into areas of labour flexibility that registered club managers thought were of particular importance, managers were asked to rate the importance of five labour flexibility variables proposed by Rimmer and Zappala (1988). Rating took place on a modified Likert scale of 0 to 10. A variable of no importance was rated 0, while a variable of a very high importance was rated at 10. The five labour flexibility variables were:

- the ability to hire and fire to suit the prevailing economic conditions;
- the ability to adjust the hours worked by employees; the ability to extend the range of tasks undertaken by employees;
- the ability to adjust wages to suit the prevailing economic conditions; and
- the ability to consult and negotiate directly with employees.

Having determined the importance placed on the different aspects of flexibility it was then necessary to determine how the managers perceived that awards and trade unions impacted on these flexibility variables. To determine the impact of awards and trade unions, managers were asked to rate the extent to which they thought the existence of awards and trade unions restricted their ability to achieve flexibility in the five areas mentioned earlier. Rating took place on a modified Likert scale with a rating of 0 to 10.

Results

The largest number of respondents to the survey were bowling clubs, which constituted 34 per cent of all clubs. The RSL/RSM/ex-services and golf clubs were the next most represented registered clubs, accounting for 21 and 20 per cent respectively. Football and surf/lifesaving clubs only accounted for 5 per cent of all clubs. The miscellaneous category of clubs, which included yacht clubs, businesses clubs, ethnic clubs etc., accounted for 20 per cent. Approximately 31 per cent of respondent registered clubs were situated in the Sydney Metropolitan region.

The rest of the registered clubs were spread over the state, ranging from 13 per cent in the Hunter region to 2 per cent in the Far West region. These figures suggest that Sydney registered clubs were slightly under-represented in this study. The variability in club turnover was considerable with a range from $0.2 million to $45.3 million. The average turnover for registered clubs in this survey was $3 million per annum. The registered clubs surveyed employed a total of 12,672 people, with an average number of employees per registered club of 29. The importance of the labour flexibility variables. It is clear from the responses that labour flexibility is valued by responding club managers. The variables considered to be the most important were the abilities to adjust working hours, to extend the range of tasks performed by employees and to hire and fire to suit the prevailing economic climate. All these variables had a mean score of over 8, indicating a high level of importance to clubs. The ability to adjust working hours was considered the most important variable. For this variable, 91 per cent of registered club managers rated the importance at over 5, resulting in a mean rating of 9.1.

This rating is to be expected, since the demand for the services offered by a registered club can be highly variable. High variability exists both within a day and over longer periods. Variability on a daily basis exists because there are particular times of a day which are quiet and other times when patronage is at a peak, for example, at mealtimes or when entertainment is provided. Variability exists over a longer period due to weekends, holidays or the occurrence of a particular event. In general, it is possible for registered club managers to plan for this variability; however, there are times, due to unforeseen circumstances, when attendance may vary significantly from the expected patronage. The ability to alter the range of tasks was given a rating of over 5 by 85 per cent of registered clubs.

This variable had a mean rating of 8.8. This is a valued feature for registered clubs. Multiskilling is highly prized and encouraged in most registered clubs. Due to the variable nature of demand, a staff member in a particular area of a registered club can often be required to work in another area. The ability to hire and fire, with 77 per cent of registered clubs giving a rating of over 5, had a mean rating of 8.2. In common with most other businesses, the ability to hire and fire staff is considered to be very important. The achievement of flexibility in this area is likely to be perceived as important in order to ensure management prerogative. The ability to consult and negotiate with employees was rated the fourth most important variable.

Approximately 67 per cent of registered club managers gave a rating of over 5 for this variable, with a mean rating of 7.7. Somewhat surprisingly, the least important variable was considered to be the ability to alter wages to suit the prevailing economic conditions. For this variable 47 per cent of clubs gave a rating of over 5, with a mean rating of 6.3. This was a surprising result for two reasons. First, registered clubs, like other hospitality industries, are a labour intensive industry and therefore wages would be a relatively high proportion of total costs when compared with other industries. For example, labour costs in clubs are approximately 26 per cent of operating costs compared with 16.6 per cent for the construction industry and 8.5 for wholesale trade (ABS, 1997). Second, the deregulation which has occurred in the hospitality industry should have made registered clubs more aware of their cost structure.

This was also an important result since the major criticism of awards is that they impose wages which impinge on the ability of business to maintain viability. But, according to the registered clubs in this sample, there were more pressing concerns in running their clubs than gaining downward wage flexibility. This lack of concern may be explained by the highly casualised nature of registered clubs. Approximately 56 per cent of the workforce in the sector are employed on a casual basis and are paid an hourly rate. Registered clubs, by adjusting the hours worked by casuals can, to a certain extent control total wage costs.

Results in Hospitality Occupation Preferences

The first set of analyses involved the set of service response styles. A principal components factor analysis of these 12 responses revealed two interpretable factors with eigenvalues greater than unity. The first factor accounted for approximately 30 per cent of the variance and loaded positively on E, F and J and negatively on A and L. This factor has thus been labelled "the avoidance factor". The second factor accounted for approximately 14 per cent of the variance and loaded on items D and J, and was thus labelled "the information-seeking factor". Each of these two sets of responses has been summed and used in subsequent analyses.

Analysis of variance (ANOVA) procedures have been used in this study so as to examine differences between these two service response styles. ANOVA procedures have also been used to examine the set of hospitality/tourism industry occupational preferences, and also the hospitality/tourism industry work context preferences. Present results from the analysis involving occupational preferences and indicate significant differences between these various hospitality/tourism industry occupations. An inspection of means here indicates the position of manager to be most favourably regarded. Other favoured roles involved professional and tourist guide. Among these potential employees the least favoured roles were plant/machine operators, labourers, service workers and interpreters. There were also significant differences found between the various hospitality/tourism industry work context preferences.

The most popular work context involved resorts, hotels, tourist attractions and bars/clubs. The least favoured contexts include caravan parks, interpreting and service industries. Principal components factor analysis has also been applied to the set of employment preferences. Two factors have been found from this analysis with eigenvalues greater than unity, accounting for 23 per cent and 17 per cent of the variance. The first factor loaded on items involving rural and light industries, the industries traditionally providing employment for the region, and was labelled traditional industries factor. The second factor loaded on items such as tourism, hospitality and retail industries and was thus labelled the hospitality tourism/retail factor. Multiple regression analysis has been used in this study so as to investigate the predictive capacity of each of the two employment preference factors and also the seek information response factor as criterion variables.

Higher levels of interest in the traditional industries employment and lower levels of interest in hospitality/tourism/retail employment were found to be significantly associated with the avoidance response style. The function was found to be significant at 0.0001. Higher levels of hospitality/tourism/retail employment were found to be significantly related to the seek information response style. This function was, however, significant only at the 0.1 level. Multiple regression analysis procedures were also applied to the hospitality/tourism industry occupational preferences, using both the avoidance and the seek information response styles as criterion variables. The function involving the avoidance response style was found to be significant.

This analysis revealed that lower levels of interest in public relations and being a professional, together with higher levels of interest in technician and labourer occupations were found to be associated with the avoidance response style. Multiple regression analysis procedures were also applied to the hospitality/tourism work context preferences, again using both the avoidance and the seek information response styles as criterion variables. Again only one function was found to be significant, involving the avoidance response styles. It was found that a lessened interest in tour operations and resorts was found to be significantly associated with the avoidance response style. Finally multiple regression analysis has been applied to the set of hospitality/tourism industry employee service quality ideals, using both response styles as criteria variables. Both analyses produced significant functions. The analysis revealed that lower levels of assent to ideals involving being calm in a crisis and neat appearance together with higher levels of assent to ideals involving being independent and being blunt were found to be predictive of the avoidance response style.

The second analysis revealed that assent to the ideal involving positive attitudes was found to be predictive of the seek information response style. This study has investigated major response styles among a sample of potential hospitality/tourism industry employees. In particular, individuals were asked to respond to a situation wherein they as reception staff were asked to react to a guest complaint about accommodation. Respondents rated preferred problem-solving response styles that could be used with the tourist making the complaint. Also measured were a range of employment preferences and service quality ideals. Perhaps the most striking finding from this study involved the isolation of two major response styles as perceived alternatives when responding to guest complaints. Reception and public relations staff in hospitality institutions were regarded as having two basic response alternatives when dealing with difficult situations: to be helpful and seek information about the problem, and to be unhelpful.

Thus these potential employees, if faced with visitor contact as part of hospitality/tourism employment, may either be helpful or on the other hand, offer no assistance or even add to the customer's sense of conflict. The latter group should engender concern among human resource managers charged with the selection of new employees. It would thus seem to be important that human resource managers should investigate problem-solving response styles in a variety of creative ways among potential staff, so as to select those individuals more likely to be involved in exchanges that lead to positive and satisfying feelings among guests.

Moreover, human resource managers may need to be more active in the dissemination of information to schools and potential employees about the employee attributes more likely to be successful in a tourism/hospitality career. This study has examined the relative attractiveness of occupations found within the tourist/hospitality industry. Clearly these potential employees preferred the prospect of employment in which they would exercise the function of a manager, a professional or a tour guide. Thus they indicated a desire for career positions or those such as tour guide wherein a high level of social interaction and knowledge were required.

While it is probably not surprising that many school leavers do not aspire to the role of labourer at the end of their school years, it perhaps should be a matter of concern to the industry that positions requiring a relatively high degree of technical skill are deemed so lowly. Again the hospitality/tourism industry may have to address a knowledge gap among school leavers and potential employees, pointing out that such technical functions are regarded highly, are important in the smooth functioning of the industry and can be both satisfying and well paid as an occupational option. Similarly, for the range of hospitality/tourism industry work contexts, the industry may need to be more diligent in regard to information packages supplied to schools and careers counsellors so that functions such as interpreting are not regarded as marginal or transitory, but rather essential in the provision of high quality service to members of various cultural and language groups. This study has found some evidence to suggest that there is a relationship between preferred work context and type of service response preferred in the context of a guest complaint.

Those individuals who would prefer the more traditional industries of the region, and not the newer and now more dominant hospitality/tourism industry, would elect for a service response style that avoided the offering of effective assistance. On the other hand those who do indicate an employment interest in the hospitality/tourism industry revealed a much more positive response style. These findings may indicate among the traditional industry supporters a disinterest and perhaps an antipathy towards tourists and tourism. Such an attitude among many school leavers if unaddressed by civic leaders and the industry, may have serious and detrimental consequences for the local industry if such individuals find hospitality/tourism to be their only realistic employment option. Those individuals who would elect for the avoidance response style preferred technical operations or labouring, and perhaps wisely eschewed areas such as public relations.

They also wished to avoid work contexts such as resorts and tour operations. However such individuals may be surprised to discover that technical staff of resorts, hotels and transportation organizations do sometimes have service encounters with visitors. Labourers also in contexts such as resorts, on occasion, have contact with tourists who sometimes try to seek out the authentic, the local resident with the "inside" knowledge of the district's attractions and regional culture. In such situations an avoidance or hostile response type can only detract from the visitors' experiences and thus the destination's reputation. Finally, service quality elements were examined together with each response style. The avoiders espoused being blunt and being independent, and rated very lowly being calm in a crisis and neat appearance. Such a configuration of elements may lend weight to the suggestion that avoiders are essentially negative in their attitudes towards tourism and tourists. Approaches such as being blunt may be regarded by such individuals as a polite way to be insulting, whereas the lessened desire to be calm in a crisis and of neat appearance may result from an interpretation that this is generally what avoiders perceive tourists as valuing most in hospitality industry staff. In contrast, those with the generally more positive problem-solving response styles elected for the global service quality dimension of positive attitudes, a dimension which seems to be lacking among the avoiders. This study has revealed results which suggest that potential hospitality/tourism industry employees see responses to the guest complaint as falling into two types, one involving avoidance and the other involving the gathering of more information as the first step in the solution of the problem. The study has highlighted a range of human resource management variables found to be associated with these two response styles. These results suggest that there are some potential employees who will respond to the guest complaint in a positive and helpful manner, and others who may respond in such a way that the grievance may be escalated and may lead to a situation in which the guest could conclude that the hotel or institution exhibits a poor standard of service quality. Such conclusions on the part of guests may have major negative ramifications for the institution and for the individual staff member. This study represents an initial step in the investigation of service quality responses to the guest complaint.

It has only investigated one type of guest complaint. Moreover the sample is derived from one particular culture and geographical region. It should be noted that further investigation needs to be accomplished in this area, focusing on a wider variety of predictor variables in a range of hospitality/tourism industry contexts around the world. In such a manner more helpful and positive responses to guest complaints can be established to the benefit of the guest, the individual staff member and the institution.

"Experience Rules" in Hospitality Industry

Given this vision, we have identified crucial actions that hospitality and leisure providers must begin taking now to prepare for an experience-based competitive landscape:

- *Uncover the unexpected.* Companies must avoid getting absorbed in only delivering what their guests ask and expect of them. Hospitality and leisure companies must act on their potential to excite, delight, and bring surprising pleasures. The key is uncovering unexpected needs and desires, and acting on them. Companies must marshal their creative resources to identify areas and innovations that cause customer excitement. Excitement quality becomes the key motivator of return visits by customers. The greatest customer satisfaction and loyalty will come to hospitality and leisure companies that build a culture of uncovering and delivering the unexpected.
- *Become agile: integrate your businesses.* Achieving success in a world where "Experience rules" will come only to those who can act quickly and with agility. This is easier said than done for enterprises with a wide range of businesses, brand assets, locations, and physical assets. It will require a centralized, fully integrated business infrastructure across business units, brands, and locations. This business infrastructure will standardize all back-of-house and key front-of-house functions, placing them on a single technology platform and implementing a common business process and organizational framework. At the same time, it must allow for great flexibility at guest touch points and in service delivery. Additionally, companies should consider whether owning all assets and operating the full value chain are indeed critical. Rather, companies should mobilize a combination of providers who can together deliver the customer's experience.
- *Pay global attention.* Success for hospitality and leisure companies will largely depend on their ability to serve an expanding variety of cultures, languages, personal tastes, and global markets. Specifically, those who aren't already doing so should: provide experiences in a manner that respects a guest's country of origin and cultural nuances; serve the local traveler when operating in a foreign market; and extend the global reach of the portfolio via direct acquisition, marketing consortia, brand sharing agreements, franchising, and organic growth.
- *Invest in your guest.* For hospitality and leisure companies, the travel experience is the platform for owning the customer relationship. It is during the experience that providers interact with their customers repeatedly over an extended period of time. Providers must combine an institutional memory of these interactions with new media and technologies to enable on-

going, two-way communication throughout the travel experience. They should begin by defining an overall guest interaction framework to deliver customized experiences to a broad consumer base. At the same time, they must begin to implement an information collection infrastructure that creates a learning cycle that inputs data continuously and in real-time from all customer touch points.

- *Rethink revenues.* Hospitality and leisure companies should begin to rethink their approaches to managing shareholder value. This is because traditional revenue streams, pricing models, and cost management will be transformed in the transition to "Experience rules". They should consider moving from the practice of revenue management into the practice of return on investment management, in which desired returns will be the basis for pricing all components of the guest experience.
- *Polish your GEMs.* Hospitality and leisure companies must transform their staff members into Guest Experience Managers (GEMs). To do so they should first create a work environment that fosters dignity, pride, and satisfaction. In addition, they should conduct training that builds a thorough knowledge of the product and service offerings and encourages the anticipation of guest needs. Reducing the costs of turnover, training, and transaction processing will be key goals. These capabilities will be increasingly important because of the high costs of training the industry's large, geographically dispersed workforce to be highly knowledgeable about customized products and services.
- *Extend the experience.* In the world of "Experience rules", the experience doesn't just begin when the guest departs from home or end upon his or her completion. For some customers, part of the fun will be the virtual experience while planning the trip or reliving the experience – for example in videos, chat groups, and Web sites. A travel game Web site or a virtual tour can deliver a sample of the excitement of being there, and interactive content will allow customers to test experiences in the comfort of their homes. Companies must powerfully convey the flavor of their experiences (and thus, their brands) online and via other multimedia outlets.

It is significant to mention that drumbeat of globalization and technological advancements is growing louder and can no longer be overlooked by today's hospitality and leisure providers. That's because consumers won't let them. Increasingly customers will demand that providers' products and services be tailored to their individual tastes. Technology innovations, particularly around the Internet, will make mass personalization possible.

During the next decade and beyond, hospitality and leisure companies will undergo a crucial transformation. They will de-emphasize standard offerings for business and leisure travelers and, instead, embrace business models that focus on individually customized travel experiences. As a result, in 2010, travel was expected to about engaging in powerful, seamless personal experiences that are carefully tailored to the tastes and demands of individual travelers.

Placement Process in Hospitality Industry

The first aim of this study was to assess Melbourne and international students' detailed perceptions of the cooperative education placements on international level. Although the expectations from placements' social climate by students of the four international institutions was similar overall, their expectations varied across specific social climate dimensions. These findings indicate detailed information about students' expectations of their cooperative education placements in industry. Unlike the various findings of the studies reviewed earlier, the results of this study indicate specific areas of differences in perceptions. Some differences in scores, notably in the involvement, peer cohesion, task orientation, work pressure, and control dimensions were evident between the Melbourne and The Hague students, and in the Autonomy between Melbourne and Strathclyde students than in other dimensions. Previous studies, although less detailed, point to similar conclusions.

Knutson (1989) and Charles (1992) for example, found that hospitality and tourism students are concerned with the issues associated with working in these industries, such as lack of challenge and lack of management involvement. It is safe to suggest, therefore, following Pavesic and Brymer (1990) and Sarabakhsh *et al.* (1989), that students' expectations of industry may affect their actual perception of the industry after their graduation.

This in turn can affect their work satisfaction and successful professional development. The second aim of this study was to find out if the Melbourne students' expectations differed from those of students from the other participating institutions. Melbourne students expected higher involvement, greater peer cohesion, more task orientation, more work pressure and greater control when compared with The Hague students. They also expected less autonomy on the job as compared with the Strathclyde students. However, in general, as can be observed the Melbourne students' expectations did not differ much from other students, with the exception of the The Hague students' expectations. This could be attributed to a few factors.

First, the The Hague students' scores could be a reflection of the different perception of the social climate of the work environment of their placements due to the different organizational socialisation processes as pointed out by Dean (1983). For example, different supportive work settings that help promote students' independence can socialise them in learning their new occupational roles on many different levels. Although the four samples were matched on the course curriculum content and the timing of the cooperative education experience, there could be some differences in curriculum delivery especially in student orientation and preparation before placements occurred.

Secondly, there could be cultural differences between the English speaking students and native language speaking students. The values attached to organizational socialisation in general could differ.

Third, the assumption that the The Hague students were fluent in English and therefore would have no problem in understanding the questionnaire could be wrong. This should be verified with translation and back translation of the WES to the Dutch language. The third aim of this study was to find out which aspects of the work environment of the hospitality organizations need to be addressed in preparing students for work experience. The differences in the work environment dimensions (involvement, peer cohesion, autonomy, task orientation, work pressure, control) highlight the need for both educational institutions and industry management internationally to address the following issues:

- reducing excessive work demands and time pressure. The hospitality industry is very labour-intensive and is perceived as demanding. Students could be briefed on the specific demands. Their placements would perhaps consist of progressively more demanding tasks, beginning with the tasks that are realistically attainable by students during the early stages of their placements.
- improving managerial support may include an increase in communication between cooperative education placement officers and supervisors responsible for students during their placements. Development of clear policies which could guide students before placements and monitoring of these policies during placements could eventuate in more student involvement in each organization's functioning and greater cohesion between students and staff.

- altering managerial control mechanisms such as rules and procedures during student placements. Managerial control mechanisms need to be applied with a greater degree of flexibility. Greater student participation in decision-making, especially in utilising their enthusiastic approaches to problem solving learned during the academic year may result in students having more positive perceptions of supervisory control.

Despite the similarities and differences between students' expectations at the international level, the question arises if these expectations will be met while the students are on their placements, or are students' expectations unrealistic? If they are not met then, as evidence by Barron and Maxwell (1993), West and Jameson (1990) and Purcell and Quinn (1995) suggests, the students may still be discouraged from entering their chosen professions after graduation. Therefore, the cooperative education experience may be a crucial factor for students in making this decision. In short, the findings just described show that students' expectations from cooperative education placements can be assessed in detail by measuring their expectations from the social climate of their industrial placements' work environment.

As Purcell and Quinn (1995) noted, the students returned from placements "...to their course more mature, with considerable insight into the industry; but this insight often crystallised in disillusion and a desire to use their experience and education to find employment in another sector of the economy" (p. 16). The assessment of the students' expectations, therefore, may help in predicting their subsequent career orientation in hospitality industries and elsewhere. While the results of the present study point to many differences and similarities between international samples, they can not be generalised beyond the samples studied. The samples were drawn from four institutions, and although they incorporated four similar courses of study, the research needs replication with varied populations and institutions. For example, data comparisons should be done based on the USA samples, since there is also close cooperation between the USA institutions and the Victoria University of Technology. Although international cross-sectional research is complex, costly and difficult to execute, this study suggests some directions for meaningful exploration of the role of students' own perception of cooperative education. As Linke (1988) pointed out "...there is no ideal structure and very little evaluative information exists to indicate clearly the practical advantages and limitations between alternative approaches with respect to the multiple outcomes expected of students, employers and staff" (p. 30).

Therefore, further longitudinal and cross-sectional research is required to assess and compare the perceptions of the work environment of various academic institutions and employers in industry. Also, there is a need not only to compare various student populations to one another over time, but also to find out if those students who stayed with the chosen industry after graduation were also the same students whose cooperative education expectations were met by subsequent experience in industry.

Counter-Arguments to the Need for Deregulation in Hospitality Industry

Despite the arguments advanced by proponents of deregulation, other commentators have argued that the centralised system was able to deliver labour market flexibility. For example, Callus *et al.* (1991) in a comprehensive study of over 2,000 Australian workplaces noted that only 6 per cent of workplace managers viewed awards as a constraint in pursuing efficiency changes and that only 14 per cent indicated changes could not be undertaken because of unions. Morehead *et al.* (1997) in an equally comprehensive study had a similar finding. They established that 9 per cent of private workplaces with 20 or more employees stated they were prevented from making changes because of awards and/or agreements.

In addition, they found that managers in 17 per cent of private workplaces stated they could not undertake changes because of employees, trade unions or union delegates. Rimmer (1991) raised objections to the assumption of wage and procedural inflexibility of the centralised system by noting there was scope for enterprise bargaining under the centralised system and that these provisions have been extensively used. As well, Rimmer (1998) and Hawke (1998) point out that awards were often augmented through informal enterprise and individual bargaining at the enterprise level. With regard to numerical flexibility, the Industrial Relations Reform Act 1993 (Cth) extended the constraints on unfair dismissal and requirements relating to information, consultation and severance pay to apply to non-award employees.

This meant that it was not awards that were inhibiting flexibility but rather legislation applying to all employees. The Workplace Relations and Other Amendments Act 1996 (Cth) which was intended to further deregulate the system through the introduction of individual contracts, known as Australian Workplace Agreements, will retain a number of standards in relation to unfair dismissal and severance pay clauses, although rights to consultation and information may be removed (Wailes and Lansbury, 1997). Work time and functional flexibility have been increasingly facilitated by many changes to the relevant provisions incorporated into awards since the 1980s. For example, there are now numerous awards which no longer specify premium payments for work during non-standard hours (Wooden, 1995). The increased numbers of casual and part-time employees have also resulted in increased work time flexibility.

The Need for Empirical Research

Lack of empirical support for the supposed benefits of increased flexibility fostered through deregulation and numerous criticisms of the post-Fordist paradigm have not prevented the promotion of enterprise bargaining amongst policy makers in Australia. A major reason may be that enterprise bargaining is consistent with a neo-classical economic approach. The neo-classical economics agenda with its reliance on market forces, adopted by the federal and state governments since the 1980s, strongly supports the pursuit of increased labour market flexibility through deregulation. Given this debate about the need for deregulation in the pursuit of flexibility, the aim of this research was to determine whether deregulation was necessary for the attainment of flexibility.

A sector of the tourism and hospitality industries was chosen for this study since the proponents of deregulation have argued that service industries are particularly concerned with the attainment of labour flexibility. Flexible work arrangements which reflect long trading hours (up to 24-hour-a-day service) are said to be necessary to ensure a competitive business environment (Commonwealth Department of Tourism and Department of Industrial Relations, 1992). Other characteristics of the hospitality sector, including fluctuations in demand, the existence of penalty rates, weekend work and work outside of "normal" hours, simultaneous production and consumption of service and labour intensity, ensure the pursuit of flexibility is a high priority for enterprises.

The Registered Clubs Sector

This study focuses on one sector of the hospitality industry, the registered clubs sector of NSW. Registered clubs in NSW which operate under the Registered Clubs Act 1976 NSW, have an unusual ownership structure and business goals. Registered clubs are unusual since they are non-profit organizations formed by groups of people who share a common interest and who have come together to pursue or promote that interest. Another unusual characteristic of registered clubs is that they are governed by a board of directors who are responsible for the formulation of policy and for ensuring that these policies are carried out by the management.

The manager/secretary, also known as the chief executive officer, is the person responsible for the day to day running of the registered club and its staff. Directors are not expected to be involved in the daily operations of the registered club nor its staff. Trade unions and industrial tribunals have been keen to ensure employees only deal with one person to avoid confusion and to maintain clear lines of communication (Registered Clubs Association of NSW, 1990). The manager/secretary is regarded by the industrial tribunal and trade unions as the employer. Registered clubs cover a vast array of interests including sporting, social, community and ethnic interests. In Australia, registered clubs are major social outlets for people and in a number of cases, provide significant funds for community projects. The majority of funds are raised through the provision of gaming facilities. In addition, clubs also serve food and beverages and in many cases entertainment is also provided to patrons.

The types of employment in clubs, which includes management, bar, kitchen and clerical staff, reflect the range of services offered by clubs. The development of the registered club industry has proceeded differently in the various Australian states and territories. NSW was, and still is, clearly the most developed state with regard to registered clubs in Australia. In NSW, there are over 1,500 clubs (40.5 per cent of all clubs in Australia), generating a turnover of over $20 billion annually and employing over 63,000 people (67.3 per cent of all employment in Australian clubs) (ABS, 1994).

Labour Market Characteristics

There are a number of awards covering both club management and employees within registered clubs. These awards are indicative of the broad range of occupations involved in registered clubs. In NSW, for example, the awards that apply to various managers and employees within the registered clubs include the club managers' and club secretaries' (state) award, the club managers' and club secretaries' superannuation (state) award, the club employees' (state) award, and the musicians' (live performance) (state) award.

Casual employment is a major component of the workforce in this sector. Approximately 56 per cent of staff in registered clubs were employed on a casual basis in 1996. A further 5 per cent were employed on a part-time basis (Buultjens, 1996a). This sector has had increasing competitive pressures placed upon it by the regulatory changes in Queensland and Victoria. In the early 1990s, clubs in Victoria and Queensland were, for the first time, allowed to introduce gaming machines onto their premises. Many NSW registered clubs, particularly in border regions, found it increasingly difficult to remain profitable with this increased competition from interstate clubs. As a consequence, a number of NSW registered clubs which profited from the patronage of customers from Victoria and Queensland have undergone a substantial reduction in income.

Another important impact on the registered clubs sector in NSW has come from the deregulation which has taken place in the hospitality industry as a whole. In most states, hotels have been allowed to operate on Sundays and introduce gaming machines. This has resulted in registered clubs losing some of their competitive advantage. In a further loss to competitive advantage, in November 1996, the NSW Government gave notice of its intention to introduce legislation which would allow hotels to introduce the same type of gaming machines as those used on registered clubs' premises.

4

Focus on Global Hospitality Industry Customers and Service Quality

"Eating, and hospitality in general, is a communion, and any meal worth attending by yourself is improved by the multiples of those with whom it is shared."

—*Jesse Browner*

Understanding Consumer Behaviour and Customer Service

The UK hospitality system has tended to rely on reactive methods of gauging customer reactions to products and services. Jones and Ioannou investigated the methods used by UK-based international hotel chains and found that some of them were inadequate as a means of tracking guest satisfaction levels. They suggest ways of systemizing customer response and hotel chain-wide satisfaction indexing, using a "scorecard" system.

The important links between customer expectations, choice and hotel guest satisfaction represent significant operational and managerial challenges and it is clearly essential to interpret guest requirements in a meaningful way. For example, Weaver and Oh undertook a survey of US business travellers and constructed a demographic profile which enabled them to compare the priorities attached to 56 hotel services and amenities by frequent and infrequent business travellers.

This kind of data can also be collated from internal information sources and Sparks reports on an Australian study of guest history data which reveals that they are widely used by hotels but that the extent of the utilization is limited. She suggests that improved usage could be obtained by:

- introducing specific guest history training modules;
- an internal service orientation that emphasizes the use of guest history information to improve customer service;
- the use of guest history data to improve guest retention rates.

Larsen and Aske apply a theatrical analogy to describe guest-customer relations and interactions. They contend that on the theatre stage, as well as in the "service theatre", customer satisfaction is dependent on the actors and their performance. The authors use a framework that draws from Aristotle's *Peri Poietikes* to review service issues in the Norwegian hospitality industry. The attitudes and behaviour of "actors" or service staff is a vital ingredient of good customer services and Sparrow *et al.* present findings from a study of food service staff that highlights many general behavioural differences between novice and experienced personnel. They conclude by offering a framework of different customer-situation contexts in which service behaviours can be tailored. Larsen and Bastiansen present an instrument for measuring service attitudes, the service attitude questionnaire, designed to capture cognitive, emotional and behavioural aspects of service attitudes. The authors use this to explore service attitudes in Norwegian private sector hotels and restaurants compared with the service attitudes of public sector workers in nursing.

Understanding Service Research and Customer Orientation

Lockwood notes that to deliver consistent quality to hospitality customers, it is necessary to be able to identify aspects of the service encounter that bring about satisfaction or dissatisfaction. In this context, he explains how to apply a technique for recording success and failure in service situations. Randall and Senior discuss the same issue and focus on a technique for detecting and preventing problems which may arise during service consumption. Sparrow and Wood concentrate on the likely effects of actions by employees and highlight the importance of eliciting the knowledge and beliefs which employees use to guide their decisions at work. They discuss the psychological techniques needed to do this and present the findings of a study in the form of "mental maps" which reflect how food service staff interpret different service situations.

The link between guest expectations, the services and amenities which are provided, and guest satisfaction, is difficult to interpret and predict. One way of overcoming this problem is to establish informal networks of intelligence by encouraging employees to talk to guests and feed back their comments. Nibblelink and Teare explain how this system operates at the Holiday Inn hotel, Brussels, in relation to fine-tuning guest services for international business travellers. In a different context, Gilmore and

Carson discuss ferry travel and passenger reactions to the services offered on British and Scandinavian operated ferries. They conclude their study by nothing the need to adapt generic offerings to suit specific routes and local customer preferences.

A similar approach has been used very successfully by Hilton International to customize its hotel services. Bould *et al.* explain the concept of "service branding" which Hilton uses to tailor its guest services to geographical and culturally different markets. Its Japanese service brand *Wa No Kutsurogi* provides an interesting example of how Hilton has packaged its guest services to appeal directly to Japanese tourists and business travellers. Hirst explains the framework which Hilton used to review and re-focus its operations so that they are "service-driven" while Larsen and Rapp and Price provide parallel case examples from a cruise ship company and licensed retailing respectively. Quality and consistency of service are increasingly viewed as a foundation for competitive strategy, especially in the budget or economy hotel sector, which, as Senior and Morphew note, has been expanding rapidly in the UK since about 1985.

Although the product is different, the concept is equally applicable to the luxury end of the market, and Chorengel and Teare explain the ethos behind Hyatt International Corporation's corporate image, its market positioning, and its philosophy of striving for excellence in service quality. A case illustration from Scott's Hotels explains the gradual cultural changes needed to embed a service quality ethos. Simmons and Teare describe the teamwork-driven structures and processes which underpin Scott's continual quality improvement effort and Hubrecht and Teare provide a strategic perspective on Scott's UK operations.

Understanding Service Concept in Hospitality Industry

In fact, the wide array of research related to service innovation has primarily focused on the definition of the "service concept" (Goldstein *et al.*, 2002). *Edvardsson and Olsson* defined the service concept as a "prototype for service, covering the needs of the customer and the design of the service". Previous research has discussed the critical role of the service concept in service design and development (*Edvardsson and Olsson*). Furthermore, Goldstein *et al.* (2002) propose that the service concept is the missing key element in service design research.

They suggest that the service concept integrates the "how" and "what" of service design while keeping both the customers' needs and strategic intent of the firm in mind. In other words, the service concept gives a detailed description of what the customer needs and how the organization will deliver the service. The conceptual background of the "service concept" in operations management literature is similar to "marketing concept". The marketing concept is the key to achieving organizational goals and involves "... determining the needs and wants of target markets and delivering the desired (customer) satisfactions more effectively than competitors..." (*Agarwal et al.*).

Firms that are considered to be market-oriented are presumed to have the capability of understanding their customers better than their competitors. Innovation plays an important role in the marketing concept because it gives the service firm the ability to stay ahead of its competitors through new market offerings. The association between innovation and the market-orientation of a firm was determined to be both positive and significant (*Agarwal et al.*). In other words, a more market-oriented firm is more likely to consider innovation, which ultimately leads to superior firm performance (*Agarwal et al., ; Han et al.*). The relationship found between innovation and market orientation emphasizes the importance of identifying customers' needs.

By understanding customer tradeoffs, service firms will have a better market orientation with a resulting improvement in firm performance. Managers when reexamining their existing service offering also need to decide which innovations will create value. For example, managers must ask themselves, which innovations not only deliver additional value to their customers but also are economically viable to the firm. Customer value can be defined as, "the customer's perception of what they want to have happen in a specific-use situation, with the help of a product and service offering in order to accomplish a desired purpose or goal". (Stahl et al.).

The hospitality industry has an abundance of options which to choose from, when determining which products and services will add value for their customers. For example, a hotel operator can offer various combinations of traditional value drivers such as price, location, and typical hotel amenities, such as pool or work-out facilities. On the other hand, new and innovative value drivers could be offered which include features such as online reservations, in-room high-speed internet access, customization of room décor, and flexible check in/out policies. Before introducing a new service innovation, hotel managers need to assess the value that it will bring to their customers.

A good understanding of value can be gained through empirical research methods, such as customer surveys. Survey research relies heavily on a customer's perception of the functionality, performance, and worth of a supplier's offerings (*Anderson and Narus*). By acquiring the vital information of why guests choose to stay at particular hotels, hotel managers are better able to understand the attributes which drive guest's purchasing decisions. Furthermore, understanding the guest's needs and desires is invaluable when determining methods for improving company image. A lack of customer preference understanding leads to problems in both product and service design (Schall). Research shows that the most successful companies are the ones which are fully aware of customer preferences and develop their services in line with targeted market needs (Karmarkar).

As a competing service firm, it is essential to not only consider the types of innovative attributes to offer but also which operational strategy must be implemented to achieve the firm's goals. Kim and Mauborgne coined the term "value innovative logic" which differs from a more conventional approach. The conventional objective is to maximize the value of industrial bound offerings while the value innovative goal is to aid the innovative aspect of the service offering (Kim and Mauborgne). Our research focuses on the value innovation logic for product and service offerings. Therefore, rather than taking a more traditional approach in determining which product and services to offer, an innovative logic approach presents options, "... in terms of the total solution customers seek, even if that takes the company beyond its industry's traditional offerings" (Kim and Mauborgne).

To develop a world view that is realistic—that conforms to the reality of the world and our role in it—we must constantly revise and extend our understanding to include new knowledge of the larger world. Louis Brandeis, one of America's great jurists and thinkers, once said that there could be no true community" save that built upon the personal acquaintance of each with each". Travel and tourism provide such an opportunity; the opportunity for individuals to gain first-hand knowledge of the larger world. Some thirty years ago, the European Economic Community was established with the objective of reconciling the enemies of two world wars.

The EEC was based on the premise that if the peoples of these countries got to know each other better, there would be less likelihood of war. One of the main cornerstones of EEC policy is freedom to travel and minimising frontier controls. The People's Republic of China, a nuclear-armed country widely regarded as a "yellow menace" in the 1960s, has in the past fifteen years become a friend. The key to a changed political relationship between the United States and the People's Republic of China has been an opening to travel and the web of relationships that have developed through cultural exchanges, conferences, sports, twinning of cities, trade and a growing set of common interests. The People's

Republic of China opened its doors to the outside world in 1978 following visits from Canadian Prime Minister Pierre Trudeau and U.S. President Richard Nixon.

Visitor arrivals have grown annually by 20-30 per cent since 1978. More than 2.0 million foreign visitors will travel to China in 1988. By the year 2005, foreign visitors are expert led to number 8-9 million. It is interesting to note that over the pat two years, the People's Republic of China has been reducing the size of its, army by a million soldiers.

Understanding Finance and Performance in Hospitality Industry

The principles of judicious planning apply equally to business finance, and the articles in this section show some techniques and skills which may be of interest to managers in the hospitality industry. Harris's article offers an example of the expanding role of technology in supporting the finance function. He proposes an approach to financial planning using computer spreadsheets and suggests that these spreadsheet models need not be large or complex, yet provide a powerful aid to management decision making. Spreadsheet design principles may be applied to financial planning and control situations such as cost-volume-profit analysis, food and beverage budgeting, flexible budgetary control, comparative analysis, stock control, credit management, cash forecasting, menu engineering, profit sensitivity analysis, pricing decisions and so on. Jeffrey and Hubbard explore the use of hotel occupancy as a primary indicator of performance and an aid to marketing planning. They contend that "occupancy data has not been analysed with sufficient rigour, or at a sufficient level of...desegregation to exploit its diagnostic potential".

It is suggested that a more rigorous approach to occupancy analysis is a useful tool in achieving high occupancy rates. The model assists in the identification of the strengths and weaknesses of the hotel's performance in relation to similar units and narrows the search for solutions to marketing and investment decisions. The inference from this article is that more systematic analysis of important generators of income, such as accommodation, may lead to greater overall performance in hospitality organizations. Damitio and Schmidgall's 1991 survey of executives, educators and students in the hospitality field sought to measure the extent of agreement of the importance of accounting skills. Respondents were asked to rate the importance of 31 accounting skills using a Likert scale both at the beginning of employment and after three years in the industry.

The research shows that "all three groups considered accounting skills to be important to lodging managers and that there is good agreement among the three groups as to the top 15 skills that ought to be emphasised in hospitality and accounting courses". The articles selected demonstrate the need for systematic financial analysis and suggest a positive relationship between analytical rigour and organizational performance. Financial analysis and decision making can be improved by the use of computer technology, but there appears to be a consensus of agreement between the hospitality industry and its education providers of the importance of accounting skills to its managers.

Understanding Hospitality Education and Training Literature

The provision of hospitality management courses mirrors the pattern of demand for "professional" managers in the industry. After the First World War, domestic science and craft courses led to National Diploma hotel and catering management courses which were controlled by the Council for National Academic Awards (CNAA). The first degree course in hotel and catering management was offered by Battersea Technical College in 1967 and the first Higher National Diploma (HND) in this discipline was available in 1969. In those early days, aspiring managers were taught craft skills by instructors who had experience in the functions of cooking, waiting, reception and other specialist technical skills. Students were expected to have a good working knowledge of those skills so as to be able to manage effectively on graduation and these courses were delivered in Technical Colleges and Polytechnics across the UK.

In the 1980s and 1990s, successive governments decided on a policy of the massive expansion of higher education and the reasons are set out in the White Paper *Higher Education: Meeting the Challenge* by Department of Education and Science (DES) (1987). There was a perceived need for more highly trained and qualified professionals who would lead the expanding industries to greater European and global competitiveness. In particular the service industries were growing at the expense of the manufacturing sector and the hospitality industry continues to expand. In 1993, the HCIMA (then known as the Hotel, Catering and Institutional Management Association) reported that there were nearly 5, 500 students enrolled on over 40 first degree courses in the management of hotel and catering operations in UK institutions (HCIMA 1993).

The rise in student numbers accurately reflects the increased importance of the industry to the UK economy. In 1996, this represented consumer spending of £36.6 billion, equivalent to 5 per cent of GDP and 2.4 million people were employed in the industry (HCIMA, 1996). The literature suggests that the strong demand for degree educated managers will continue. The creation of new universities from polytechnics in the early 1990s has increased the number of institutions in higher education and has heightened the competition for the provision of hospitality education. Arksey *et al.* (1993) suggest that "by the year 2000 Britain will have transformed its élite universities into a system of mass higher education".

Although there is a firm commitment to mass higher education in the UK, Ashworth and Harvey (1995) remark that there are no guidelines for achieving this expansion in an affordable way. The implications are that each HE institution is required to manage its dwindling public funding more efficiently and its success depends upon the business skills of senior staff, many of whom are career academics. Greater market awareness encourages many vocational HE organizations to be more "customer-centred" but there are issues as to whether their customers are students, parents, employers, governments or perhaps society at large. It is difficult to generalise about students on hospitality management courses in the UK, but many are from middle-class backgrounds, perhaps with parents who are in the business. The reasons for espousing the hospitality business vary from those with a genuine interest to others who enrolled on a course because of worse than expected A level grades.

Many are outgoing and social young people whose interests in the industry may have been stirred by a love of cooking or a fascination with staying in hotels. Experience suggests that these "second-best" students have little realistic knowledge of the industry to which they aspire, and may be disappointed by its demands. The professional stage or work placement which is an integral part of most hospitality management courses tends to mature students to "real life", and may sour them forever against the industry.

This may be due to inadequate support given by institutions, who are seen by some employers as supplying motivated and cheap labour for the busy season. Academic staff are sometimes criticised because of their lack of industry experience and their rigid, outdated curricula. Many academics are intelligent, hard-working and well-meaning, but unfortunately others are narrow and closed in outlook. Increasing demands for research, teaching and administration have raised stress levels of many academic communities. For academics who teach as well as acting as in an administrative or co-ordinating capacity there is a need to combine the skills of academic abstraction, the ability to teach and personal organization as well as bureaucratic competences.

In many cases, these tasks are constrained by shortages of capable support staff or outdated administrative and technological systems to cope with ever larger student numbers. Further, it may be suggested that effective academic abilities (including abstraction, attention to detail, "hair-splitting") are not always found in conjunction with personal organization skills (such as planning, delegation, prioritising tasks). Professorial types are often caricatured as intelligent, disorganized and absent-minded. The problem of staff who become subsumed in an organizational system is, however, probably no worse in academia than in other settings.

The people that succeed are often those who either are able to cope or can adapt and improve the system. Academic institutions, like hospitality firms are heterogeneous and tend to be conservative and functional in their outlook. The strength of the status quo is so great in HE that greater innovation often occurs in those institutions which are less rigidly structured and established and where radical solutions are necessary for organizational survival.

Current funding arrangements make it difficult for newer universities to aspire to research-based objectives with reducing resources and they must look to other income-generating methods such as targeting overseas students, summer/short courses and consultancy. The effects of these survival tactics tend to deflect attention away from the task of vocational institutions to provide high-quality courses which fit graduate students to enter that profession as well as augmenting their general education.

Understanding between Service Quality and Customers in Hospitality Industry

The main function which a hospitality organization's members must perform is the delivery of quality services to its customers. Eight articles from the *Hospitality Research Journal* discuss how employees can best deliver quality service to the organization's customers. Barsky (1996) suggests that customers may be excellent sources of information for management on how the organization can provide quality service. Through surveys and focus groups, customers can help management determine which service areas are most in need of improvement. Management may also choose to create an internal service-quality audit which can identify errors and determine their frequency, assign costs of fixing (or not fixing) the error, and identify the steps to prevent them.

Luchars and Hinkin (1996) described an example of such an audit conducted at a full-service hotel to determine the cost of errors in transactions at the front desk. The most common error was failure to post late charges to the guest's folio, which cost the hotel an estimated $250,000 per year. This internally and externally derived information can assist management in its endeavours to satisfy customers. Gunderson *et al.* (1996) defined customer satisfaction as, "a guest's post-consumption judgment of a product or service that can, in turn, be measured by assessing guest's evaluation of a performance on specific attributes". The authors' research revealed that business travellers were most concerned with the tangible aspects of housekeeping (e.g. room amenities) and the intangible aspects of the front desk (e.g. receptionists' willingness to provide service). Being able to provide services which customers prefer is obviously a starting point for providing customer satisfaction. A relatively easy way to determine what services customers prefer is simply to ask them. Travellers who Greathouse stopped at visitor information centres rated cleanliness of room, value for price, friendliness of staff, and security of property as some of the most important attributes of a hotel.

Understanding between Education and Training in Hospitality Industry

McIntosh (1992) has pointed out that tertiary level hospitality and tourism education is a relatively recent phenomenon, originating with the 1920s US extension programmes to assist those interested in planning and managing their own hospitality businesses. In contrast, hospitality/ tourism degrees in Pacific Rim countries developed much later, but are currently flourishing with expanding numbers of specific programmes and majors, and adjustments to course content to reflect global and local trends (Wells, 1996).

However, Wells contends that a fundamental question is the contribution such education makes to delivering an effective workforce. Similar concerns were expressed by Morrison (1994) who argued that expansion in the number of hospitality degree places has been driven by student, rather than industry, demand. The vast majority of employment opportunities in the industry do not require the intellectual capabilities of competent graduates and the match between type of employment and expectations of graduates is often incongruous. Morrison contended that if a relatively small number of quality, skilled operational managers are required by industry, then that is what should be produced.

The finding that 54 per cent of first-year hospitality students from four Australian universities expected to start work in trainee/junior management/ supervisory positions also lends weight to Morrison's concerns (Davidson, 1996). Perhaps the solution to this dilemma is more involvement of relevant stakeholders in hospitality/tourism curriculum design. Shepherd and Cooper (1995) identified these stakeholders as students, tourists, educational institutions, government, media and the tourist industry. They noted that the implicit nature of tourism as a diverse and complex activity among such stakeholders necessitates taking account of their views, actions and influences on education and training.

The importance of stakeholder groups in hospitality/tourism curricula is also implicit in a framework developed by Ritchie (1995) for designing and developing tourism/hospitality management programmes. Criteria emphasised include sensitivity to industry needs, balance between economic development and environmental protection, building on and developing skills of faculty members, location where tourism is a significant component of the local economy, and a balance of conceptual material and practical experience. The importance of integrating "hands-on" experience into a more formal educational framework (Shepherd and Cooper, 1995) is also advocated by King (1994b) who reviewed the development of hospitality/tourism co-operative education, defined as a pedagogical process involving a relationship between educators, industry employers and students.

The espoused benefits of this approach are that students are introduced to the working environment of their chosen industry, develop awareness of supervision, management, motivation, and decision making, apply academic knowledge in employment situations, and learn to accept individual responsibility by working as part of a team. King concluded that the sound philosophical principles of co-operative education are essential for hospitality/tourism education and that urgent action is needed in Australia to protect earlier advances made.

In addition to incorporating stakeholder needs, cultural factors are also important in curricula design. King (1994c, p. 38) contends that "no body of knowledge can be right for all places and all seasons because knowledge alters as the society it supports changes". He criticised lack of acknowledgement shown for social, cultural, biological and physical landscapes in which tourism operates and argued it is imperative to provide professional education in a national context. Go and Mok (1995) demonstrated the importance of cultural factors in examining hotel and tourism management education in Hong Kong and the influence of the Chinese cultural context in which such education takes place; while Echtner (1995) examined the challenges facing developing nations when designing tourism education programmes. She concluded by advocating a three-pronged approach: professional education, vocational training and entrepreneurial development. In the context of Kenya, Sindiga (1994) also called for further training and extension services so that increased indigenization can proceed in a country where high levels of foreign ownership and control have resulted in foreign domination of hospitality/tourism management positions.

As Sindiga (1994, p. 45) points out, "training is the transition between formal education and the needs of occupation and employment". Dowell (1995) discussed the role of training in the Australian hospitality industry and concluded that the link between productivity and training investment is at the enterprise level. Studies of effective Australian service sector enterprises show they devote more attention to training and deliberately attempt to recruit more highly skilled and qualified workers than their less effective counterparts. Also in the Australian context, Robson (1995) echoed Dowell's support for training. He described the work of the National Employment and Training Taskforce in encouraging demand for trainees and delivering simple access for employers to traineeships.

Peacock (1995) also recognized recent advancements made in Australian training systems which provide significant opportunities for expansion into hospitality/tourism training in the Asia Pacific region. He argued that rapid economic growth of Pacific Asian countries has increased demand for education and training which they cannot meet. The challenge will be a commitment to quality, and creative and flexible delivery of these services.

REFERENCES

Bond, H. (1995), "Frequent-guest programs build brand loyalty", *Hotel and Motel Management*, Vol. 210 No.3, pp. 23.

Enghagen, L., Hott, D. (1992), "Students' perceptions of ethical issues in the hospitality and tourism industry", *Hospitality Research Journal*, Vol. 15 No.2, pp. 41-50.

Hamilton, A.J., Veglahn, P.A. (1992), "Sexual harassment: the hostile work environment", *The Cornell Hotel and Restaurant Administration Quarterly*, Vol. 33 No.2, pp. 88-92.

Kipps, M., Middleton, V.T.C. (1990), "Achieving quality and choice for the customer in hospital catering", *International Journal of Hospitality Management*, Vol. 9 No.1, pp. 69-83.

5

Towards Hospitality Warehouse Management and Logistics Solutions

"Hospitality is the practice of God's welcome by reaching across difference to participate in God's actions bringing justice and healing to our world in crisis."

—*Letty M. Russell*

It is interesting to note that hospitality industry presents an interesting sector in which to examine the interaction of pressures and influences which lead to the creation and reinforcement of gender segregation. Casual and part-time jobs, demanding "gendered" tacit skills which reflect patriarchal domestic divisions of labour, clearly attract female applicants and discourage males. Women's concentration in these "supplementary-earner" jobs reinforces "male breadwinner/female dependency" relations in the home. Their presence in *patriarchally-prescribed* contingent jobs—chambermaids rather than porters—similarly reinforces the patriarchal dynamics of gender segregation and wider norms and values relating to gender roles and socialization. Their presence and presentation in *sex-typed* occupations such as hostesses and bar staff in particular establishments, also reinforces gender difference and thus, patriarchy. A comparison of the gender structure of hospitality industry occupations in a range of European countries suggests that jobs mainly done by women in one country (for example, restaurant table service or bar work in UK) may be male-dominated occupations in another (for example, Spain or Greece), but an examination of such divisions of labour invariably reflect cultural gender norms, most significantly, women's relatively low labour market participation and exclusion from the public sphere. Management jobs in hospitality reveal the interaction of the three dimensions which, it is argued, determine the gendering of occupations.

The industry has been becoming progressively more sophisticated, competitive and complex in the increasing range of services it provides. One of the side-effects of this has been the demand for an increasingly professional management, which has been reflected in the proliferation of degree and diploma-level courses in hospitality management in developed countries. In the UK, the first degree-level course in the subject was introduced in 1964 and by 1994, it was possible to do such a course at 40 UK higher education institutions. Over two-thirds of the students on such courses are women. It might be expected that the proliferation of such vocational education opportunities would have improved women's occupational profile in the industry. Crompton and Sanderson have hypothesized that the increasing importance of professional credentials in the hospitality industry might lead to increasing female penetration of career occupations, from which they have previously been conspicuously absent, although previous research indicated that female degree- and diploma-holding entrants to the industry are considerably less likely than their male counterparts to embark on a career trajectory designed to lead them into mainstream management, and that initial inequalities of access are reinforced by subsequent early career moves. Research carried out in 1993 reinforced the earlier findings.

An *alumni* study of 712 degree and HND students who completed hotel and catering management courses at 30 UK educational institutions in 1989 revealed that women were less likely than men to have been given the opportunity to develop supervisory or management skills as part of their undergraduate industrial placements, more likely than men to have had difficulty in obtaining suitable employment, less likely than men to have developed careers in the industry, less likely than men to have been given the opportunity to acquire recognized post-experience qualifications, more likely than men to be under-achieving professionally, less likely than men to perceive that they had "a great deal of autonomy" in their current employment, less likely than men to have a strong possibility of promotion in their current employment, more likely than men to express dissatisfaction with their career to date. The most unambiguous indications of persistent obstacles to equal opportunities were the differentials in rewards. The average wage of the highly-qualified women in this cohort who were currently employed in the hospitality industry, more than three years after graduation, was £11,562, whereas the average wage for their male peers was £14,816. These differentials were reinforced by differences in fringe benefits, with men in the commercial hospitality sector significantly more likely than women to be entitled to valuable "perks" such as company cars, free or subsidized meals, low-cost housing, private health insurance, company share ownership schemes and product discounts.

These findings reflect the wider picture. Rubery and Fagan have pointed out that women managers in hotels and catering earn below average wages for *women* as a whole, quite apart from being well below average in relation to *managers'* wages. The findings suggest that highly-qualified women in hotel and catering management have different experiences of early career development than their male counterparts. They are more likely to have had negative experience in their supervised work experience year, more likely to have difficulty in obtaining the kind of job they want, less likely to have jobs which offer them intrinsic satisfaction and good career prospects and finally, less likely to have "professional" salaries with accompanying fringe benefits.

The "qualification lever" seems to have been somewhat less effective than Crompton and Sanderson predicted. Why? The survey cohort consists of males and females with similar qualifications, acquired at the same time, virtually all in full-time employment, surveyed *before* the onset of family-building and career breaks. There was some evidence that males in the sample tended to have clearer career plans, but the differences were minimal. There was virtually no difference in the distributions of women and men at first destination after completing their courses, not much difference in their distribution throughout the industry (although women were slightly more likely to be employed in public sector catering, which is generally characterized by less requirement to work "unsocial" hours than the commercial sector). It is significant to mention that customer demand is driving today's supply chain. Globalization, outsourcing and the increasing number of order channels are impacting the way you match demand to inventory—so how do you balance the two? Manhattan Associates' Distributed Order Management solution enables seamless customer order fulfillment by providing inventory visibility, sourcing, allocation and delivery scheduling at each stage of the fulfillment process—and across your entire supply chain—in real time.

Manage Multiple Order Fulfillment Channels: Customer demand is constantly changing, products are flowing from factories to distribution centers around the world, inventory availability is fluctuating by the hour and customer orders are strewn across divisions and order channels.

We can help you adapt to these changes by providing a single view into customer orders and supply.

With Manhattan Associates' Distributed Order Management solution you get real-time visibility into your inventory pipeline, so you can have complete control over orders, suppliers and worldwide trading partners.

Dynamic Sourcing and Allocation: With our Distributed Order

Management solution, you know what you have in stock, what has been committed and what is scheduled to arrive at your warehouse. Using configurable rules, our solution aggregates orders as they are placed, considers your global inventory—including in-transit shipments and purchase orders—and then optimally matches demand to the supply within or outside your enterprise. This dynamic sourcing capability makes it possible to improve order execution speed, accuracy, fill rate and ultimately customer service. Manhattan Associates' Distributed Order Management solution is built on a standards-based, pure Java (J2EE) platform. The solution, which works with warehouse and transportation planning and execution systems for fulfillment, also integrates with your existing ERP and supply chain execution software.

Approach to Warehouse Management

If you want to take your warehouse operations beyond basic picking, packing and shipping—look to Manhattan Associates for a fresh new perspective. Our Warehouse Management solution provides insight into your inventory, your operational processes and your people, so you can achieve optimal efficiency and productivity—taking your warehouse operations to a new level of excellence.

Move Goods and Information Through Your Warehouse at Maximum Speed

Experience faster and more efficient flow of goods through your warehouse. With our solution, you can decrease inventory, improve order fulfillment, reduce order cycle time, eliminate chargebacks and exceed customer expectations to optimize execution of your distribution center operations. Streamline receiving and shipping to facilitate cross-docking and expedite back-ordered product. Track every unit down to the lowest level of detail, including country of origin, lot number, serial number and date code. With cycle counting capabilities, it's possible to eliminate annual physical counts that can shut down operations. Our technology includes built-in RFID and EPC technology to ensure ongoing compliance with the top 100 retailers' guidelines. It also supports full compliance with dynamic routing initiatives.

The result is improved shipment planning and accuracy, optimized order fulfillment processes and enhanced in-stock position. With the ability to handle single-byte and double-byte languages, various units of measure and international currencies, management of your global supply chain becomes straightforward.

Leverage the Power of Integration

Maximize your warehouse operations with Manhattan Associates' integrated Warehouse Management solutions—Warehouse Management, Labor Management, Slotting Optimization, Load Management, Billing Management and Performance Management. Or streamline your entire supply chain by implementing our Integrated Logistics Solutions™ for source-to-consumption execution and optimization.

Finance, Strategies and Performance in Hospitality Industry

Another major issue is the current financial practices and strategies utilized by mangers in the hospitality industry. Sheel analyses the relationship between a firm's capital structure, its cost of capital, and its stock value as well as the impact of earnings information on common stock returns. Gu focuses his attention on the hospitality investor by reviewing the risk and return on investment in three sectors of the hospitality industry. Findings show that the casino sector was the best performer, followed by the restaurant sector, and then the hotel sector.

The overall financial performance of a property is of importance to investors, managers, employees, and sometimes even guests. Van Dyke and Olsen compared the performance variables of highly profitable hotel operations with those of marginally profitable or losing operations. Five key variables (occupancy rate, rooms sales as percentage of total sales, rooms department labour cost percentage, food cost percentage, and property tax percentage) were found to have a significant relationship with total or consolidated profitability. These variables can be computed relatively easily and can assist the manager in ascertaining the relative financial health of the property. Most managers of financially successful properties develop and follow a long-term strategic plan. Once the strategy is in place, managers must continually scan sectors of the environment, which are appropriate to the intended strategy, in order to identify trends and changes within each sector. West found that firms espousing low cost or differentiation strategies performed significantly better than firms that focused on one segment of the industry. These higher performing firms also engaged in significantly higher levels of environmental scanning.

Managers must have a clear understanding of the strategic direction of the firm in order to be able to react positively to environmental changes. If, for example, a competitor lowers its prices, management must be able to determine if a matching price reduction is in line with the firm's overall strategy. Haywood describes the key elements of a comprehensive cost management strategy which would assist management with this decision. In addition, Shaw defines the key factors for a pricing decision as demand, competition, and cost: demand sets the ceiling, cost sets the floor, and competition determines where on this continuum the actual price will fall. If, in our example, the competitor does not lower its price below our costs, we may for a time want to follow suit and lower our prices too.

The above pricing example is indicative of a short-run management decision. Whether or not a property should become part of a franchise is an example of a long-term, strategic decision. Poorani and Smith examine whether bed and breakfast owners perceive the need to join a franchise. Although the owners have unmet marketing and sales needs, franchisers have not yet persuaded the owners that they can fulfil these needs effectively. Powers suggests that reservation systems technology, which can create worldwide reservation networks for independent and small chains, will adversely effect the growth of franchising in the lodging sector.

Other forms of technology are continually changing the way the hospitality industry operates. Chervenak believes that high-speed, high-capacity fibre optics will link the world and change the way hotels communicate with their guests. Interactive, three-dimensional televisions will change how and what guests view in their rooms, while private videoconferencing networks will change the way business is done. One need only examine the impact the Internet has had on the world to agree that technology is one of the most important issues facing the hospitality industry today.

Integrated Logistics Solutions Enterprise Agreements in Hospitality Sector

Globalization, outsourcing, special fulfillment requirements, fluctuating transportation costs, increasing regulations—today's supply chain landscape is filled with new challenges, growing complexity and increasing competition. To help you overcome these challenges, Manhattan Associates developed Integrated Logistics Solutions™—a source-to-consumption solution that offers a fresh new perspective on the supply chain. Integrated Logistics Solutions enables companies to optimize supply chain execution by streamlining operations and transforming the supply chain into a single, well-coordinated business process. So you can maximize value throughout your entire supply chain and extended enterprise to boost overall corporate performance.

Connecting Every Link in the Supply Chain

Developed for companies of every size and across multiple industries, Integrated Logistics Solutions can be implemented as an integrated whole for maximum value or may be deployed as individual point solutions.

Either way, our best-of-value solutions can help you reduce costs and target opportunities for continuous improvement.

- Warehouse Management. Optimized warehouse management, workload planning, labor resource management, space utilization and billing reduce costs while increasing productivity and customer service. Integrates with current enterprise systems, such as RFID, radio frequency (RF), material handling and voice-enabled systems.
- Transportation Management. Integrated procurement, planning and execution, load management analysis and optimization capabilities allow shippers and carriers to manage their entire transportation network for optimum resource utilization and profitability.
- Distributed Order Management. Real-time order lifecycle management and supply-demand balancing across the entire distributed supply chain improves order fulfillment, accuracy and fill rate performance regardless of sales channels, geography and multiple distribution centers.
- Trading Partner Management. Business process synchronization across the trading partner network, with secure electronic exchange of critical documents, enables global visibility and extension of execution capabilities to suppliers, hubs, carriers and customers.
- Reverse Logistics Management. Comprehensive Web-based returns processing capabilities reduce administrative burdens, provide inventory visibility and boost net asset recovery by automating every aspect of the product return and disposition process, regardless of disparate technology systems.
- Performance Management. Support the entire logistics platform by providing a dashboard that monitors and scores supply chain performance based on Key Performance Indicators (KPIs). Flexible reporting delivers results in a user-friendly format. Event management functionality alerts users to exceptions for rapid problem resolution.
- Carrier Management. Driver&Load®, Drop&Swap®, Fuel&Route®, Profit Analyzer and Load Analyzer solutions designed to put carriers in the driver's seat of asset utilization and profit maximization.
- RFID in a Box®. Eases deployment to meet supply chain requirements and EPC compliance. A highly configurable Integration Platform enables connectivity with existing systems.

Implementation and training reduce risk and speed time-to-value. Provides single-source convenience for RFID software, hardware, middleware, tags, antennae and readers.

Manhattan Associates' Integrated Logistics Solutions is further enhanced by services that help you assess, generate and measure the return on your investment. Whether you require a quick implementation, 24-hour customer support, complimentary hardware or hands-on training courses—our service offerings dramatically increase the value of our solutions and impact throughout your organization.

Enterprise Agreements in Hospitality Sector

The existing level of flexibility under the centralised system is a likely explanation for the lack of formal enterprise agreements in the sector. At the time the survey was conducted no registered club in NSW had an enterprise agreement registered with the NSW IRC. Registered clubs have had the opportunity under Section 11 of the Industrial Arbitration Act 1940 (NSW) to enter into a formal enterprise agreement if they so wished. Since the introduction of the NSW Enterprise Agreement Amendment Act 1990 (NSW) there has been an opportunity for registered clubs to enter into such agreements without the involvement of a trade union. Given the increasingly competitive environment in which registered clubs operate, and the perceived importance of the penalty rates issue, it is somewhat surprising that not one registered club had entered into a formal enterprise agreement.

Despite the lack of formalised agreements there were a number of registered clubs (28 per cent) which had entered into informal enterprise agreements. It appears this may be an underestimate of the actual number of clubs which had an informal agreement. As discussed previously, a minimum of 39 per cent of registered clubs stated they negotiated, individually or collectively, with employees, while 75 per cent negotiated with management. Both these figures were greater than the number of registered clubs which stated that they had an informal enterprise agreement. The results from this study indicated registered club managers believed that the most important areas of flexibility were work-time flexibility, functional flexibility and numerical flexibility. Procedural flexibility and wage flexibility were considered less important in the management of clubs.

In rating the impact or restriction of awards on the different areas of club flexibility, managers indicated that, on average, this impact or restriction ranged from low to moderate. There were wide discrepancies in the ratings amongst registered clubs, ranging from some club managers indicating that they were severely restricted to other managers reporting no restriction. The other important finding was that the most valued flexibility variables, functional and work time flexibility, were two of the least affected by awards. The perceived impact or restriction of trade unions on registered club flexibility was not as great as awards, with slightly lower ratings for all variables.

The ratings for unions followed closely the pattern for award ratings, which suggests registered club managers perceived awards and trade unions operating in tandem. The ratings for the impact of trade unions also indicated wide discrepancies amongst registered clubs, as ratings for awards did. Taken together the ratings for the impact of awards and trade unions, despite the variability between registered clubs, suggests a number of registered clubs have substantial levels of flexibility under the centralised system. This level of flexibility suggests that the proponents of deregulation are not correct in assuming the centralised system prevents the attainment of labour flexibility and that there may be few benefits arising for the hospitality industry from the deregulation of the industrial relations system in Australia.

6

Training Technology and Vocational Work

"The mind is not a hermit's cell, but a place of hospitality and intercourse."

—Charles Horton Cooley

Successful companies such as Chrysler Corporation, RJR Nabisco, Catapillar and Bethlehem Steel have accepted the responsibility of educating their employees with the most efficient and effective methods and tools available on the market. Executives interviewed gave two consistent reasons for using cutting-edge multimedia technologies in training: effectiveness and efficiency. Newer forms of technology and programmes, compared to traditional learning techniques, offer more flexibility, ease of access, learning level variety and immediate feedback.–Using computer-based multimedia technology and high-quality programmes has decreased training costs and the amount of inaccurate information given to customers.

In addition, easy-access training has increased the motivation to train. Customer service, employee knowledge, employee morale and sales are also increased with the use of this delivery system. Having training needs that are comparable to those of the hospitality industry, these companies serve as an example of how large organizations can manage and deliver training better by using computer-based multimedia technology.

As organizations review the costs incurred by employee development, concern is rightly focusing on the costs of continuing to use traditional training methods and low-quality or inappropriate training programmes. According to telephone interviews with hotel and restaurant executives representing companies employing 1,500 or more employees, the costs of training are difficult to track. It is the belief of these executives that ongoing training is necessary but near-impossible to evaluate.

The tracking task is arduous owing to internal inconsistencies of training delivery, high turnover rates and individual needs of employees. Managers of individual units often select programmes, training methods and instructional tools according to budgets, time, and talent available. In addition, individual units may have employee needs that are unique; therefore, training techniques and the needs of employees may be unit specific, meaning that what works for one unit may not work for another. Computer-based technology has been successfully used for improving training, customer service and the management of information in many firms.

For example, Holiday Inn analysed the needs of properties both domestically and internationally and, as a result, multimedia computers were purchased and incorporated company-wide. To date, training based on individual need, time available to train and delivery talent for Holiday Inn is managed by multimedia technology. Scheduling training is co-managed by both trainers and employees via their desktop computers. Training executives send messages via e-mail and public training programmes electronically.

Employees enrol in classes or request programmes to be delivered to their desktop computers by e-mail. Programmes are then delivered to the desktop at the time selected by the employee. After this, employees type their name and social security number and training begins. Employees interact with the programmes by using touch screens, the keyboard, and the mouse so as to respond to multiple choice questions or essay questions. Users are presented with educational programmes that are rich in colour, sound, text, animation, graphics and special effects.

According to Holiday Inn' regional director of franchise service and training, Tom Bernard, multimedia delivery and instructional programmes will reduce the learning curve for employees and provide more consistency in Holiday Inn' training program...on site training will also reduce travel and other costs associated with traditional training. Holiday Inn along with others, like Marriott, Brinker International and McDonald', are using multimedia training technologies to provide cutting-edge training that is both more effective and more efficient than traditional techniques.

Computer-based Multimedia and Other Technology Defined

The use of several media devices electronically controlled by the use of a computer is known as computer-based multimedia. Systems used to manage reservations, video check-outs, multiple phone lines, facsimile machines, smart cards and voice mail are all examples of technology with a multimedia emphasis. In the realm of training technology, computerized systems and programs that manage instructional programme delivery, accessibility, and tracking of user interaction are known as multimedia training. These programmes often provide training that is enhanced with electronically controlled graphics, animation, text and audio.

The strength of the technology is that it merges traditional tools that are stand-alone and manually operated into a system that requires one operator, the user, and one programme to deliver the information. Multimedia systems are not without their disadvantages. Costs associated with the purchase of hardware, software development, user acceptability, upgrades to hard- and software, maintenance, and system and software training are in themselves significant barriers to investment cost.

It has been said that multimedia is only a feasible option for large firms because of this, and it is the view of some that little has been done by software and hardware companies to provide comparable services to smaller firms. This adds to the scepticism about, and low acceptance of, multimedia technology in the hospitality industry as a whole.

Determining Appropriate Training Delivery Methods and Tools

While technology may offer much more control and flexibility to both trainers and trainees, it can only be viewed as a tool of programme implementation. The system will only deliver programmes of high quality if the multimedia designers are experienced in learning theories, knowledgeable about instructional design, and familiar with what electronic systems can and cannot do. If the designer is to do his or her job, training executives must first determine: the information that is to be delivered; the variety of needs of their employees; and the training budget.

The first step in determining what information is to be delivered requires a clear understanding of corporate goals. Owing to the unique attributes of firms, most off-the-shelf programmes are too general and narrow in scope; therefore, most training packages need to be custom designed. Costs associated with custom development often limit flexibility in terms of how the programme can be delivered. Second, firms must consider the learning levels of the audience and the individual challenges associated with training. Owing to the diversity of educational, cultural and experiential backgrounds, information is likely to be synthesized differently.

Hence, instructional designers must develop courseware that uses: vocabularies based on educational level examples for communicating material that are familiar to the cultural group; and material that is sequenced according to the experiential backgrounds of the learning group. Until the backgrounds of the audience are known, it is difficult to design instruction for their needs. Third, costs associated with delivery have to be considered. Unfortunately, costs are often the driving force behind training, placing it first in the training delivery decision process instead of last. Most hospitality firm training executives agree that the unresolved issues with regard to training include, but are not limited to, the following factors:

- the background of the trainee;
- the quality of the programmes delivered;
- the relative flexibility of the programme delivery format;
- the high costs associated with traditional programme delivery; and
- the problems of tracking both effectiveness and costs of training.

A new approach to training is needed that will give both the deliverer (employer and trainer) more control over costs and a return on training investments, and the employer a higher quality learning experience. The question is why are the majority of hospitality firms continuing to use traditional training techniques when more innovative, more efficient and more effective delivery systems and methods exist?

Sample and Survey

The sample comprised 300 hospitality food service training executives randomly selected from the database purchased from American Society of Trainers Directory (ASTD). Database selection was made of hotel, restaurant and resort firms specializing in the production, service and delivery of food. Human resource directors, directors of training and vice-presidents of human resources were targeted respondents. Executives were asked to identify their position, level of firm, number of employees, and type of food services offered. Accompanying the demographic information was a 8.5in. x 7in., 15-page survey (each page counted as one, printed on front and back). Respondents were asked to identify the types of training methods, tools and the quality of each.

They were also asked whether training is tracked, whether learning levels of trainees are considered before training programmes are selected, the languages in which training is offered, and to identify the most innovative form of technology currently used for training. Lastly, respondents were asked to identify positions and departments that were not receiving adequate training and, if they felt that training in their firm was inadequate, to indicate possible reasons for this.

Research Questions

The purpose of the study was to discover the following:

- What are the current methods of training used in the food service sector?
- What are the current training tools used to deliver training in the food service sector?
- Does opinion of training methods vary significantly according to position of respondent, level of
- What would respondents recommend to improve training if they believed improvements were needed?

Methodology

Descriptive statistics and analysis of variance was used to analyse the survey data using SPSS for Windows and Duncan' Multiple Range test, to identify group differences. The level of significance was established at the $p < 0.05$ level, although some differences thought to be significant at the $p < 0.10$ level are also presented. For the purposes of a larger study, questions in the survey were compared to a variety of independent variables. These included position of respondent, level of organization (local, regional, national and international), type of company, total sales, total number of units and services offered. For reasons of clarity, the findings presented here focus on the descriptive statistics and selected significant differences found using analysis of variance (ANOVA). These tests were applied to the independent variables of position of respondent and type of company they represented, and their respective answers to the 30 survey questions.

Company type was identified as "firms offering management services to other firms", "firms managing only their own properties", and "firms that manage their own properties and offering management services". Type of company is identified as 1 = management firms, 2 = management own properties and 3 = manage own properties and others. Positions were identified as 1 = directors of human resources, 2 = directors of training and 3 = vice-presidents of human resources. A full report of additional significant findings using analysis of variance and Duncan' multiple range test is currently under review.

Results

The first wave of responses produced a return rate of 46 per cent (139 returned surveys). Non-respondents were mailed a second copy of the survey, which resulted in 11 additional responses for a total of 158 returns. However, four were unusable, lowering the total return to 146 or a 49 per cent overall return rate. The opinions of directors of human resources (DHR) differed significantly from vice presidents of human resources (VPHR) with regard to how often lecture-pupil (classroom style) training is actually used.

Furthermore, the opinions of DHRs differed significantly from the opinions of directors of training (DT) on this issue as well (F = 0.0182). Significant differences between the two positions with regard to the effectiveness of the most frequently used training technique (method), lecture-pupil, and the opinion about the most popular method of training is in question. The effectiveness of this training method is based on the opinions of DHRs, VPHRs and DTs, with VPHRs having the lowest opinion of the method and trainers having the highest opinion of the method. The significant findings were the most robust of those presented in this study (F=0.0010). It is interesting to note that although firms choose this training technique more frequently than any other, the opinions expressed of this technique (method) tended to reflect the lowest rating, "ineffective". Type of company also produced significant findings at the 0.10 alpha level with regard to frequency of use of textbooks and manuals as training tools and training people in groups as opposed to individualized training. The significant findings between respondents representing firms that offer management services only, firms that manage only their own properties, and firms that both manage their own properties and offer management services to other firms.

The differences of opinion were discovered between firms managing their properties only and those firms that manage their own properties as well as offering management services to other firms (F = 0.0715). The difference relates to the second most popular training technique, the use of textbooks and/or manuals as stand-alone training systems. The findings for firms that offer management services only and firms that manage only their own properties (F = 0.1003) relating to the use of group training, or training employees in a large group setting as opposed to offering individualized training. Firms offering management to other firms use it only occasionally, while firms that only manage their own properties hardly ever use it. Not surprisingly, the results indicate that traditional training techniques and tools are widely used in the industry.

Classroom-style (lecture-pupil) training is the most often used for large groups. One-on-one training such as on-the-job or shadowing a more experienced employee is the training method most used by smaller firms. Tools used to deliver training were also of traditional format; texts and manuals were most often selected, flip charts and overhead transparencies were the second most often used, and the third most often used tools were videotapes. The most innovative form of technology used overall, regardless of size, is videotape; however, this tool is made available to management and corporate executives and less available to wage-level employees. It is also more available to employees of large companies than to employees of small firms. Most wage-level employees are trained by on-the-job training, management by class-room style, executives in small groups by outside professional services (conferences, sponsored training at universities/other, or private consultants). Differences in opinion with regard to the ranking of effectiveness and efficiency of training methods and tools is evident.

Generally, the higher the rank of the respondent in the organization, the higher the opinion of the current, traditional training methods and tools used in their firm. Managers at the property level, who are often the ones closest to the customer and responsible for planning training, delivering training, or both, had lower opinions of both the methods and delivery tools. It should be noted that when respondents were asked whether training was tracked, directors of trai ing (DR) and director of human resources (HR) reported differently, with HRs reporting positively and DR reporting negatively. No significant differences were noted in opinions relating to levels of organization or type of services offered. However, respondents of companies of varying size (numbers of employees) reported differences with regard to the effectiveness and efficiency of training methods. Respondents representing firms with employees numbering 1-50 ranked on-the-job training as their first choice of method.

Most also ranked it as the only method of training used. Firms with the largest number of employees (250 or above) ranked classroom-style training as the most effective training method and ranked on-the-job and videotape training second and third, respectively. When asked what type of training would be preferred, DTs wanted computer-based equipment and programmes, management requested more time to improve the current training programmes in place and executives reported that plans were in place for improving training overall, both current programmes and the development of new ones. The barriers or obstacles to providing tracking and to more innovative programmes and tools for the user are mentioned as being:

- lack of time;
- high costs; and
- the short life-span of current computer technology (outdated hard- and software).

The hospitality industry offers a wider range of quality products and services with every passing year. The US workforce demographics reflect an increase in diversity of race, educational and experiential backgrounds, which serve as further reasons to make a commitment to providing training that is current, efficient and, most importantly, effective. This study confirms that training methods and tools used to train employees are not as effective or efficient as they could be. It also confirms that the continued use of traditional training formats such as classroom-style lectures accompanied by textbooks and manuals is supported by upper levels of management but with reluctance by those who deliver training.

For property-level managers or training directors, more innovative training methods are being requested. These respondents said that the reason for the reluctance to upgrade training technology is lack of time and high costs; however, the majority reported that lack of communication and commitment from higher levels of management (corporate) were additional reasons for the absence of innovative training technology. Further research on ways of improving training management in the hospitality industry is needed. Investment in different forms of technology both to deliver and to manage this important function will help to identify methods, tools and systems that can meet corporate budgetary and training goals and improve customer service. As new and innovative training delivery systems appear on the market, hospitality firms would be wise to analyse the costs versus the short- and long-term benefits of computer-based technologies.

Industry Perspectives and Vocational Work in Hospitality Sector

It is significant to mention that work experience requires a triangular partnership, and industry occupies one side of that triangle. While industry may subjectively perceive itself to be a worthwhile partner, it is worth looking at how various commentators objectively perceive the industry in training and employment terms. At a general level, Keep (1990, and in Storey 1989) notes overwhelming survey evidence that places the UK at or near the bottom of the international league of training provision. Handy et al. (1987) show that, while leading employers in West Germany, Japan, and the USA spend up to 3 per cent of turnover per annum on training, on average employers in the UK spend only 0.15 per cent.

Keep (1990, and in Storey 1989) analyses the factors that inhibit the extension of training and observes that managers in the UK have themselves had comparatively low levels of formal education and training. Both the HCTC (1993) and Guerra and Peroni (1991) estimate that, in the UK, approximately 10 per cent of managers have a specific qualification, and that 94 per cent of those employed in the tourism industry have no recognised qualification. Ireland follows the trend in this respect. The level of formal training among owner/managers is considered low (CERT 1992). Keep suggests that, as a consequence, they are likely to accord a low priority to the training and education of their subordinates.

Guerra and Peroni (1991) have a similar view from a European perspective. Given the prevalence of small, family firms, the owner often manages the many functions of the firm. Such entrepreneurs tend to look on training more as a cost than as an investment, especially as they have often reached the top of their small firm by working their way up (e.g. waiter—head waiter—small entrepreneur) and their training is mostly experience based. Keep suggests that an educated workforce may even be regarded as a threat, as a more self-reliant workforce would be incompatible with traditional styles of management. However, the HCTC (1993) believe that, based on their research, there is a strong correlation between employers' satisfaction with employees and the extent of employees' qualifications.-Keep concludes by commenting that international competitive advantage is likely to turn upon the skills, knowledge and commitment of an enterprise's employees, and points out that the economic consequences of a failure to invest in the human resource "are deemed to be dire".

He suggests that, instead of the "vicious circle" the aim should be to emulate the "virtuous circle" of Germany, for example. Keep's relatively pessimistic view of the hotel and catering industry contrasts with but also complements Hayes (1989), who argues that those countries that invest in all their people, and not only the most talented, also have the most successful economies. Sir Christopher Ball, (in Tuckett, 1991) concurs by commenting that most nations recognise today that the quality of the education and training of the workforce is the single most important factor in determining economic competitiveness. Learning pays, says Ball, and he argues that experience and common sense tell us that the obligation to train the whole workforce cannot be met merely by relying on market forces and the self-interest of employers. Ball (in common with the CBI, 1989) argues that this obligation to train is a role for government through:

- leadership (create a culture of learning);
- financial incentives (resources are available to support priority groups—those with the fewest advantages and the most needs).
- legislation (create an entitlement to education and training for all);

In his opinion, the task is to change our learning practice from the "vicious" circles of 1990 to the "virtuous" circles of the twenty-first century

(Ball, 1990), that are quite similar to Keep's "virtuous" circle for Germany. Tuckett (1991) agrees that what is needed is the creation of a culture of learning. To achieve it government, employers, trade unions, education and training providers and individuals will need to change attitudes, change practices, and reorder priorities. No single measure will secure the culture change necessary to create a learning society, but taken together, and accompanied by a real increase in investment by individuals, employers and government, Tuckett believes that these will do much to increase a learning work force. In contrast, Miller *et al.* (1991), argue that the lesson the UK Government has drawn from the experience of central planning and intervention in the 1960s and 1970s is that it does not work, and that effective training strategies are best designed, undertaken and funded by employers.

Cooper and Messenger (1990) agree, pointing out that the demand for, and the change in, education and training for the hotel, catering and tourism industry in the UK is occurring against a background of government handing over responsibility for training to industry at regional and local level. From an industry perspective, the national vocational qualifications (NVQs) in the UK require the recording of work-based learning, and provide a sign that industry is beginning to take learning at work much more seriously. As the pace of industrial and technological change quickens, so learning becomes of central importance to work organizations. Such developments should make work experience easier for industrial organizations to manage, encouraging them to develop more effective ways of using placements for learning purposes, although not necessarily under the aegis of the NVQs.

Case Study: Results of Career Profession Study on Iris Graduates in Hospitality Sector

Remarkably, similar proportion of respondents are employed within the tourism industry and outside the industry (48 and 46 per cent, respectively). In the original study, 73 per cent of respondents were working inside the industry and 27 per cent were employed outside the sector. This suggests that there is a high drop-out rate from tourism/hospitality employment in Ireland. A number of potential reasons for this are explored later in the paper. Four per cent of those currently working outside tourism are also pursuing further study: of these, one is employed as a cleaning supervisor, one as a social worker and one is working in the electronics industry. The remaining six per cent are unemployed and are seeking work either in or outside the tourism industry.

Of those who are working either in or out of the tourism industry, the vast majority are employed on a full time/permanent basis: 86 per cent of those in tourism and 94 per cent of those outside the industry. Amongst those working in tourism-related areas, 21 (57 per cent) are employed in management positions (six GM or MD hotel, three deputy GM hotel, two restaurant manager, two sales and marketing manager, two catering manager, one HR manager hotel, one GM golf club, one commercial manager magazine, one development director, one conference and banqueting co-ordinator, one reservations co-ordinator).

Of the remainder, seven are self-employed (bar, restaurant, hotel, catering), two are senior receptionists, two are airline personnel (cabin crew, supervisor), two are lecturers, one is an accountant (bar/hotel), one is an accounts administrator and one is an assistant supervisor in a travel agency. A breakdown of the job category by level of current qualification demonstrates that there is a greater representation of those with degree-level qualifications employed in senior management positions within the tourism industry.

Those employed within the tourism education sector are the most qualified. Finance is the job function most frequently undertaken by those employed in tourism; 72 per cent of respondents reported that they always or often perform tasks in this area. Food and beverage (69 per cent), followed by sales and marketing (65 per cent) are also carried out regularly. The fact that front office/accommodation functions are less frequently conducted suggests that as people progress in their careers in tourism they are likely to perform less of this role. The lower frequency attributed to personnel/training may indicate that this is regarded as a more specialist task within the sector. Those working outside the tourism industry are involved in a variety of different areas, including education, finance, retail and healthcare.

While a direct comparison between the level of qualification of those working inside and outside the tourism industry is not feasible given the small sample size, it is evident that those employed in the education sector are the most qualified group in both segments. Moreover, it is worth noting that a higher number of masters and degree level qualifications have been obtained by those who now work outside the tourism industry, matched by a higher number of diploma holders within the industry.

Gender

It is pertinent to note that relationship between employment status and gender. The majority of men (61 per cent) have chosen to remain in the tourism industry, whilst only two-fifths of women are currently employed in the sector. Over half of female respondents work outside of tourism, compared to just 35 per cent of men. The fact that women exhibit a greater tendency to leave the tourism industry may be linked to the unsociable nature of the work, which is often incompatible with family life. It may also be related to difficulties associated with achieving equal opportunities within the sector because women are less likely to be recruited, developed and rewarded as career staff with senior management potential (Purcell, 1993). There is no major difference in annual gross salary between those who work within the tourism industry and those who are employed outside the tourism sector for the lower salary ranges. Twenty-three per cent of those employed in tourism earn less than 25, 000 and 17 per cent earn between 25, 001 and 30, 000.

The corresponding figures for those working outside the tourism industry are 22 per cent for both salary ranges. A more obvious difference is apparent further up the salary scale. Thirty-one per cent of those working inside the tourism industry earn between 30, 001 and 40, 000, whilst only nine per cent of those outside of tourism are in this bracket. However, the opposite is true for the 40, 001 to 50, 000 salary range, as only nine per cent of those working in tourism are in this range, compared to 26 per cent of those outside of tourism. Furthermore, whilst only three per cent of those employed in tourism earn between 50, 001 and 65, 000, 25 per cent of those outside the industry are in this salary range. In contrast to this pattern, a greater percentage of those working in tourism are in the highest salary bracket (17 per cent compared to 3 per cent outside).

On closer inspection, it was found that the vast majority of this 17 per cent are self-employed/proprietors, whilst the three per cent from outside the industry is related to the retail sector. Thus, it is clear that, with the exception of the self-employed tourism workers in the 65, 001-70, 000+range, those outside the industry tend to fare better in terms of gross salary. There was no noteworthy relationship between age (i.e. length of time working) and earning potential. However, further insights are gained when annual gross salary range is cross-tabulated with gender and original level of qualification. There is a greater representation of men in the higher salary brackets. Thirty-eight per cent of men are in the 55, 001-70, 000+range, compared to only 12 per cent of women. Regarding the different qualification levels, it is clear that those respondents who had originally graduated with a certificate are significantly under represented as the salary scales increase; seven per cent are in the 55, 001-70, 000+category, while the corresponding figures for diploma and degree graduates are 21 and 24 per cent respectively. The employment benefits received by employees are summarised. Staff discounts are the most widespread employment benefit within the tourism industry, received by 79 per cent of employees.

This is consistent with the nature of the industry where there is scope for employers to provide *inter alia* reduced rates for hotel rooms or concessions for restaurants and leisure centres. The provision of a pension scheme is the most commonly received benefit amongst those working outside the industry, noted by 82 per cent of employees. The fact that fewer respondents from within the tourism sector (64 per cent) receive a pension is perhaps indicative of the often more impermanent nature of the work.

The other most notable difference between those working inside or outside the tourism industry relates to the use of leisure facilities: understandably, this is listed as an employee benefit by 43 per cent of those employed within tourism compared to only 11 per cent of those from other sectors.

Job Satisfaction

Respondents were also asked to give feedback regarding the importance they attributed to a variety of different factors with respect to job satisfaction. Employees from both sectors rank interesting/challenging work and salary as their top two priorities. Ability to combine work/home life, freedom to organize own work and job security are the next most important factors for those involved in tourism. However, the items outlined by those outside the industry differ slightly: job security is also noted within the top five factors, but hours of work and location comprise the remaining two. The work/home life issue was a recurring theme throughout the study and was frequently referred to by those involved in the tourism industry.

Leaving the Industry

Respondents who are currently working outside the tourism industry were asked to indicate which factors had contributed to this decision. Unsuitable/unsociable working hours coupled with poor remuneration are the primary reasons given by those who have left the industry, cited by 60 and 55 per cent of respondents respectively. Along with work/life balance, these issues were referred frequently to throughout the entire study. Just over half of respondents to this question indicated that they had left the industry in order to achieve a broader range of experiences.

Poor career structures (27 per cent) and the unchallenging nature of the work (21 per cent) within the industry were also noted as contributory factors. When those employed outside the industry were asked if they would return to the industry, the majority were either negative (61 per cent) or unsure (26 per cent) in their response. Respondents were also questioned regarding the factors that would encourage people to return to work in the tourism industry. There were 34 responses to this question, and respondents listed more than one factor: 44 per cent of these noted sociable working hours (quality of life/family life), 32 per cent cited better remuneration, 18 per cent mentioned owning their own business and 6 per cent referred to improvements in management practice/structure within the industry.

A further 26 per cent said there were no factors that would encourage them to return to work in tourism. Regarding the factors that would prevent respondents from returning to work in the tourism industry, there were 39 responses and respondents listed more than one factor. Seventy-two per cent of these referred to hours of work, 59 per cent cited remuneration, and 23 per cent mentioned the industry structure (in terms of management and ownership). Other responses included the lack of prospects/promotion opportunities within the industry, insufficient training and staff development, and the unchallenging nature of the work as well as seasonality/insecurity.

Working Abroad

Respondents were asked to identify whether they are currently working abroad or whether they had worked abroad since 1996. The majority (64 per cent) had worked in Ireland only, 10 per cent had worked abroad, and 26 per cent had worked in Ireland and abroad. Respondents who had worked abroad or were still abroad were asked to list the most important factors which had led them to do so; there were 27 responses to this question, with some respondents noting more than one factor. Almost half of these (48 per cent) referred to a desire to experience change and gain additional knowledge, 41 per cent of respondents were encouraged to seek work abroad by the conditions of employment (money, etc.) and opportunities available, while 31 per cent were motivated by travel. Respondents were asked to describe the differences between conditions of employment in Ireland and abroad.

There were 25 responses to this question and respondents listed more than one difference in some cases. Almost half (48 per cent) referred to superior remuneration (pay/benefits) and perks (medical, maternity) offered abroad, 22 per cent cited more favourable hours of work, 22 per cent also cited better quality management/HR/training, 15 per cent noted a more positive image of the industry (recognition and respect), seven per cent highlighted opportunities for promotion, while 28 per cent reported conditions to be the same or similar. Regarding the factors which would encourage those still working abroad to return to work in the tourism industry in Ireland, responses were similar to those identified by those working outside the tourism industry generally: salary, hours of work (office-based), own business, a more modern approach to management practices and none.

Career Progression and Plans

Respondents were asked if they had changed jobs since the previous study was undertaken: 68 per cent reported moving jobs at least once since 1996, indicating significant mobility. The average number of job movements was evenly divided between those currently working in and outside the tourism industry – approximately two for both segments. Respondents were asked to specify any factors that might have curtailed their career progression in the tourism industry, whether personal, job-related or education/training-related. There were 49 responses to this question and some respondents identified more than one factor. Almost two-fifths of respondents (37 per cent) felt that their advancement within the industry was hampered by the need to achieve a balance between work and home life: this was particularly obvious for female respondents who consider that the number of hours people are expected to work, coupled with their unsociable nature, are not compatible with family life. Other factors identified as having inhibited career progression include pay-related issues (22 per cent), personal/lack of interest (18 per cent), owner/management structure (18 per cent), scarcity of opportunities/ promotions available (8 per cent), lack of experience/training (8 per cent), variety/unchallenging (4 per cent).

A further 10 per cent reported that there were no factors that had impeded their career development. Respondents were also queried regarding their views on management jobs within the tourism industry as a career option; there were 64 responses to the question. Twenty-seven per cent noted the frequency of long and unsociable hours within the sector, while 22 per cent cited the relatively poor remuneration provided. Sixteen per cent focused on the personally demanding nature of the work, describing it as both physical and stressful. A further 14 per cent referred to the limited opportunities available within the industry and the difficulties associated with attempting to progress therein: there is a perception that the industry operates as a "closed shop", where jobs at managerial level are commonly retained for family members. Five per cent of respondents (all female) indicated that they had no interest in taking up a management position and an additional five per cent (both male and female) suggested that they would need to be involved in the ownership of the business.

It should be noted that even though several respondents highlighted positive aspects of the industry (e.g. great position, excellent opportunity, interesting, good variety), these are usually qualified by one or more of the negative aspects discussed above. The need for managers within the tourism/hospitality sector to be multi-skilled and flexible was also frequently expressed: this reflects the "hands on" nature of the industry, where management is expected to become involved in general operations as well as performing more executive functions. Respondents were asked to specify where they hoped to be working in five years time. Thirty-five per cent expressed a desire to remain in their current position or move to a similar role. Almost a quarter of respondents (24 per cent) aspired to become self-employed or involved in their own business. A further 23 per cent would like to assume managerial responsibilities within the tourism sector.

Education and Training

Respondents were asked to provide information regarding any additional education qualifications they had achieved since 1996. There were 33 responses and some respondents listed more than one course. Qualifications ranged from masters' and degrees in tourism/hospitality management, to diplomas and certificates in areas such as marketing and health and safety. Respondents were also asked to provide details of any training programmes they had undertaken since 1996. There were 29 responses, with some respondents listing more than one course. These training programmes covered topics such as information technology, first aid and food management and hygiene. It is clear from the analysis that even though there is an interest in ongoing education/training, there is not a high uptake of formal postgraduate courses amongst those employed in the tourism industry. When queried regarding the factors that might prevent individuals from pursuing further courses, there were 64 responses to the question.

For the majority of respondents (66 per cent), the most significant prohibitive factor is time, whether work-related, family-related or personal. Just over a third (34 per cent) expressed financial concerns, including the actual cost of enrolling in a course, potential loss of earnings if not working full time and additional childcare expenses that may be incurred. The emphasis by respondents on time and money suggests that employers are unwilling to release staff to engage in additional education/training and provide financial support towards the cost of such programmes. Thirteen per cent of respondents felt the location of courses (e.g. Dublin) and lack of availability in their local area were restrictive factors, while a further eight per cent stated that they had no interest in undertaking a course. These findings are consistent with O'Mahony and Sillitoe's (2001) study regarding the perceived barriers to participation in tertiary education among hospitality employees; namely, informational, situational, financial, institutional and dispositional. In light of the factors that may deter people from participating in further study, respondents were asked to recommend the most appropriate methods of course delivery: there were 65 responses to this question. Over half of these (55 per cent) suggested that courses should be offered on a part-time basis, 35 per cent proposed a block release system and 28 per cent were in favour of distance and e-learning.

Respondents also remarked that courses should not be "time-fillers" and should ideally be work-related with practical/hands-on application and productive outputs. In this respect, a definite balance between theory (academic) and practice is recommended. Regarding the level of contact that tourism management graduates have with their respective colleges, respondents were asked to classify this on a scale of "regular" to "never".

Over half of respondents (57 per cent) have no contact with their former college, 25 per cent are rarely in contact, 14 per cent have some level of communication while only four per cent describe their contact as regular. Amongst those who are in contact with their college, the most common forms of communication are alumni associations (magazines and newsletters), recruitment of existing students, as well as various informal exchanges. The lack of formalised contact between colleges and their graduates represents a wasted opportunity for networking and industry involvement in tourism/hospitality programmes.

Methodology for Analysis: Job of Controller in Hospitality Industry

The data was collected as part of a biennium survey performed by the Hospitality Financial Technology Professionals (HFTP) Research Institute at the University of Houston. The survey focuses on the compensation and benefits, as well as, the job characteristics and demographics of the HFTP membership. The association of HFTP is the predecessor of the International Association of Hospitality Accountants (IAHA) founded in 1952. The *IAHA* was the organization surveyed in many of the previous studies already citied. Based in Austin, Texas, HFTP is the professional association for financial and technology personnel working in hotels, resorts, clubs, casinos, restaurants and other hospitality-related businesses.

The association provides continuing education and networking opportunities to more than 4,000 members around the world, and produces the premiere hospitality technology shows HITEC and ONHTEC. HFTP also administers the examination and awards the certification for the CHAE and the Certified Hospitality Technology Professional (CHTP) designations. Prior to the HFTP Research Institute doing the survey in

2002, the 2000 compensation and benefits survey was commissioned by HFTP and carried out by an independent research firm. The reported results (Hassmiller, 2000) will be referenced as part of the analysis. In 2002, a random sample of the HFTP membership was used (Countryman and DeFranco, 2002). Eight hundred and sixty-one HFTP members were randomly selected to participate in the survey. A stratified sample was used to insure that appropriate portions of the HFTP membership were surveyed. Those not involved directly in the hospitality industry such as educators and vendors were also excluded, even though they are members of HFTP. This survey was mailed to participants and they were asked to return the completed surveys in the postage paid envelope provided. Out of the 861 surveys mailed out, 272 were returned for a response rate of 31.7 per cent. In 2004, an online or web survey was used (Countryman *et al.*, 2004).

This allowed for the entire membership of HFTP to be surveyed or at least those that opted to receive e-mail correspondence from HFTP. Seven hundred and eighteen responded to the 3, 149 e-mails sent out, this is a response rate of 22.8 per cent. The e-mail directed respondents to a web survey. In relationship to the two surveys, participants of the 200 survey were asked to project their salary and bonus for that year since the survey was done during the middle of the year. Participants of the 2004 survey reported actual salaries and bonuses for 2002 and were asked to project them for 2004. Because of the overlap in surveys for the year 2002, therefore, only actual numbers for 2002, which were collected from the 2004 survey, were used in regards to salaries and bonuses reported in 2002.

Unlike some of the early studies mentioned in the literature review, this research chose to focus on those who just have the title of controller and does not include corporate controllers or division/area controllers. The Statistical Package for the Social Sciences (SPSS) was used for the data analysis. Means and frequencies were computed for the various profiles. *T*-tests and chi-square tests were used to determine if statistically significant differences existed between different profiles. *T*-tests were used to test for significant difference between means and chi-square tests were used for the frequencies. General sample characteristics and demographics are presented in which shows that the respondent pool is very diverse in terms of age, gender, annual household income, and education level.

A snapshot of travel frequency, the type of hotel room stayed in, and nightly room rate for the sample. A majority of the respondents had traveled in the last three months, taken 1-3 trips during the last 12 months, and paid nightly room rates between $40 and 100. The sample was divided into two segments based on the following classification scheme. Respondents who report that that more than 50 percent of their trips requiring hotel stays are business related are considered to be business travelers. A total of 169 respondents were classified as business travelers. Respondents who report that more than 50 percent of their trips requiring hotel stays are leisure related are considered to be leisure travelers.

A total of 691 respondents were classified as leisure travelers. Those respondents who were split equally, 50 percent business and 50 percent leisure were categorized as business travelers. This resulted in a total of 239 business travelers and 691 leisure travelers. Next, we explain the results of the innovative hotel choice experiment.

Innovative Hotel Choice Modeling Results

The primary analysis approach associated with DCA is the estimation of the MNL models based on a maximum likelihood estimation technique (*Ben-Akiva and Lerman*). Recall that each respondent had to evaluate eight choice sets, each containing two descriptions of hotels along with the option of not choosing either. Statistical details about MNL model estimation is described in extensive detail by *Ben-Akiva and Lerman* and *Louviere et al*. A more applied description of DCA and MNL mo del estimation is provided in *Verma et al.* and *Verma and Plaschka*. *Louviere et al.* and *Ben-Akiva and Lerman* recommend that when estimating MNL models, experimental variables can be "effects-coded" to accurately estimate the relative impact on respondents' choices. The estimated MNL model for this study was statistically significant at the 5 percent level. The relative impact of each experimental attribute on hotel choice decisions. Recall that we are only focusing on the innovative attributes that were included in the original broader dataset.

Therefore, all results presented ignore the non-innovative attributes that were also included in the study. The estimated ^{2} weights for the innovative attributes are standardized to be between "zero" and "one" based on the highest and lowest part worth utility of an attribute. By transforming the data linearly, it is easy to compare and contrast the impacts of each attribute to one another. We estimated the relative main effect by subtracting the highest and lowest ^{2} weights for a given attribute (Louviere *et al.*). The main effects allow us to compare the overall impact of changing the levels of innovative attributes in hotel choice against each other. The numerical results are shown to depict graphically the hotel choice patterns. It is important to reemphasize that the results provided are determined from the innovative constructs only; all other options were not included in the calculation of the estimated standardized weights.

The relative main effects of all experimental attributes and the relative impact of each of the levels. Among these three constructs, "hotel type" accounts for 61 percent of the relative weight, followed by "customization" with a relative weight of 27 and 12 percent from "technology". The main effect for each attribute was determined to give a more detailed insight into hotel choice criteria. For example, within the "customization" construct, the attributes with the smallest main effects are the option to customize room décor and the option of flexible check in/out. In addition, the availability of internet reservations has a small overall effect in comparison to the other technological attributes.

A larger main effect for type of hotel became apparent when respondents were selecting a midrange to upscale hotel in comparison to an economy hotel. The relative impact of each level of the "hotel type" attributes. For business travelers choosing an economy hotel, motels were the most preferred type of hotel. While those who were selecting a midrange to upscale hotel preferred standardized hotel chains with independently operated boutique hotels following close behind. In comparison, the most popular hotel type for leisure travelers selecting economy hotels were boutique hotels.

In addition, leisure travelers choosing among upscale hotels most prefer boutique hotels operated by a recognized chain. Overall, boutique hotels were a strongly preferred option across both customer segments. The relative main effects for the "technology" attributes are shown. For business travelers, providing internet access has the largest impact on hotel choice while for the leisure traveler it is the availability of a business center. While it may appear counterintuitive that leisure travelers' hotel choice is being influenced by a technological offering such as a business center, possible reasons for this perceived anomaly are described below: first, recall that these reported main effects are relative comparisons to one another.

A business center may be the most preferred technological option, but when compared to other innovations such as childcare and in-room kitchen amenities it no longer has the largest impact. Second, leisure travelers may want a business center available to them because it provides benefits such as email checking, copying, package delivery, and other facilities which a leisure traveler might also value. Both segments ranked the option of booking hotel reservations via the internet as a low priority probably because internet reservations are no longer "order winners" but a necessary requirement. Furthermore, those respondents selecting amongst economy hotels, consistently weighted the availability of technological innovations more heavily than when selecting a midrange or upscale hotel.

This would suggest that the hotel choice of travelers staying at economy hotels is swayed more from offerings of technological service innovations than travelers staying at midrange or upscale hotels. The main effects for the "customization" attributes. Across all hotel and traveler types, available childcare facilities, in-room kitchen facilities, and pet policies have the largest impact on hotel choice. Respondents deciding on economy hotels placed a greater emphasis on all the customized service options in comparison to the other types of hotels. Once again, implying that travelers choosing among economy hotels make their choices based on the innovative offerings the hotels provide. Academic and managerial implications. First, the results present the tradeoffs made by hotel guests.

Secondly, by examining the tradeoffs made by hotel guests, in terms of innovative service offerings, we are able to enhance the design and development of a service concept. Lastly, by pinpointing which innovative attributes have an impact on hotel choice; managers will be able to judge how, operationally, they should deliver such innovative services. Past research and anecdotal evidence suggest that service innovation, in general, has a positive impact on customers' choice and can result in increased revenues for a firm. IBM's innovative service program is just one example of the financial benefits that can be realized from implementing service innovation.

Our study, demonstrates the impact of including innovation within a hotel's service concept. The type of hotel has the largest impact for both business and leisure travelers' hotel choices. We also find service innovation to have a larger impact on guests who are selecting economy hotels in comparison to midrange or upscale hotels. Furthermore, innovative service amenities, such as technological improvements and customization features, have a stronger impact on leisure travelers' hotel choices in comparison to business travelers; while hotel type has a larger effect for business travelers' choices.

Overall, we found across both customer segments that innovation does matter when selecting a hotel. Recalling the three broad categories of hotel innovation presented in our study – hotel type, technology, and customization we can infer the following results. First, hotel type contributed to the majority of hotel choice. In particular, business travelers' decisions were found to be guided more by hotel type when compared to leisure travelers; and midrange to upscale hotel selection were influenced more by hotel type than economy hotel selection. Second, the technology option, specifically the booking of hotel reservations via the internet, has the smallest impact on both business and leisure travelers' hotel choice.

Third, the customization construct's greatest impacts came from available child care, pet accommodation, and the inclusion of in-room kitchen facilities. Within each construct, tradeoffs were apparent for both business and leisure travelers. First, hotel type contributed to a significant portion of hotel guests' choices. The boutique hotel, the innovative option, stood out as a preferred choice among other more traditional alternatives. Independent boutique hotels were the second most popular hotel type for business travelers staying at midrange and upscale hotels and it is the most popular type for leisure travelers staying at economy hotels. Also, leisure travelers selecting from upscale hotels prefer boutique hotels operated by a recognized chain more than the other hotel options.

A recognized chain boutique hotel was a secondary preference for leisure travelers selecting from mid-range hotels. Second, business travelers, across all hotel types, are more greatly influenced by the technological offering of in-room internet access. The availability of a business center was next in priority, followed by internet booking reservations. In contrast, leisure travelers, across all hotel types, are more greatly guided by the presence of a business center, followed by in-room internet access. Once again the smallest impact emanated from the internet reservation bookings option.

Lastly, the preferred customization options included service offerings such as on-site child care, pet friendly policies, and in-room kitchen facilities rather than flexible check in/out and customized room décor. By examining the tradeoffs made by hotel guests, we are able to gain a better understanding of what types of innovative service offerings determine a traveler's hotel choice. The customer tradeoffs we have identified play an important role in the design and development of a hotel's service concept. We have to remember that a service concept acts always as a mediator between the "what", customer needs, and the "how", operational capabilities of service design must be aligned. Additionally the study emphasizes the "what" for the service concept but does not specifically test the "how".

However, a thorough understanding of customers' desires will allow experienced managers to more easily infer which operational capabilities are necessary to implement such innovations. For example, the popular hotel type option of a boutique hotel conjures up such operational questions as: what layout and facility changes would be necessary? What staff training would need to be conducted? What service amenities would be needed to constitute a boutique hotel to would be guests? Another example, in-room internet access, brings forth operational issues such as: what infrastructure costs are incurred from adding technological services? What price level would the hotel need to charge for the access or can it be complimentary? Would managers need to hire information technology staff for dealing with internet-related problems? Or would managers need to train the current staff to handle such problems?

Similarly a flexible checking option might require implementation of a more complex hotel reservation and labor scheduling system. Therefore, while we have not statistically tested the influence of innovative service offerings on operational strategy formulation, we are still able to make inferences regarding operational issues which might arise from implementing various service innovations. Numerous managerial implications can be drawn from our study. First and foremost, our study assists hotel managers in understanding what service innovations might have the greatest impact on potential guests' choices. This understanding will enhance the design and development of hotel service. In addition, it will focus manager's efforts around the innovations which are most important to guests.

Through the provision of customer choice patterns, managers will be more adept at improving their operational planning and decision-making. Ultimately, the end result will be a better-devised operational strategy formulation that is sensitive to the preferences of customers. Furthermore, the results presented in this paper can be used to develop a decision-support model which can assist in conducting "what-if" type of analyses. The managers can evaluate the relative values and willingness to pay for each proposed service innovations prior to making huge investment of money and effort (*Verma et al.*).

While our study provides a detailed outlook of the tradeoffs made by hotel travelers and the design and development of a hotel's service concept, there are limitations in our conclusions. For example, as in most studies, our data represents only one snapshot in time. This limits our ability to draw conclusions on the long-term impact of service innovations. In order to address this issue, a longitudinal study would be required to track and compare the impact of guests' choices over time. Also, our data are limited to the hotel industry and one geographic market, the US, which presents issues concerning the generalizability of the results. Studying hotels in a variety of countries, for example, would undoubtedly yield different service preference results.

Thus, cross-cultural, horizontal and vertical industry sector studies would enhance the generalizability of the results. Despite the inherent limitations of our study, we have presented a solid first examination of the impact service innovation has on customer's choices and the operational issues which arise from implementing such service innovations. In summary this paper offers both academic and managerial contributions through the examination of innovative service tradeoffs made by hotel guests.

Our goal was to contribute to the service management literature by presenting an innovative-specific industry sector perspective when it comes to adding new services into the core service concept. We also presented a managerial tool for hotel managers to utilize when deciding which service innovations to implement. Finally the results can be used in formulating an operational strategy which aligns with hotel guests' values and preferences. By understanding the service innovation tradeoffs made by customers, a service concept can be designed more effectively yielding into a firm's much more profitable and sustainable operational strategy.

7

Other Issues in Hospitality Management and Service Organizations

"When I sell liquor, its called bootlegging; when my patrons serve it on Lake Shore Drive, its called hospitality"

— *Al Capone*

SEXUAL HARASSMENT IN HOSPITALITY AND SERVICE ORGANIZATIONS

It is significant to note that inherent characteristics of service organizations create a prime breeding ground for sexual harassment. By its nature, the service production process is inextricably linked to the close involvement of the customer, and behavioural norms are often set around satisfying a customer's expectations; preferably exceeding those expectations. In addition to the intra-organizational strains resulting from the "normal" conflicts between different hierarchical levels and departments, the service organization has to deal with three categories of workers: back-stage staff, front-line personnel, and participating customers. The constant interaction between these groups is therefore a constant source of stress and conflict.

The service workplace is largely populated by women, especially at the lower levels. Service employees tend to be young and have little formal education. Their position in the workplace is often weak: young women are less confident when dealing with people in authority, and feel less important than any other group of employees in the work place (Aaron and Dry, 1992; Hamilton and Veglahn, 1992; Laudadio, 1988). Due to the lack of legitimate, coercive, reward, or expert power, the service worker may have to rely on referent power; that is, to be socially attractive and friendly with the customer. One author knows of a young girl who was told on starting as a waitress to "wear her skirt as short as she would feel it comfortable".

Research by Eller (1990) clearly indicates that more men and women experience sexual harassment in the hotel industry than do individuals in society-at-large. Woods and Kavanagh (1994) also found that hospitality managers perceive sexual harassment to be pervasive within the industry. The hospitality industry may be particularly susceptible to incidents of sexual harassment due to the ambiguity of "hospitality service", the unusual hours and conditions of work, the interaction of persons in the delivery of service, and the importance placed on appearance—which focuses attention on people as sexual beings. In many customer contact roles in the service sector, "sexiness" is a part of the role itself, the "job flirt" is encouraged as a part of the service style (Hall, 1993) and there may be a thin line between "selling the service" and "selling sexuality". We found from our hospitality survey of personnel directors that 80 per cent responded that the dress code was important with 39 per cent allowing very short skirts and 38 per cent not allowing trousers. Interestingly on being asked if safe "flirting" with customers was part of the job for your service staff 7 per cent agreed it was and 39 per cent were neutral. Outlets such as TGI Fridays utilise training schemes which encourage flirtation as a means of increasing the amount spent and repeat business. This is not an easy situation to manage. MacKinnon (1979), for example, defines the role of the waitress as requiring "constant vigilance, skillful obsequiousness, and an ability to project the implication that there (are) ... sexual possibilities for the relationship while avoiding the explicit 'how about it' that would force a refusal into the open".

While management may implicitly or explicitly encourage customer contact staff to use their personality (sexuality) to please the customer, the staff themselves may also actively exploit their assets for their own interests. The following quotation (Cook, 1996) from a London waitress demonstrates some of the contradictions of the role: Everyone I know wears shorter skirts ... especially on Saturday nights—because you can guarantee better tips ... I suppose you are slightly willing to compromise and I'm not as feminist about it as I know I should be. But unfortunately men tip and women don't. An emphasis on the quality of customer service, which is normally regarded as a positive feature of an organization, may leave staff feeling unsupported and vulnerable if they are expected to respond in a reasonable and friendly manner to customers who overstep the mark. Hochschild's (1983) classic study of cabin attendants showed the stress associated with having to keep smiling regardless of the way one is treated by customers.

Sosteric (1996) reports a case study of staff in a night-club whose morale and quality of service went down when they were no longer allowed, in the name of improving customer service, to support each other and use aggression and rudeness to deal with obnoxious behaviour or sexual harassment from customers. Unlike office and manufacturing work places where an employee works virtually without interruption from outsiders, hotel employees usually have close social contact with co-workers, supervisors, customers and suppliers. Moreover, hotel employees work long, irregular hours and experience periods of intense activity balanced with slack periods. These long hours often involve night, evening and even holiday shifts. In an environment of heightened—almost forced—social interaction (particularly in smaller hotels with shared employee accommodation), a prime breeding ground exists for the existence of sexual harassment.

Guidelines for Inter-Vendor Cooperation and Systems Integration

On June 27, 2002, nine prominent hotel industry technology leaders from around the world, meeting over a two-day period prior to HITEC, have formed an initiative to break through the current impasse on systems integration and productivity at Chicago. The initiative, known as Hotel Technology—Next Generation (HTNG), aims to define a new approach to providing systems and technology services at the property, brand, management company and ownership levels. The group concluded that the hotel industry is fundamentally dissatisfied with the effectiveness of current technology options and their preparedness to address future business needs. The primary causes of this dissatisfaction were:

- lack of effective inter-vendor cooperation and systems integration
- poor adoption of modern technologies.
- drawbacks in the current technology financing process

Equally, there is a lack of recognition within large segments of the hotel community of the importance of technology in hotel management, and the industry has been unable to communicate a common and consistent vision of its requirements to the vendor community. The HTNG initiative aims to define a new approach that will facilitate the development of next-generation, customer-centric systems that will better meet the needs of the global hotel community. Commencing with the development of specific architectural and business guidelines, HTNG will work to promote closer vendor working relationships, system interoperability, and the development of new service-delivery models. HTNG has produced a white paper, "A Path to Achieving Next-Generation Technology for the

Hotel Industry," available by e-mail, that details the group's analysis and recommendations, including a set of proposed guidelines.

It has also launched a campaign that will, starting at HITEC, seek to determine the level of support among industry participants, and to obtain feedback on its initial findings. "The objective of Hotel Technology—Next Generation initiative is to respond to the technology needs of the hotel industry," says Jim Yoakum, a member of the HFTP Technology Hall of Fame and former Chief Information Officer of Marriott International and later, Choice Hotels International. "Hopefully, it will lead toward establishing inter-vendor cooperation and systems integration, creating a much-needed customer-centric platform within our industry."

About Hotel Technology—Next Generation

Launched by nine prominent hotel technology industry leaders during a two-day meeting held prior to HITEC 2002, Hotel Technology—Next Generation (HTNG), aims to define a new approach to providing systems and technology services at the property, brand, management company and ownership levels. HTNG aims to facilitate the development of next-generation, customer-centric systems that will better meet the needs of the global hotel community. Commencing with the development of specific architectural and business guidelines, HTNG will work to promote closer vendor working relationships, system interoperability, and the development of new service-delivery models.

Case Study Examples of International Hospitality Management

This section provides an overview of approaches to IMD using three case studies, with data obtained from the second phase interviews. The company approaches will then be discussed and appraised against the four key criteria outlined in stages one and two of the framework.

Company A

This airline company's approach to IMD is dictated by central business strategy in line with overall corporate strategy. Historically, this UK company used to operate a strong ethnocentric recruitment strategy. Currently, international recruitment and selection is undertaken within the organization with structured and rigorous graduate recruitment, selection and training. Training occurs annually, and there is a pool of talent for senior and global management potential. The company recruits approximately 30-40 graduates per year and an international posting early on in the training period has recently become integral to the general management programme.

This enables future managers to gain international experience early in their careers and clearly indicates the link between the development programme and succession planning. The company does not have a formal IMD programme but recognizes the need to offer the opportunity to work abroad both for personal development and to fulfil the international staffing requirement. The past ethnocentric approach meant that the majority of key positions abroad were filled by British employees or parent country nationals (PCNs). However, recent policy changes have resulted in an increasing number of host country nationals (HCNs) in management positions. This allows local employees better career opportunities within their small units and reduces the cost of expatriation to the company. Third country nationals (TCNs) are also being used increasingly to fill key foreign positions.

This implies a shift to a geocentric approach to international recruitment. Managers can choose to follow two types of international careers: the individual expatriate or the lifelong expatriate. The former are posted abroad for two or three assignments to gain experience of managing their own unit and of different cultures. These placements generally last between six and nine months; on repatriation their experience leads to further career progression within the company. The latter group are professional expatriates who simply transfer from country to country maintaining similar positions at each move. These lifelong expatriates would traditionally stay overseas for years and sometimes experienced transition problems on repatriation. Because of this, the company is encouraging more frequent, shorter-term international assignments, while utilizing the career development process to identify individuals who are capable of placements on this basis. Expatriate assignments are not seen as an essential part of the career progression, but the global ambitions of the company mean that managers are expected to retain a flexible attitude to overseas postings. There are no formal selection criteria for international assignments, the main criteria being similar to those for national placements, namely a proven record of competence in technical and managerial areas of expertise.

A sophisticated database is used to track career moves. It is supplemented by a company newsletter containing details of all vacancies worldwide; in fact this is considered to be the main vehicle for international transfers. Attractive salary and benefits packages are offered to expatriates, and it is not uncommon for an individual to visit the country (with family if appropriate) to enable a final decision as to the suitability of the placement. The company also offers individual cultural awareness and language training using tailor-made courses dependent on individual training needs and type of assignment.

Company B

Company B, a US-owned hotel multinational, has no formal IMD programme, although it has recently relaunched its graduate management scheme with a more international focus. International positions that become vacant are communicated across the company using a computerized personnel database, and all those interested are invited to apply through the local unit personnel department. The company fully supports individual development needs and has a rigorous approach to training and development, inextricably linked to business objectives. An appraisal system in place aims to identify potential managers who wish to transfer to international positions. Prerequisites for these international postings are a minimum of five years with the company and proficiency in at least two languages. In addition, selection criteria, such as adaptability, international background and mobility, are stated as essential attributes. Extra training is offered to candidates working overseas in order to develop competences, for example cross-cultural awareness and country culture familiarization.

The sophistication of the computerized database and the consistency with which the vacancies are communicated to staff enable the company to operate a geocentric recruitment strategy. The company stated, however, that intra-regional transfers were most common, thus it could be implied that it was operating a regiocentric strategy. The company is committed to "developing truly international managers" but it states certain barriers to this as being visa/work permit difficulties, inappropriate management style because of lack of cultural understanding and awareness, and a low supply of potential international candidates. The newly launched trainee management scheme hopes to help solve this problem and a key selling point within this is the "global nature of the industry and the international opportunities it can offer" (company brochure).

Although the company does not operate a formal international development programme, it does not consider this to be a weakness. It believes the development opportunities it offers are such that, if individuals are competent and motivated to succeed at an international level, the internal human resource systems in place will support them to achieve this.

The focus is very much on staff making full use of the resources and opportunities available to them through international developmental opportunities which include both long and short-term assignments. It is clear that the issue of developing managers for international assignments is very high on the corporate agenda.

Company C

Company C is a Japanese-owned multinational hotel company whose approach to IMD is three-dimensional. The first initiative is the corporate management development programme which was developed in the early 1990s. The company had no real succession planning system in place at that time while it pursued an active international expansion programme and it realized that, unless it addressed the issue, it would risk demand outstripping supply. At the time, it identified the main weaknesses within the system as being: no identifiable IMD programme; existing programmes lacked credibility; the need to attract good calibre graduates; and, finally, no centralized recruitment system causing fragmented decision making.

In designing its new approach, the company wanted the programme to be dynamic, novel and aimed at attracting and keeping the best people, while at the same time being exacting and tough to ensure quality. Therefore, it was proposed that a programme of active recruitment specifically designed to attract potential management should be introduced, with a ten-year training and development programme culminating in a general management position. The programme would encompass a tailor-made foundation year (depending on previous experience), placements in progressively more senior management positions, part-time study for an MBA qualification, designated project assignments throughout the training period and, most importantly, placements in at least three countries to encourage mobility, cultural empathy and global business awareness.

Entry to the programme is dictated by specific criteria—a formal qualification, total mobility and competence in at least one other language, and the target age for the programme is 21-26 years. The programme is open to both external and internal candidates with a proven record of achievement. Although the programme appears highly structured, the speed and ease with which trainees will progress through the different stages vary in practice. Performance is rigorously assessed throughout and, although utmost support is given to help progress, trainees need to reach high standards at each stage. In order to help support the young trainees through this steep career path, a mentoring system is actively used. Although at present the programme focuses on general management positions, there are plans to expand it to include other functional areas such as marketing and information technology. While fully committed to this programme, the company wanted to ensure that other future potential managers who did not fit into the previously described programme would also have a development route to general manager status with international experience. Another two systems, therefore, are in place. Short to medium-term supply and demand for international positions are dealt with through a combination of appraisal, succession planning and a computerized global transfer system. Each hotel in the company produces a six-monthly labour plan which includes anticipated requirements and proposed sources of recruitment. Potential talent is identified through the appraisal system and entered into the succession plan which identifies the individual's current position and their desired future position in six months' time. Hotels in a region will use this plan as part of their selection strategy.

The global transfer system is a worldwide database which tracks and provides information on key senior positions across the world, widely communicating the opportunities available, and encouraging international mobility and promotion or transfer opportunities. The third dimension to the company's approach is its most recent. Aimed at senior executives in hotels, this programme is used to identify the required development needs and potential of general managers of the future. Criteria for acceptance on this include: completion of basic management skills programmes; excellent appraisal reports; international mobility; and good written and spoken English.

The company hopes to get to the point where every executive manager has been on this programme before being a general manager. This rigorous assessment programme is based on identified key competences or dimensions for general managers. These have been chosen by assessing current general managers in terms of what makes them successful. Candidates participate in a rigorous, five-day assessment centre exercise, run by senior company managers and psychometric specialists. Candidates receive feedback on their future development needs. The programme identifies one of the following scenarios for each candidate:

- competence at current level but not capable of development to general manager level;
- capability for general manager level but many/few development needs identified;
- capability for general manager level at next position.

Service Innovation and Customer Choices in the Hospitality Industry

Customers, in a number of industries, are constantly bombarded with run-of-the-mill product and service offerings. As a result, customers both desire and more often demand innovative alternatives. In response, many service-oriented firms are striving to integrate novel features into their product-service offerings. Even product-oriented firms have noted the benefits of adding service innovation to their business strategies. For example, during recent years, IBM, a predominantly product-oriented firm, generated over half of its total revenue from services. Yet, only 15 percent of IBM's research and development budget was being allocated to services (Fitzgerald, 2005). Realizing this discrepancy, IBM recently realigned its strategy and business plan emphasizing service-based innovations.

The new strategy was a resounding success. With one of IBM's innovative service programs adding over $300 million to last year's total revenue (Fitzgerald, 2005). The benefits of service innovation are apparent. What is not as clear is how managers should decide on which innovations to implement. In some cases, innovative service offerings are necessary just to maintain a firm's current market share. This phenomenon suggests "... that some innovations may merely raise the cost of doing business without a significant economic benefit, other than to preserve current business and without providing a competitive edge..." (*Reid and Sandler*). However, other innovations may enhance service differentiation and induce financial gains.

Thus, it is important for managers to implement innovations which are not only desired by customers but also are economically beneficial to the firm (*Reid and Sandler*). Hospitality firms, such as hotels, are an ideal example of a market which could benefit from the implementation of service innovation. First, from a customer's perspective, the hospitality market is perpetually inundated by many similar, often easily substitutable service offerings. This can cause difficulties for hotel managers as they attempt to differentiate an individual hotel from its competitors (*Reid and Sandler*). One solution to this challenge may be to offer new and innovative features to customers. Secondly, the hospitality industry is rapidly changing due to accelerations in information technology (*Olsen and Connolly*). Managers will need to make proactive changes which focus even more intensely on customer preferences, quality, and technological interfaces in order to stay competitive in such a dynamic environment (*Karmarkar*). Thirdly, travelers today do not exhibit, as in past decades, a truly brand loyal behaviour.

Travelers instead are choosing to patronize hotels that offer the best value proposition under existing budgetary constraints. (*Olsen and Connolly*). In order to add value to the guests' experience, hotel managers and marketers must meet the challenge of determining which services are preferred by hotel guests (*Olsen and Connolly*). Once a manager understands customers' preferences, the challenge then becomes prioritizing those preferences which add the greatest value to the hotel's existing service offering. The purpose of this study is to explore customer tradeoffs for service innovation. The paper will examine the addition of innovative offerings and its relation to the hotel's core service concept. The service concept encompasses both the "how", in other words, the operations content, and the "what", the marketing content, of service design as well as the integration of the two (*Goldstein et al.*).

In other words, we will examine the innovative service preferences of hotel guests, while also exploring how these preferences align with the strategic intent of the firm. Aligning customer preferences with operational strategy is important because operational constraints make it impossible to implement all options of innovative service offerings. Instead, hotel managers need to develop an understanding of market preferences prior to the addition of new services. This type of knowledge will enable managers to select innovative offerings that are most beneficial to the firm and that will truly have an impact on customer's choices.

Finance and Accounting in Hotel Management

For a start, you will know by now, or be pretty certain of, your estimated overheads. These must include rent, rates (an ever-increasing burden to most businesses), insurances, a provision for wages and possibly National Insurance, and an estimate of energy costs, even though some of these may be variable (e.g. the place must be heated and lighted even when you are not busy, although the kitchen will be using less power). It is essential that nothing is left out and that the figures you compile are as accurate as they possibly can be. It may, at this stage, be comforting to bear in mind the happy fact that, as you become more successful (busier, that is), the proportion of these fixed overheads against earnings will decline. But that is some way ahead yet. The thing to stress here is that you must include everything, even costs like telephone and stationery. As a very rough rule—and this can be only a merest guide, because such 'rules' will vary between one type of place and another—your fixed overhead should eventually work out at about twenty per cent of your turnover, staff costs up to forty per cent of turnover (much less if you do a lot of the work yourself) and materials, food and drink about thirty-five per cent of turnover, but this depends very much on whether you are buying in most of your food or preparing fresh food from the start.

However, that is still in the future. You need accurate costs because the trade works on gross profit, from which your net profit can be deduced. And at no time include VAT in any calculations. At the end of this chapter I have gathered together some calculation tables for working out various profit, mark-up percentages and VAT-inclusive selling-prices which you will find useful, as well as self-explanatory. The prime aim when you first open your doors should be to cover your variable costs by the prices you are going to charge. Obviously you are going to have to cover all your costs eventually, but if you see a reasonable return just on the variables—food, staff and so on, you are also contributing towards your fixed overheads. But there is a danger here of underpricing your business. This is a very real danger for the newcomer for, although it would be silly to price yourself out of the market at the outset, you have already decided the sort of operation you are going to run, the sort of clientele you hope to attract and the sort of prices for similar businesses locally, and it is a mistake to try to undercut all and sundry. If you undercut overmuch, you will be forced to increase your charges at a later stage, and customers do not like this one bit, for they rarely understand—and why should they?—the complexity of restaurant charges. Once again, begin as you mean to go on.

A restaurant not far from our own business made the mistake of too-low prices when it first opened. It did, indeed, attract customers, including some of mine, but all of them said that no place could stay in business too long on those prices in this day and age. It actually became a bit of a joke but, alas, the joke was on the owner, who soon had to shut his doors as the enormous hoist in prices which he was eventually forced to make lost him most of his hard-earned reputation. It is a warning all should heed. This is easier said than done. The mark-up—the price you are going to charge for your meals—depends on local factors as well as costs. And the mark-up is not necessarily the same on all foods sold. It is just not practical to establish a rule for your gross profit margin applicable to everything you sell. You are bound to have to vary the charge depending on whether it is a first, a main or a sweet course, otherwise customers will find themselves paying ludicrously low or unacceptably high prices on dishes which are simply not worth either.

So once again your common sense will have to do battle with your fiscal policy. Thus your overheads may well dictate your mark-up policy, but your customers alone have the say in whether they stay away or come regularly. In fact, mark-ups tend to be thirty-three, forty or fifty per cent throughout the trade. It may be easier here if we look for a fifty per cent gross profit as our example. At this figure, if you spent, say, Rs. 500 a week on food and drink, you would have to sell it for Rs. 1,000. Your overheads for that week must then be deducted, preferably both the fixed and the variable, which, again let us say, comes to Rs. 300. This is all well and good, but advice on, or examples of, sums tends to go wrong when you are dealing with the fickle public. The sales figure is merely notional, because you will have no idea that you can attain such sales until you have been in business for quite a time.

So at the start you are going to be groping in the dark with your mark-up, which may have to be very much greater if you are not achieving the sales target, in order to cover the overheads. What on earth do you do? You grin and persevere; that is what you do. And providing the amount you charge for your meals and drinks seems to be right to you, taking into account all local restaurant charges on which you have done research, as well as your style of service, the setting and so on, you will not go far wrong. If you are successful, and you have got the sums right, you may even be able to reduce charges slightly to give you an edge over the competition. But you must be careful—customers like 'special offers' but they abhor very large swings in prices, especially upwards. So your pricing, or sales, policy has to be reasonable for what you are offering, taking into account all your overheads.

Spend-per-Head

This brings us to the need to estimate in advance the amount per head that you expect your customers to spend. This is an essential estimate. It is no good saying you are going to take Rs. 1,000 a week just because you need to take that amount of money in order to stay afloat. Such a figure depends not only on 'getting 'em through the doors' but on a sensible appraisal of the service and food you are providing. Only you can estimate that. 'Spend-per-head' is very important indeed, and yet I have come across a great many people who run restaurants who have never actually estimated that and have no idea what the figure is.

In our own restaurant we knew exactly what the average was: at the end of each week I divided the takings by the number of 'covers' we served. I strongly advise you to do the same. It is an easy but instructive exercise. And remember: exclude the VAT. Some restaurants charge for set meals on the basis of the main dish. This practice, which is common and quite fair, has the slight disadvantage in that customers who want just one dish resent paying for others they do not wish to eat. Our own way round this problem was to offer all dishes priced individually, from starters to pudding, and with the main course inclusive of vegetables.

But we also offered a three-course meal, taken from the main menu, at a price slightly less than the three dishes added together. We found this was very popular, especially at lunchtime. There is nothing original about this idea, but it came about because of a close study of our market. It is a typical example of what I mean about a reasonable pricing policy coupled with flexibility and maximization of profits. It so happened, that in our country restaurant in the south, we became known not only for the quality of our food but for the reasonableness of our lunches, which attracted the retired 'gentry' and (we liked to think) the professional man with a little more time to spare than his junior colleagues. That was the market we aimed at, and it was a market in which we were totally successful. For most of the retired, older customers, it quickly became apparent to us that lunch was the main meal of their day, but for the most part they seemed content with just the one dish, although many of them always had a pudding if it appealed to them. Hence, in our place, the three-course menu was born as an experiment. It became enormously popular—it was balanced, well cooked and presented and at an acceptable price. As a result we moved, almost unconsciously, into the situation of selling three dishes when before we had sold only one. Our lunch 'spend-per-head' moved from an average of Rs. 5 to Rs. 8 almost overnight. Our costs remained virtually the same.

Back to Our Sums

The complexity of book-keeping, whether double or single entry, and the need for various 'ledgers' to go with them are quite often beyond the capability of the ordinary, smaller restaurateur, especially when he starts up in business and there do not seem enough hours in the day. I would therefore urge you to ask your accountant to set out, plainly and simply, exactly what he would like to see and how you should keep the necessary records. This will not in the long run cost anything more than his normal fees, because, as we pointed out before, it will save him time at the end of the year, and therefore you money, if everything he wants is neatly documented in the way he finds acceptable for his own method of working.

The first 'book', in my opinion, is something akin to the Kalamazoo or Lamson Paragon VAT ledger, which actually does, a number of things, by no means all of them to do with VAT. Into this book you can enter every cash or cheque transaction made: on the left-hand pages are columns into which you can put all takings, and on the right hand are columns in which to record all payments.

This is so blindingly obvious, and so easy, that, if the worst came to the worst, you would need very little else. It is a good idea to make time—say, every week—in which to enter all these items. They do not, in the case of receipts, obviously have to be itemised bill by bill—totals will do, either for the whole day or for the morning and evening services. By splitting the service, for instance, you have a record for yourself of any differences between lunches and dinners.

It is of no interest to the tax people, the VAT officers or even your accountant, but it does form a record for yourself, takes no extra trouble and allows you to see more clearly where you are going. On the right-hand pages you must record all your outgoings and to whom they were paid. Include everything. In this way you will have an absolute record, and it will be useful not only to you and the authorities but to your accountant and the bank. It is a daily record of the business, and from it you can take any information you subsequently require. You can use the various columns you will find in the book for purposes designated by you: perhaps a column for cash and another for cheques paid to you, perhaps a column for food costs and another for drinks.

Be guided by your accountant: he is the expert, you are not. But the use of each column is simplicity itself. And in any event, this is the book that the VAT inspectors will want to see, and they truly *are* experts. But what this general ledger does not contain is any information regarding money owed to you or money you are going to have to pay out in the future. It is merely a record of what has happened, not what is going to happen. Neither does it contain any standing orders which you have authorised your bank to pay on your behalf, perhaps for rates, hire purchase, equipment on lease and so on. Nor does it contain depreciation figures which will be needed to work out your annual accounts, or any assets in terms of stock, buildings, equipment and so on. On the other hand, you are asking, what more must I do? The man or woman who is a fiend at figures will be keeping many more 'books': petty cash, a bought ledger, a non-bought ledger, a cashbook, a sundry debtors ledger, a takings book, a wages book.

There is no end to the paperwork. You must call a halt, otherwise you will be swamped. Most of these records are for larger businesses, where, perhaps, the owner has plenty of time to do the bookwork while employing staff to look after his customers. This is a curious state of affairs, you may imagine. Surely, I hope you will say, I should be the person who is looking after the staff and the customers? I cannot look after both and still remain sane. Very true. Well said. Get someone else to do it, someone who knows, understands and enjoys it. Early on in this book I mentioned this point. The world is actually full of people who understand figures—retired accountants or their 'moonlight' clerks, bank managers or their 'moonlighting' tellers or assistants, men and women who have worked in accounts offices in local firms and other businesses, and many quite reliable people who advertise in the local papers, perhaps mothers of school children who have had experience of book-keeping, who cannot work full time but need a little pin money and an interest outside the home.

The service they can provide will be well worth the money and, above all, it will free you to work where you are most needed-earning money by attracting customers, not by keeping records. But, having said that, I must urge you to get *regular* help. The odd occasion is no good. Once a week is ideal, as the work may then take about an hour, or, say, three or four hours a month. But do not get too far behind. That is a certain way to muddle. It can also be dangerous. And if you cannot get help, set aside a very definite time each week in which to do the books; make it sacrosanct, and it will very quickly become a habit.

Leave it too long, skip a week, say, 'The end of the month will do', and it won't. By that time you will be in despair at the work you have to catch up. However, whether you do all your own accounts, or whether someone else does, it is essential that every bit of paper be kept. Your office will quickly resemble some vast waste-paper bin, I know, but you must be able to prove, if required, where the money has gone and on what it has been spent. So keep, preferably in separate files, the following:

- All suppliers' delivery notes, invoices and receipts.
- All bank statements relating to the business (keep your own money in a separate bank account).
- Bank paying-in books. (Try not to use single paying-in slips.)
- Cheque-book stubs.
- Cancelled cheques. (Ask the bank to return them to you with each statement.)
- Copies of your own bills, whether for customers paying cash or for invoices you have perhaps sent to company clients.
- Receipts for all cash purchases. (Always remember to ask for a receipt, however small the amount.)

The mountain of paper may depress you, but it will impress accountants, tax and VAT inspectors.

Fair Dealing

Above all, I would urge you at this point to ensure that your pricing policy is fair and honest. So I will tell you a perfectly true story of what happened to my wife and me when we started our research before we opened our first restaurant. We went to see a very successful restaurant-owner in Glasgow, who was flattered that we had asked his advice. During the course of the conversation we told him we thought it best to start with a 'set menu' in which everything, except coffee, was included, whatever choice they made. He was absolutely horrified. 'The punters won't thank you for that,' he told us flatly. 'Price everything individually. I'll give you an example. Are you going to have a speciality cheese, say?' We were puzzled. 'What do you mean by a speciality cheese?' Asked my wife humbly.

The man sighed patiently. 'You know,' he said, 'something like Camembert, Stilton, that sort of thing.' You will make up your own mind. All I can say in my own defence is that a great many of our customers have commented pleasingly on our bills, which come to exactly what they reckon they will be, and we based a reputation on it—no hidden extras is, I think, fair and honest, and the system of charging for every single thing (whether it be butter with bread—a common practice in my part of the world—or extra for courgettes in place of, say, fresh broccoli) is something which I find unpleasant. I also think it is unnecessary and shows that the restaurateur is not doing his job properly.

Taking Stock

The idea of all these records is not, however, just to please those three people, and all the others who will take an interest in your business. They are to help *you*. The net profit figure at the end of every month is all-important. It will show you how your business is progressing. From the records you have kept, you can draw up a monthly trading account and a profit-and-loss account. And to do this properly you must try, at least for the first few months or even a year or more, to do a stock-take on a certain day. This is not as complicated as it sounds. In a small business it should take no rime at all, and you will very soon get used to it. Basically you need to know, on that certain day, the value of everything you hold by way of food, drink and so on. You must estimate what is left in bottles, of course, but cases of beer, wines and spirits are easy enough, as you can refer quickly to your invoices from your suppliers. Do not forget food in the deep-freeze or in the storage cupboards and larders.

In practice, these should be comparatively similar each month, unless you have been drastically over-buying, in which case the monthly stock-take is going to be helpful in another direction too. Overbuying is in reality a waste of money. Your stock-take should reveal a more or less constant figure, certainly when averaged out over a year.

A Monthly Balance Sheet

You take this stock-take value as your starting-off point at the beginning of a monthly period, and to it you add all your purchases during the new month, along with all your other expenses, such as wages, phone bills and so on. You then enter the value of your stock at the end of that monthly period. This will give you a *gross profit* (or loss, probably, in your first few months). Against this figure of Rs. 1,500 you can then set your sales figure for the month.

So if your total sales for the month are, say, Rs. 3,000, you have a gross profit of Rs. 1,500. To get a *net profit* (or loss), you now have to add in your overheads. Of course, this is pretty basic stuff, and by making it more complex, i.e. adding in more information or breaking down the payments and overheads, you can make it more informative, perhaps even including the money you pay yourself, thus making your income tax easy to calculate at the end of the year. There are no hard-and-fast rules, but remember to exclude VAT from *all* figures, as it forms no part of your personal or business income. It is essential that VAT be kept separate from all calculations; you should pay it directly to HM Customs and Excise, less your own deductions as allowed under VAT regulations. The disadvantage is that, although this monthly balance sheet seems to be a pretty healthy one, it does not necessarily include, say, the actual cash you have received in your sales figure.

This could lead to an unbalanced view of things. You may well have paid out cash for certain items, or because some suppliers want cash in advance or on delivery. Some of your customers may be business clients who pay late the following month, but your sales figure has included them for ease of calculation. So even, if on paper, your business seems to be doing quite well, you could still run out of actual cash at the bank sometime in the future. That is where a cash-flow forecast comes in.

Only this time it is going to be a lot more accurate than the first one you did. So an update is required and, if necessary, a visit to the bank manager to ask for a future overdraft to cover any shortages which loom on the horizon. You will now have definite figures to put in at least for your first month's trading. If you do that regularly, you can foresee any trouble ahead and help yourself as well as pleasing your bank manager.

Breaking Even

Important to you at all times is the break-even point, and you should calculate this in advance. It is at least something you can do in your early days, or even before you open, as the figures can be based on a fair and reasonable knowledge or guess. The break-even point, fairly obviously, is when your sales are yielding just enough money to cover the cost. Before this is reached, you are trading at a loss; when it is exceeded, you are making a profit. Simple as that. In the restaurant trade your projected sales should be based on the number of meals you need to serve multiplied by the average spend per head, a question we have dealt with earlier, in order to cover all your fixed and variable costs.

The costs are almost certainly known to you, certainly the fixed ones, and, as I said above, you should be able to guess the variables until your trading pattern is established and you have evidence for them. The only problem is the sales. But it is also fairly obvious when calculating your break-even point that, if your total costs are going to be, say, Rs. 2,350 a month, to use the example on p. 165, you must sell 1,000 meals at a price of Rs. 2.35, 500 meals at a price of Rs. 4.70 or 250 meals at Rs. 9.40. This, once again, is where your market study comes in—just what is the price band (and therefore the type of person) at which you are aiming? You know you cannot guarantee to get all those customers in that first month, or even in subsequent months, but at least with an idea of a break-even point you can see what you need to achieve in terms of sales, and by how much you are either topping the figure and making a profit or dropping below it and making a loss.

If you are clever enough, you can even draw a neat graph and update it every month on the known figures of your costs and your sales.

VAT

Now, what you have been waiting for all this time—a word about VAT. We have already mentioned the need to do your books regularly, and nowhere in this more important than in keeping your VAT records. VAT returns are due every quarter, and if you leave them until the end of three months, you are creating for yourself a whole load of trouble. The VAT officers' powers are draconian and, although most VAT inspectors I have met are courteous and helpful when they call to inspect your books, the enforcement officer, should he have to call, is anything but. VAT regulations seem to change regularly and by the time this book is published will almost certainly have changed yet again, probably more than once, as eager Customs and Excise officials invent new rules or bring within their grasp more ways in which they can impose their dreaded fifteen per cent. Basically, everything you sell as a restaurateur has a fifteen per cent tax on it, even though some of the foods you buy do not.

This is not a treatise on VAT—that would take a whole library to house—but, broadly speaking, unless you are in the business of selling cold food as 'take-aways' (but not drinks or ice-cream or confectionery), you are subject to that fifteen per cent. This can make life difficult for delicatessen/coffee-bar operations which might sell a range of items, some VAT-free, some not. The other problem is the fact that most food outlets deal mainly in cash, and the VAT inspectors are especially attuned to such a situation, which offers plenty of scope to cheat them out of their money. The teams of inspectors specialise in certain trades and industries and can spot attempts to cheat a mile away if the books somehow do not 'add up', not in a fiscal sense but in comparison with other businesses.

On the other hand, it should be said, and said fairly, that you are not actually cheating the VAT system, you are cheating the public at large who have paid you their fifteen per cent share, willingly or unwillingly, in the knowledge, they presume, that it will be passed on automatically to HM Customs and Excise. There is an important principle here: it is not your money, in effect; it is money taken from someone else under false pretences if you do not pay it over to Customs and Excise, which is why the regulations are so strict. In any event, the VAT inspectors are sadly lacking in any tendency to argue the point-they want their money, and if they do not get it promptly and correctly, they have the power to penalise you heavily, as well as putting in the bailiffs without further ado. It is no bad thing, then, to stay on the right side of HM Customs and Excise and call on them whenever you want a point clarified.

They are usually very keen to ensure that traders do not get into any trouble, and most are reasonably understanding of genuine errors or omissions, providing it does not happen too often. On one visit by the usual two inspectors I was chided for my poor book-keeping and my ignorance about claims I had incorrectly made and which they disallowed. But they then pointed out that I had failed to claim on some other items, and within a few days a substantial cheque arrived from the VAT office in settlement of my own errors. Some years later the boot was on the other foot, and the two inspectors found a shortfall of Rs. 1,200 in their favour, which I had to pay within thirty days.

It was very bad news and not something I would like to happen to anyone else, even though both inspectors recognized a genuine error and told me as kindly as possible that no one trying to cheat with their VAT would have been foolish enough to do what I had done. There is no argument worth making against any decision they make, as they always have the whip hand, and the corruption commensurate with such absolute power means that 'awkward customers' are not likely to be forgotten but marked forever in their files. As background to the extraordinary jargon you will have to face (jargon which only a Civil Servant allowed to run riot with the English language could have invented), the VAT you pay on the goods and services you buy for your business is called 'input tax', and the VAT charged on the goods and services you supply to your customers is called 'output tax'.

You claim relief on the input tax by deducting it from the output tax, paying over the difference within twenty-eight days of the end of the quarter's accounting period. If, however, the input tax claim is greater than the output tax debt, as sometimes happens, for understandable reasons, that money is paid to you by the VAT office once you have filled in the quarterly form. There are penalties for late return of forms, as there are for virtually every infringement, honest or otherwise, of the regulations. There are three classes of goods and services: exempt, on which no VAT is payable such as insurance; zero-rated, on which VAT is payable in theory but not in practice, such as books, food and so on: standard-rated, on which VAT is charged at fifteen per cent.

It is unlikely that the nuances of these differences will affect your own business, but they are of importance to, for instance, exporters. It is an offence not to register for VAT, as it is for registering late, so once again, ask their help if at all in doubt. Mistakes can be very expensive. If you buy a ready-made business but intend to trade it down below the level at which VAT becomes compulsory, you must first de-register for VAT, and until you have done that, you must continue to charge, and pay, VAT. This can be particularly applicable in 'seasonal' businesses if, for instance, you are going to operate in a tourist area and may be open for only part of the year.

There are regulations (inevitably) which may mean you should have registered for VAT because your quarterly turnover has exceeded Rs. 8,000, even though your annual turnover may be less than the Rs. 23,000 'floor' at present (1988) in force. The VAT inspector has to be convinced that it is not increasing success on your part but that the business really is 'seasonal' and not open all the year, or, if open, is trading down very considerably during the other quarters.

Many business people make a point of paying the money due for VAT into a special deposit account at their bank, where it earns interest before it has to be paid to HM Customs and Excise in one lump sum. Other people say the money is better off helping their own cash-flow situation. The policy you adopt is entirely up to you, but if it is the second, please make sure you actually do have the money every quarter to pay over, and have not spent it on something else. Now, we know that this chapter has been far from exhaustive, and we hope that the quantity of paperwork will not depress you, but some personal understanding of the complexities of simple book-keeping is absolutely essential.

Insurance

Earlier in this chapter we made a passing reference to the need to include insurance costs in your overheads. What particular insurance do you need? Obviously you must be covered against the normal disasters which could threaten your business: burglary, flood, fire and so on. Remember, your business is your only source of income, and insurance should be effected to cover loss of any income in the event of a disaster, as well as re-building costs etc. You will also have a quantity of expensive equipment, furnishings and fittings—do not under-estimate the *replacement* costs of such items. You can also insure against loss of profits if something terrible happens. But perhaps most important of all, you must have public liability insurance, which will cover you against claims made by staff or the public who, say, trip over a carelessly placed carpet or slip on the proverbial banana-skin or perhaps get burned by having very hot soup poured over them accidentally. The best course is also the simplest: find a reliable insurance broker and take his advice. He is an expert, and he is also highly unlikely to urge you into unnecessary expenditure, especially if he is a member of the British Insurance Brokers' Association.

REFERENCES

Brownell, J. (1993), "Women ity managers: perceptions of gender-related career challenges", Vol. 11 No.2, pp. 19-32.

Burgess, C., Hampton, A., Price, L., Roper, A. (1995), "nternational hotel groups: what makes them successful?", *International Journal of Contemporary ity Management*, Vol. 17 No.2/3, pp. 74-80.

Chung-Herrera, B.C., Enz, C.A., Lankau, M.J. (2003), "Grooming future ity leaders: a competencies model", *Cornell Hotel and Restaurant Administration Quarterly*, Vol. 44 No.3, pp. 17-25.

Collins, G. (1991), "Selecting POS systems for table service restaurants", *FIU ity Review*, Vol. 9 No.2, pp. 36-51.

Getty, J.M. (1996), "The use of peer evaluations in group projects: benefits, applications, and what students think of them", *ity and Tourism Educator*, Vol. 8 No.4, pp. 44-6.

Grau, J., Borchgrevink, C.P. (1993), "Doing more with less: utilizing hidden resources", *ity and Tourism Educator*, Vol. 5 No.4, pp. 67-9.

Gregg, J.B., Johnson, P.M. (1990), "Perceptions of discrimination among women as managers in ity organizations", Vol. 8 No.1, pp. 10-23.

Ingram, H. (1996), "Clusters and gaps in ity and tourism academic research", *International Journal of Contemporary ity Management*, Vol. 8 No.7, pp. 91-5.

Johns, N., Lee-Ross, D., Ingram, H. (1997), "A study of service quality in small hotels and guesthouses", *Progress in Tourism and ity Research*, Vol. 3 No.4, pp. 351-63.

Kriegl, U. (2000), "International ity management. identifying important skills and effective training", *Cornell Hotel and Restaurant Administration Quarterly*, Vol. 41 No.2, pp. 64-71.

MacVicar, A., Brown, G. (1994), "Investors in People, at the Moat House International, Glasgow", *International Journal of Contemporary ity Management*, Vol. 6 No.1-2, pp. 53-60.

Meyer, R.A., Schroeder, J.J. (1989), "Rewarding non-productivity in the ity industry", Vol. 7 No.1, pp. 1-12.

8

Towards Business Development and Service Improvement in Hospitality Industry

> "Be kindly affectioned one to another with brotherly love; in honour preferring one another; / Not slothful in business; fervent in spirit; serving the Lord; / Rejoicing in hope; patient in tribulation; continuing instant in prayer; / Distributing to the necessity of saints; given to hospitality."
>
> —*Bible*

It is significant to mention here we intend to review hospitality research concerning the broad theme of business development and service improvement. This theme is divided into five sub-themes: market sensitivity and competitiveness; segmentation, branding and service customization; service quality and customer retention; product design and internal marketing. Journal articles from 1990 to June of 1997 were used in this study. Abstracts of most of the articles can be found on the WHATT CD. The objective of the study is to provide practitioners with suggestions and ideas for business improvement. Millions of dollars of research are referenced in this article.

The results of the research are not proprietary, but available for all to use. For practitioners, the article will explain the management implications of the research. For academics, the article provides an overview of current research by area and presents suggestions for future research.

Theme 1: Market Sensitivity and Competitiveness

The research in the area of market sensitivity and competitiveness tended to be on yield management and positioning. The yield management research was grouped into two general issues, pricing systems to increase yield and the choice of market segments that would create the highest yield. The positioning articles discussed the use of perceptual maps as a strategic tool. The methodology used in the positioning articles could be applied to most hospitality companies, giving good information for strategic planning. The yield management articles are broken up into conventional yield management articles and methods for choosing the market segments that will create the highest yield. Griffin (1995) provided an overview of yield management and identified a number of critical success factors for yield management systems.

Among these are several environmental factors that relate to booking patterns, price sensitivity of market segments, and the distribution channel's tolerance for differential pricing. Jeffrey and Hubbard (1994) developed a model of occupancy performance that can be easily applied by hotel managers and others with access to hotel occupancy data. The model looked at two fundamental aspects of a hotel's occupancy performance: the proportionality component, which includes the effects of regular and periodic demand fluctuations, and the competitive components, which include local and unique forces. Bull (1994) investigated the contribution a hotel's location makes to the market value of the hotel's rooms. This methodology makes it possible to put implicit price-location contours on an area map.

The study also has implications for area growth that may affect the contribution of a property's location to its room rate. Weatherford (1995) cited the importance of incorporating a guest's length of stay into the room allocation decisions. He claimed proper use of the length of stay dimension can increase revenue by up to 3 per cent. One of the problems with most yield management systems is that they only look at room revenue. Quain (1992) introduced profit analysis by segment (PABS). PABS takes into account room and non-room revenue to determine the value of different market segments. As yield management matures in the hotel industry, more robust models will be developed that take into account total guest expenditures and the long-term value of the guest.

In developing yield management systems it is important that customer retention be included in the model. Maximizing revenue today has little value if it drives off tomorrow's customers. Dev *et al.* (1995) cited the need for managers to monitor the implications of their marketing strategies. The authors stated that managers need to examine the attributes that consumers use to differentiate one hotel brand from another and illustrated how managers can do this by using multidimensional scaling to build perceptual maps. Kim (1996) used perceptual maps to show how customers perceive food and beverage at competing hotels. Kim also developed ideal points to show how a hotel can change its attributes to gain a better position *vis-à-vis* its competitors.

The methodology used in the study could be used to position different product or product groups of a hotel or restaurant. Shaw (1992) investigated price from a strategic positioning viewpoint. She explained how price has both a strategic component and a tactical component. Shaw stated a positioning approach focuses first on price levels, then on actual price decisions for a specific product. Shaw's approach to pricing could help a brand achieve a desired position, which then could be validated through one of the perceptual mapping techniques.

Theme 2: Segmentation, Branding, and Service Customization

In fact, it is no secret that different customer segments want different product attributes. Commissioned sales people want hotel rooms with a free telephone, while upscale business travellers want expedited check-in. Thus, one of the first decisions for a company is to decide what segments it wants to target. This will determine the company's marketing mix. As segments grow and decline, a company must constantly review its segmentation strategy, looking for viable segments that are compatible with the company's objectives and products.

After a company chooses a target market, the company must position itself in the marketplace *vis-à-vis* the other companies that are going after the target market. Two ways of accomplishing this positioning are through branding and service customization. This section looks at research on segmentation, branding, and service customization. The segmentation research identifies product attributes that create value for market segments. This information is useful to companies targeting these segments or companies who may have a marketing mix that is valuable to these segments.

It is always advisable to replicate segmentation studies using data from customers. Owing to time and regional differences, the wants of customer segments can vary. The segmentation research also presents a variety of research techniques that can be used to give greater insight into what the segments desire and the importance they put on different product attributes. Shaw *et al.* (1991) investigated product attributes of hotel convention services that create satisfaction among meeting planners. The authors went beyond just looking at the mean ratings of the attributes. They developed a multivariate approach to analysing the data, which could be applied to similar survey data to provide rich information. Several studies looked at specific segments. For example, Wight (1996) researched ecotourism and divided it into two market segments: general consumers interested in ecotourism and experienced ecotourism travellers. Her findings are useful for resorts that are interested in catering to this market. Callan (1996) compared UK leisure travellers with business travellers on their importance ratings of hotel attributes. Makens (1992) investigated catering to the family market at resorts. The article provides some case studies of resorts that have children's programmes. For more studies that looked at specific segments. Conjoint analysis gives insight to the importance that customers place on different product attributes.

Several studies provided examples of how conjoint analysis can be used in segmentation studies. Hu and Hiemstra (1996) used hybrid conjoint analysis to measure meeting planners' preferences in hotel selection. Becker-Suttle *et al.* (1994) used conjoint analysis to explore restaurant benefits sought by seniors and non-seniors. The use of neural networks, a type of artificial intelligence, is becoming a popular segmentation technique. It is often used in data mining tools to discover relationships between customers, identifying customer segments that might not be apparent to the marketer. Mazanec (1992) illustrated the usefulness of neural networks by segmenting tourists.

Branding: Customers develop brand images, or a set of beliefs, about where each brand stands on different product attributes. One of the trends in the hospitality industry is to use brands that have a positive brand image, rather than a company's own products which may have little brand image. For example, many hotels and catering companies in the USA are using kiosks to sell Starbucks Coffee, which has a strong brand image.

ARAMARK, a contract food service company, franchises Burger King and Pizza Hut outlets even though they have the ability to produce products that have a similar quality. Hotels are contracting out their food service to local providers and chains that have a strong image. Thus, brand management is an area that is emerging as an important marketing area. The research on branding was scarce, indicating a need for future research in this area. Hallam and Baum (1996) surveyed hotel managers in North America and the UK to gain perceptions of why hotels may contract out portions or all of their food and beverage operations.

One of the major reasons cited in the study was that a branded or well-known operator could help attract more accommodation guests. Thus, managers saw a branded restaurant as an amenity that was valued by the lodging guests. Connell (1992) looked at the benefits and problems of branding in the hotel industry. He used the rebranding of Forte after the acquisition of Crest as a case study. Effective guest history systems now make it possible to customize guest service. Unpublished research by Bowen and Shoemaker found that customized services were one the most important attributes to luxury hotel customers. Ritz-Carlton used guest history very effectively to produce customized services (Partlow 1993). Dev and Ellis (1991) presented a guest history management model and explained how it could be used to customize service for repeat guests. Customization of services can create a competitive advantage by increasing guest loyalty.

Theme 3: Service Quality and Customer Retention

A distinction can be made between two types of quality: product features that enhance customer satisfaction and freedom from deficiencies that increase customer satisfaction. The first type of quality, product features, adds to the cost of the product. Customers must be willing to pay for either the added costs of additional product features or these features must make them more loyal. For example, lettuce and tomato is found only on McDonald's more expensive hamburgers. Hotel rooms on concierge floors have more features than standard rooms and command a higher price. La Quinta Inns offers free local telephone calls to encourage loyalty among salespeople.

The expectations of guests are formed by company image, word of mouth, the company's promotional efforts, and price. A guest paying $35 for a room at a Motel 6 or Formula 1 will have different expectations from a guest paying $250 for a room at a Four Seasons Hotel. The person staying at the budget hotel may be perfectly satisfied. The room features meet their expectations. The first type of quality, product features, relates to guest expectations. People staying in a budget hotel may perceive it as the best quality motel for less than $40.

They are not comparing it to a Four Seasons Hotel. Both the guests of a Motel 6 or Formula 1 and a Four Seasons Hotel will expect the room to be free from deficiencies. For example, guests at the Four Seasons and those at the budget hotel are both likely to get upset if they return in the evening to rooms that have not been made up. There is another way to view quality. A distinction can be made between technical and functional quality. Technical quality refers to what the customer is left with after the customer-employee interactions have been completed. For example, technical quality relates to the guest room in the hotel, the meal in the restaurant, and the car from the rental agency. Functional quality is the process of delivering the service or product (Grönroos, 1982). While the service is being delivered, customers go through many interactions with the firm's employees.

A guest makes a reservation, is greeted by the door attendant, is escorted to the front desk by a bellperson, checks in with the desk clerk, and is escorted to the room. The experience of checking into a hotel is an example of functional quality. Excellent functional quality may make up for a room that is not quite up to expectations. If functional quality is unpleasant, a high-quality room might not overcome the guests' previous dissatisfaction. For a good introduction to service quality see a series of articles by Johns (1992a, 1992b, 1993). In these articles he presented a comprehensive overview of quality management in the hospitality industry. Partlow (1993) provided a comprehensive overview of how Ritz-Carlton won the Malcolm Baldrige Award. In the article, Partlow presented an overview of Ritz's quality management program.

Later, Partlow (1996) focused on the human resource practices that support TQM. Heymann (1992) provided a ten-point model for quality management. A service quality audit can identify problems when a firm is first developing a quality management programme or it can be used to audit an existing programme. Luchars and Hinkin (1996) developed a service quality audit that can be used to identify errors and determine their frequency, assign costs of fixing (or not fixing) the errors, and identify steps to prevent them. They provided a case study of a New York hotel to illustrate their service-quality audit. SERVQUAL developed by Parasuraman *et al.* is one of the most popular instruments for measuring service quality.

Knutson *et al.*(1991) adapted SERVQUAL into a specific instrument for hotels. They tested the reliability of their instrument, LODGSERV, and found it to be a reliable instrument. Later Stevens *et al.* (1995) developed DINESERV for measuring service quality in restaurants. Barsky (1992) discussed a theoretical model of customer satisfaction and then tested the model using a survey instrument. Using his survey instrument, he was able to support his hypothesis that intent to return will be positively related to customer satisfaction. One desired outcome of service quality is customer retention. The following research investigated customer retention. Dube *et al.* (1994) used conjoint analysis to show the overall utility of seven service-quality attributes that all bear significantly on customers' intent to return.

The authors' methodology provides managers with information that will help justify (or not justify) the costs of improving quality. Toh *et al.* (1991) researched the effectiveness of frequent-guest programmes in hotels. They found many of the programmes were not effective in creating repeat customers. The authors provide insights on how the programmes could be improved. Buttle and Bok (1996) provided an overview of Fishbein's theory of reasoned action. They found two predictor constructs: attitude towards the act, and subjective norm jointly explain about 65 per cent of the intention to stay in a hotel on the next trip.

Theme 4: Product Design

A company must build a service delivery system that provides product attributes desired by its target market. The articles on service design were on both the macro and micro level. Some articles looked at the overall design of a hospitality operation, while other articles looked at specific issues. This section will first review the macro articles and then discuss the micro articles. Pannell Kerr Forster Associates (1993) concluded that hotel design factors can be summarized into three areas: market factors including customer requirements, competitive influences and trends; impact of new technology enabling new services or increased levels of comfort to be available and leading to improvements in construction techniques and choice of materials used; and statutory requirements affecting the design and construction of buildings and specific legislation relating to hotels. Verma and Thompson (1996) illustrated how discrete choice analysis can be used to design business concepts based on the importance that customers place on different product attributes.

The researchers use delivery pizza as an example, but the technique could be applied to the development or design of any concept. Several articles looked at the development of new products. Jones (1995) applied Scheuing and Johnson's model for new service development to flight catering. His research found that airlines lack many of the systematic procedures suggested by Scheuing and Johnson. Shoemaker (1996) looked at how customers develop a series of actions regarded as necessary or appropriate for a service transaction. Variations from the script can be a source of dissatisfaction.

Thus, when developing new service delivery systems, companies must assist customers in developing a new script. Miner (1996) presented a customer focused approach to developing new products in a restaurant. The six stage process includes product ideas, initial evaluation, consumer reaction, sensory testing, field testing, and product introduction. Another set of research looked at the design of special projects. Goldman (1993) discussed the importance of concept selection for independent restaurants. He discussed the different external factors that affect concept selection. Makens and Bowen (1996) discussed merchandise opportunities for restaurants.

Design consideration for restaurants wanting to implement a merchandising programme include space to merchandise the products and storage space. Bowen and Morris (1995) looked at the design of a menu to increase product sales. They found that menu design in a sit-down service restaurant may not be as effective in selling products as previously thought. Monteson and Singer (1992) explained how spas can add value as an amenity in a destination hotel or resort. They gave advice on how to manage and market a spa properly, so it creates maximum value for the guests and adds to the bottom line of the hotel. Conner (1991) focused on how renovations could capture the original glitz and glamour of the hotel, while making the hotel operationally efficient. Conner provides specific examples from design renovations in New York City. Knapp (1991) provides a case study of the renovation of the Sheraton Palace in San Francisco.

Theme 5: Internal Marketing

The hospitality industry is unique in that employees are part of the product. When people think of marketing, they usually think of efforts directed externally towards the marketplace; but a hotel or restaurant's first marketing efforts should be directed internally to employees. Managers must make sure that employees know their products and believe that they are good value. The employees must be excited about the company they work for and the products they sell; otherwise, it will be impossible for the guests to become excited. External marketing brings customers into the hotel but does little good if the employees do not perform to the guest's expectations.

The sub-themes identified in the research relating internal marketing include culture, service orientation, empowerment and listening. An internal marketing programme flows out of a service culture. A service marketing programme is doomed to failure if its organizational culture does not support serving the customer. It is difficult to establish an effective culture in a permanent organization and even harder to establish a culture in a temporary organization. Meudell and Gadd (1994) looked at the establishment of a culture in short-life organizations. The authors used an organizational beliefs questionnaire to investigate the National Garden Festival Wales' organizational culture.

This article built on earlier work by the authors on short-life organizations. If management expects employees' attitudes to be positive towards the customer, management must have a positive attitude towards the customer and the employees. Too often organizations hire trainers to come in for one day to get their customer-contact employees excited about providing quality customer service. The effect of these sessions is usually short-lived because the organizations do little to support the customer-contact employees.

A company must develop policies and an organizational structure to support its service orientation. Barsky (1996) described how to build a system to deliver world-class service. In the article he provided numerous examples from hospitality firms, including a sample of a guest survey. Barsky also provided examples of how to map the customer cycle. At the heart of this process is a step that redesigns exiting processes based on both customer and employee input. The second part of this step is to develop employee programmes that support the new processes. Shimko (1994) explained how existing decision-making polices, coupled with the manner in which organizations reward conforming behaviour, may result in polices that prevent employees from providing optimal customer service. King and Garey (1997) looked at how the organizational context in which a service encounter takes place affects employee interactions with customers, and resulting guest satisfaction.

They found that stress-related factors including a bureaucratic climate were negatively related to guest satisfaction ratings. Dienhart *et al.*(1991) and Dienhart *et al.* (1992) investigated factors that might influence restaurant employees' degree of service orientation. The authors developed a questionnaire that was administered to supervisory and non-supervisory employees. The results of the research suggest that increasing employee's job involvement, job satisfaction, and job security could assist in improving their overall service orientation. Perhaps one of the most important research areas of internal marketing is the management of listening. Employees have the potential for collecting information directly from the guests.

Through proper training and information collection systems employees can provide more information than market research costing tens of thousands of dollars. However, for these systems to work, employees must trust the organization. Good communication between employees and managers not only provides good customer information, but it also supports a service culture by identifying management problems and solutions to those problems. Several researchers investigated the area of listening and communication. Brownell (1994) focused on the importance of managers creating an environment that fosters good communication between employees and management. She stated, "The vision of strong listening environments may foster practices and attitudes that become the most important tools managers bring with them into the twenty-first century". Sparks (1994) found that customers evaluate the quality of the service, in part, on the manner in which information is communicated by employees.

Thus, part of customer satisfaction is dependent on the ability of employees to listen to customers and communicate with them. Empowerment has been associated with a number of benefits including increased employee and customer satisfaction. The increased customer satisfaction comes through better complaint resolution, ability to customize products, and more responsive service. One problem in the implementation of empowerment can be lack of management support. Most of the research on empowerment dealt with the process of empowering employees. Brymer (1991) presented a framework for implementing employee empowerment and also provided some guides which will help measure the results of empowerment.

Lashley (1995) provided an overview of the benefits of empowerment and illustrated how different hospitality companies have implemented empowerment. Lashley (1997) later provided frameworks for employee empowerment and called for research to investigate the tradeoffs between employee empowerment and improved organizational performance. Sparrowe (1994) proposed that investments in psychological empowerment among hospitality employees seem worthwhile, as satisfaction with promotion opportunities should rise and intent to leave should decline.

Thus, empowerment can not only lead to guest satisfaction, it can also result in employee satisfaction. Through market analysis, perceptual maps are developed providing insights into attractive market segments. Much of the research in the area of market segmentation focused on the importance different market segments place on product attributes. The target market determines the design of the product. Quality management ensures that the product is being delivered at a level which will create repeat business. Quality measurement validates that the quality management system is working. The quality measurement also monitors changes in wants and expectations of the target market. Changes in market expectations or wants can be met through product redesign. Thus, the link between quality measurement and product design indicates an ongoing process of shaping the product to meet the needs of the target market. Since employees are part of the product, they need to be included in the design of service delivery systems.

Employees that deliver good service also contribute to the quality of the organization and will be included in the quality management process. Finally, quality impacts on brand image. Customer retention is one of the objectives of most businesses. The brand image, service customization, and internal marketing all affect customer retention. At the heart of this model is the target market or customer. When a company chooses a market segment that can create value for the firm, then the firm must deliver a product that creates value to the market segment.

The literature reviewed in this article will help hospitality managers gain insight into the process of choosing the right target markets and delivering value to their target markets.

Customers and Service Improvement in Hospitality Industry

The concept of mass customization has emerged in part, from a decade of debate centred on the mass production of inexpensive, commodity-like products or services (the assembly line approach) on the one hand and premium-priced, individually-tailored and highly differentiated offerings on the other. Hart' observes that much of the power of mass customization, like total quality management before it, lies in its visionary and strategic implications. Its application should enable companies to produce affordable, high-quality goods and services, but with shorter cycle times and lower costs.

The key dimensions of his diagnostic framework for assessing the potential for mass customization are: customer sensitivity, process amenability, competitive environment and organizational readiness. Taylor and Lyon discuss the application of mass customization to food service operations and its likely adoption in a rapidly maturing marketplace. A compatible step is for management to create an appropriate form of internal customer orientation and Stauss notes that a deliberate and sustained effort is needed to create a climate that promotes a customer's viewpoint of work activities, processes and non-standardized support services.

Customer orientation also implies a readiness to measure, and where necessary improve, the quality of service and support in keeping with customer expectations. Lee and Hing assess the usefulness and application of the SERVQUAL technique in measuring service quality in the fine dining sector. They demonstrate how easily and inexpensively the technique can be used to identify the strengths and weaknesses of individual restaurants' service dimensions. A periodic audit of customer service deliverables might also be usefully conducted and Congram and Epelman recommend the use of the structured analysis and design technique (SADT). This enables service providers to review the processes in which they participate, identify, implement and review improvements in service delivery and rethink aspects of the service package.

The interpersonal aspects of service delivery are potentially the most difficult to audit and improve. A useful starting point is to undertake a programme of job analysis for service staff to identify the best fit between tasks, behaviours and personal attributes. Papadopoulou *et al.* identify the dimensions of a higher customer contact food and beverage operative's job as perceived by managers, supervisors and operatives and examine within-source and between source-differences in perceptions. Their study confirms the versatility of job analysis as an organizational and diagnostic tool. Among other uses, it depicts the dimensions of a job, the related personal qualities and experience and the training implications.

In most cases, it is also helpful to profile ideal combinations of age and experience for different service roles, especially as the industry relies heavily on younger workers. Corporate level concern about service quality issues has stimulated interest in employee empowerment. In theory, empowered employees will be more committed to ensuring that service encounters satisfy customers as they have the necessary discretion and autonomy to "delight the customer". Lashley explores the implications of empowering employees and provides a framework for understanding managerial motives in selecting different forms of empowerment and their consequences for achieving improvements in customer service quality. To support empowerment and other customer-led initiatives, training and development is needed. Clements and Josiam outline a step-by-step procedure to evaluate both the costs and the benefits of any training proposal.

Their approach utilizes a financial analysis model for identifying the dollar value of both performance outcomes and training costs. While interpersonal skills development and support is needed for service staff, supervisors and managers need to make appropriate decisions and Gore examines some of the theoretical models of decision making derived from the field of psychology and considers the related implications for training in decision making.

Research Methodology

Analysis Approach

An effective method for determining the market-based relative value of various features of a service (e.g. hotels) involves modeling customer preferences in response to experimentally designed service profiles. This approach, commonly known as probabilistic *discrete choice analysis* (*DCA*) has been used to model choice processes of decision-makers in a variety of academic disciplines, including marketing, operations management, transportation, urban planning, hospitality, and natural resource economics (*Louviere and Timmermans,* ; *Pullman and Moore,* ; *Verma et al.,* ; *Verma et al.,* ; *Verma et al.*). Statistical models (e.g. Multinomial logit (MNL) models, nested logit models), developed from a *DCA* study, link service attributes to customer preferences. Therefore by describing a service in terms of appropriate attributes, *DCA* can be used to predict relative market impact of various service offerings (*Danaher*). Recent papers by *Verma et al.* and *Verma et al.* review *DCA* literature and provide guidelines for designing and conducting *DCA* studies of services. Rather than repeating here what has already been detailed in various publications, we only briefly describe the *DCA* method.

Discrete choice experiments involve careful design of service profiles, in this case, a specific hotel and choice sets (a number of service alternatives) in which two or more service alternatives are offered to decision-makers and they are asked to evaluate the options and choose one (or none). Each subject in a *DCA* experiment typically receives several choice sets to evaluate (e.g. 8-32 sets) with two or more hypothetical services to choose from in each set. The design of the experiment is under the control of the researcher, and consequently, the decision-makers' choices (dependent variable) are a function of the attributes of each alternative, personal characteristics of the respondents, and unobserved effects captured by the random component (e.g. unobserved heterogeneity or omitted factors).

For a detailed theoretical and statistical background of DCA please refer to *Ben-Akiva and Lerman*, *Louviere et al.* and *McFadden*. DCA applications based on choice experiments typically involve the following steps:

- identification of attributes;
- specification of attribute levels;
- experimental design;
- presentation of alternatives to respondents; and
- estimation of the choice model.

Past studies have shown that in general, the market share predictions generated from the statistical models (e.g. MNL) based on *DCA* are extremely accurate (*Ben-Akiva and Lerman,* ; *Louviere et al.*). Subsequently we describe our implementation of DCA within the context of business and leisure hotel travelers in the US.

Hotel Attributes and Experimental Design

Prior to finalizing the experimental attributes and levels with the discrete choice customer survey, we conducted extensive qualitative research (*Verma et al.*). We interviewed managers from economy, mid-range and upscale hotels and several business and leisure hotel customers. Based on qualitative data and a review of academic and practitioner's literature on the topic, we identified five broad constructs of hotel attributes to be varied in discrete choice experiments. They are – hotel type; price; loyalty/

frequent user programs; eating options; office facilities and technology options; customization options; and hotel amenities. Each of these constructs was further expanded into attributes (each with two or more levels). However, in this paper we will only focus on the innovative constructs: hotel type, technology, and customization for ease of understanding and clarity.

Each of these constructs is considered to be innovative because each involves offering services which are not traditional to the industry. The "hotel type" construct consisted of three attributes: economy, midrange, and upscale. Each attribute was represented by four of the six experimental levels: motel, bed and breakfast inn, independent boutique hotel, standardized hotel affiliated/operated by recognized chain, boutique hotel operated by a recognized chain, and convention style hotel. The "technology" construct was described by three attributes: internet access in room (none, free, $5 or 10/day), business center (not available; full-service and centrally located; multiple business kiosks, in-room printer, fax, etc.), and availability of internet reservations (yes, no).

The last construct, customization, includes different alternatives which match a person's life-style. Customization was described by five attributes: ability to bring small pets to room (yes, no), availability of flexible check-in/check-out times (yes, no), ability to personalize in-room décor (yes, no), childcare (not available, fee-based nanny and/or kids club for infants and up to 12 years old kids), and in-room kitchen facilities (none, coffeemaker, microwave, refrigerator, and full-kitchenette). After finalizing the list of attributes and their experimental levels, we designed 64 orthogonal profiles that allowed us to reliably estimate the main effects of all the hotel attributes described above (*Verma et al.*). To enhance the realism of the task, a full-profile approach was used in presenting the choice sets (*Green and Srinivasan*), i.e. each profile shown to the respondents simultaneously described some combination of all the attributes.

Within the actual survey three hotel profiles (one economy, one mid-range and one upscale) were shown to respondents at the same time and they were asked to choose one hotel (or neither) which varied from each other on numerous attributes simultaneously. Each respondent evaluated eight hotel choice-sets. In addition to the hotel choice task, the survey instrument included several questions about respondents' past hotel visits as well as demographics. We pre-tested the survey with 25 randomly-selected hotel customers to ensure ease and comprehension of the task, as well as to ensure reliable data collection methods.

Average time for completing the entire survey was approximately 20 minutes and respondents did not indicate difficulty in comprehension.

Sampling Frame and Data Collection

The population of interest consisted of business and leisure travelers who stayed in economy, mid-range or upscale hotels. To obtain a representative sample (or as close to it as possible) we acquired from a third party vendor a reliable electronic mailing list of 4,000 potential respondents with residences scattered across the United States from a well-reputed marketing research company. The mailing list contained a sample of respondents balanced according to US census data validated by various demographics criteria. Each of the potential respondents received an email invitation to participate in the survey from the lead researcher. By participating in the survey, a respondent had the ability to participate in a raffle to win one of the ten gift certificates for $100. From the initial list of potential respondents, approximately 2,500 chose to participate in the survey.

Approximately 40 percent of the respondents answered negatively to the screening question (have you taken a business or leisure trip during the last one year which required a hotel stay?) and were not allowed to continue with the survey. At the conclusion of a three-week data collection period, a total of 930 respondents completed and returned the survey (each received a second email reminder). Since there was no indication of any response bias, the analysis presented in this paper is based on survey data collected from all the respondents.

9

Quality Management and Services Management in Hospitality Sector

"Hospitality is the practice of God's welcome by reaching across difference to participate in God's actions bringing justice and healing to our world in crisis."

—*Letty M. Russell*

Explaining Service Quality and Customers in Hospitality Industry

A summary of the articles on the themes of service quality and customers is provided. Through effective human resource management an organization can create an environment which encourages and rewards employees for providing quality service to guests. In order for this to occur, management must know what quality service entails and how it can be properly measured. Getty and Thompson conducted research geared towards creating a reliable and valid instrument to measure customers' perceptions of delivered quality. In addition, Bojanic and Rosen used an instrument for measuring service quality SERVQUAL to examine the association between service quality as perceived by customers and its service determinants. Management attempts to measure service quality not only from the guest's perspective, but from the employee's as well. It is important for management to be able to quantify the interpersonal skills required by employees in service positions. In two separate studies, Samenfink utilized a self-monitoring scale to determine the theoretical characteristics required of employees to be successful in the service encounter. Once the service encounter is complete, attempts can be made to measure the customer's overall satisfaction. Barsky created his own definition of customer satisfaction along with a practical approach to facilitate its measurement. Almanza *et al.*, on the other hand, used Albrecht and Bradford's service attribute matrix to determine attributes leading to customer satisfaction. All of these models, scales, and surveys used to measure service may seem redundant, but in order to provide quality service it is imperative to know what quality service is. How management defines quality service is insignificant; how the customer defines it is paramount. Once management is able to identify and provide quality service, the next step is to attempt to attract customers to serve. Measuring how a customer makes a choice between hospitality products is a bit more difficult than some of the other measurement methods previously discussed. The customer's choice of a hospitality product frequently involves trade-offs among multiattribute product alternatives, and a majority of the attributes, such as location, brand name, image, ambience, and amenities, are difficult if not impossible to measure quantifiably. Lewis *et al*. along with others, have used conjoint, or trade-off, analysis to measure customer's choice preferences. Determining customer preferences is important to an organization's success. However, those of us in the hospitality industry must attract customers in the first place. Knowing who the customer is and how to reach him/her is therefore essential. The methods management use to reach its customers depend on the type of customer sought. Vogt *et al*.examine how meeting planners use personal sources of information, such as prior experience or the advice of others, when making their client's travel arrangements. Conversely, Mihalik *et al*. compared published sources of information used by Japanese and German international travellers when determining overseas vacation destinations. In order to reach and attract customers successfully, management must also be aware of the prevailing dynamic socio-demographic characteristics. Francese warns that managers need to realize that the post-baby-boom hospitality consumers will be few in numbers, tough in spirit, pragmatic, and technologically aware. On the other hand, Lago and Poffley address the demographic variability among the elderly with respect to health status, income, and family structure. In either case, awareness of the differences between demographic groups can assist management in identifying the needs of individuals in those groups in order to provide them with quality service.

Understanding Brand Loyalty in Hospitality Industry

Brand loyalty has been described as a behavioural response and as a function of psychological processes (Jacoby and Kyner, 1973). That is, brand loyalty is a function of both behaviour and attitudes. Repurchase is not sufficient evidence of brand loyalty – the purchasing practice should be intentional. Brand loyalty includes some degree of commitment toward the quality of a brand that is a function of both positive attitudes and repetitive purchases. Generally, more than one brand is offered of the same product within a given product category, and a buyer has to choose one of these brands at the moment of purchase. Today, many products and services are sold as branded products and services; this shows the great confidence placed in the effectiveness of branding. In general, the brand chosen at many previous purchases has a high probability of being bought again on subsequent occasions (Reichheld, 1996). Holiday Inn was one of the first to introduce a branded service to the hotel business. By using the brand name to assure travelers of uniform service standards, experience, and consistency, Holiday Inn was able to capture a repeat customer base. To attract different market segments and respond to a variety of customer needs and budgets, Holiday Inn extended its product line from economy (Holiday Inn Express) to upscale (Crowne Plaza). This branding strategy helped Holiday Inn increase occupancy and revenue as some of the lodging segments have become saturated (Seacord, 1996).

Importance of Brand Loyalty

Loyal customers are best for hospitality firms because they are easier to serve than non-loyal customers, and they provide higher profitability. Reichheld in his book, *The Loyalty Effect*, explains the advantages of brand loyalty as follows:

- *Continues profit*. The advantages of customer loyalty are long-term and cumulative. The longer a customer remains loyal, the more profit a business can get from that single customer.
- *Reduces marketing cost*. Businesses have to invest money to attract new customers, such as advertising. For loyal customers, these costs are eliminated or minimized.
- *Increases per-customer revenue growth*. Customer spending tends to increase over time. For example, a customer who repeatedly stays at the same hotel becomes more familiar with the hotel's full product line, such as gift shops and banquet rooms. And that customer will be likely to sample other product lines of the company, thus helping the company achieve a larger share of customers.
- *Decreases operating cost*. For a loyal customer, the front desk clerk does not need to spend time entering data into the computer – instead she/he retrieves the loyal customer's existent data. Loyal customers' familiarity with the company's products makes them less dependent on its employees for information and service, thus decreasing servicing cost.
- *Increases referrals*. Satisfied customers recommend the business to friends and others. Referrals are a vital source of new

customers, and customers who show up on the strength of a personal recommendation tend to stay longer.

- *Increases price premiums*. Brand loyal customers pay more for a brand because they perceive some unique value in the brand that no other alternative can provide, and they are less likely to be lured away by a discount of a few dollars. Many people will pay more to stay in a hotel they know than to take a chance on a less expensive competitor.
- *Provides competitive advantage*. As consumers become loyal to a brand, they become less sensitive to a price increase. The company can maintain a price differentiation over the competition because of the product's ability to satisfy their needs.

Factors Contributing to Brand Loyalty

In order to increase the brand loyal customer base a hospitality firm should explore the factors that create brand loyalty. Then, tactics or strategies need to be developed and implemented by all levels and functions of the organization. For each customer, the reason for brand loyalty may be different. However, loyal customers generally show these common behaviours: making repeat purchases, trying other product lines of the company, showing resistance to the pull of the competition, giving referrals, providing publicity, and serving on advisory boards (Bowen and Shoemaker, 1998). The following paragraphs summarize the factors that create brand loyalty.

Awareness

The first step toward loyalty begins with the customer's becoming aware of the product (Aaker, 1991). At the *awareness* stage, a potential customer knows that the brand exists, but the bond between a customer and the product is low. At this point, a brand-name may provide the awareness of the product because brand names offer value to the consumers by helping them interpret, process, store, and retrieve large quantities of information about products (Aaker, 1991). Awareness can be enhanced in a variety of ways such as advertising, direct mail, trade press, word-of-mouth communication, and promotion activities (Grover and Srinivasan, 1992). The more the customer is aware of the product, the greater the possibility that she/he will purchase the product. Hospitality companies need to expose their products to more consumers to create and increase brand-loyal consumers who will buy their product wherever it is available. The more places the customer can buy the product, the more often that customer will become a new customer of the same product in another marketplace (Lewis *et al*., 1995, p. 655). Holiday Inn benefits from being the number one chain in terms of size in the USA dominating 34 percent of the business-travel market (Aylsworth, 1996).

Reputation

Selling high-quality products and commanding premium prices increases the *reputation* of a firm; thus, developing brand loyalty. In order to build and maintain a reputation, the promised quality of goods or services must be delivered. Having a good reputation increases a firm's sales, attracts more customers because of word-of-mouth activity, and cuts customer departures (Rogerson, 1983). For a firm expanding its product line, a well-known brand can facilitate user acceptance of the new product (Aaker, 1991). Sellers who develop a reputation for high quality can often command premium prices (e.g. Ritz Carlton).

Image

One of the first steps in maintaining customer brand loyalty is to build and sustain a positive brand *image*. A strong brand image is important to brand owners because the brand name distinguishes a product from the competitors' products. The image includes colors, symbols, words, and slogans that convey a clear, consistent message and not simply the name (Berry *et al*., 1988). The brand image plays an important role in product choice because consumers attempt to reinforce their self-image by buying products that are congruent with their self-image. For example, a consumer may drive an Alfa Romeo rather than a generic brand because the Alfa Romeo reflects the style and flair that the consumer sees in his or her personality. The consumer may perceive that one brand is more desirable than its competitor's solely because of the difference in image (Schiffman and Kanuk, 1991).

Promotion

While *promotion* is the biggest reason consumers initially try a product (Grover and Srinivasan, 1992), if tied to something positive, such as a new or better facility or a new product, it facilitates brand loyalty. Promotions can be used to develop cost leadership or differentiation, and can be used to create loyalty through switching costs (Grover and Srinivasan, 1992). For instance, many credit card companies discourage existing users from switching by offering them incentives or better deals (e.g. lower APR).

Perceived Quality

A brand should represent a credible guarantee of quality to the consumers (Aaker, 1991). Once the consumers are persuaded that the brand offers what they expect, they stay with the brand. Brand names provide a symbolic meaning which assists the user in the recognition and decision-making process. A consumer will choose a familiar name becausebrand names carry higher *perceived quality*. Brands generally deliver the quality they promised. Customers feel comfortable with brand versus unbranded products. That is why brand-leading products consistently command a 10-to-15 per cent price premium over their competition (Elliott, 1996). Customers may also see this price difference as a quality indication.

Innovation

Innovation allows the brand to remain up-to-date and demonstrates an unceasing attentiveness to the changes in customer taste. To keep pace with changes in the marketplace companies should meet and exceed customer needs and wants. Studies show that successful new brands are typically more distinctive, novel and superior in comparison to established brands (Nowlis and Simonsen, 1996). When companies make innovations to their products they have to consider customers' perceptions and attitudes. Customers may not approve the new ideas or products. If new additions or products, are so different from the existing core product, consumers may not make the proper connection between the new product and the mature brand, and thus may not transfer the brand's positive attributes to the new product (Aaker and Keller, 1990).

Brand Extension

Carrying the brand into new categories that fit well with its concept and image will help companies increase customer brand loyalty (Aaker, 1991). When the brand's associations and perceived quality can provide a point of differentiation and advantage for *brand extension*,the extension will be successful. However, there is a risk that an extension may damage the core brand by weakening its associations or its perceived quality. If customers want to buy a new product, they will prefer a familiar brand. They already know the brand and have the same performance expectations with the new product. If they do not get what they expect, they may switch to the new brand. The reason for the product extensions in the hospitality industry (e.g. Courtyard by Marriott) is to better meet more heterogeneous consumer tastes. From a marketing perspective, this is a way to reach different market segments. When a company uses a brand name that has already been established, some risk associated with new products may be eliminated. For brand names with high customer value, such as Holiday Inn, Ramada, and Marriott in the hospitality industry, brand extension has been a good tool for marketing and growth potential. Marriott estimated that adding the Marriott name to Fairfield Inn increased occupancy rates by 15 percent (Farquhar, 1990).

Satisfaction

The relationship between *satisfaction* and brand loyalty has been observed in several studies. Fornell (1992) examined 27 different businesses and found strong correlations between satisfaction and loyalty (e.g. 0.66 for television broadcasting). Fornell further found that loyal customers are not necessarily satisfied customers, but satisfied customers tend to be loyal customers. Highly satisfied customers are much more loyal than satisfied customers – any drop in total satisfaction results in a major drop in loyalty (Jones, 1990). Xerox conducted a study for satisfaction using a five-point scale: 5 (highly satisfied) to 1 (highly dissatisfied). The relationship between the scores and actual loyalty differed greatly. Customers giving Xerox fives were six times more likely to repurchase Xerox equipment than those giving fours (Reichheld, 1996).

Customer Background

Customer background characteristics may also contribute to brand loyalty (Morgan and Dev, 1994). Higher income customers may stick to one premium brand because they perceive it as a contribution to their social status. Some brands carry images or symbolic meanings that may provide social value for them. The higher household income, the less switching is expected because customers can exercise their preferences independently from monetary considerations. For instance, customers with more income can afford to repeat purchase of familiar lodging brands despite limited availability and wide price variation. As previously stated, the reasons for being brand loyal (e.g. brand image) may be different for each customer. Some firms offer trial discounts to attract new customers, whereas others offer loyalty programs to retain their current customers. The next section discusses in detail how loyalty programs have an impact on brand loyalty.

CRM in Business

In this day and age the use of internet sites and specifically e-mail, in particular, are touted as less expensive communication methods, compared to traditional methods like telephone calls. This revolutionary type of service can be very helpful, but it is completely useless if you are having trouble reaching your customers. It has been determined by some major companies that the majority of clients trust other means of communication, like telephone, more than they trust e-mail. Clients, however, are not the ones to blame because it is often the manner of connecting with consumers on a personal level making them feel as though they are cherished as customers. It is up to the companies to focus on reaching every customer and developing a relationship. CRM software can run your entire business.

From prospect and client contact tools to billing history and bulk email management. The CRM system allows you to maintain all customer records in one centralized location that is accessible to your entire organization through password administration. Front office systems are set up to collect data from the customers for processing into the data warehouse. The data warehouse is a back office system used to fulfill and support customer orders. All customer information is stored in the data warehouse. Back office CRM makes it possible for a company to follow sales, orders, and cancellations. Special regressions of this data can be very beneficial for the marketing division of a firm.

Teamworking in Performance Management

Much of the literature on performance and quality management emphasizes that hospitality organizations can continuously improve their businesses through more effective analytical techniques and through people. Teamworking is a force for co-ordination and communication and is of particular use to the hotel sector where inter-departmental conflict is a characteristic feature (Dann and Hornsey, 1986) and negative images of employees affect job performance (Palmer and Lundberg, 1995). Although hotels are traditionally grouped into functional departments, Nebel *et al.* (1994) propose a re-engineering approach in which hotels group tasks into coherent business processes such as customer communication, product development and problem resolution. Hotels may not wish to espouse such radical solutions, but the literature suggests that empowerment can offer benefits for hotels. Lashley (1995) advances teamworking in hospitality as a means of empowerment and continuous improvement and cites examples such as the Accor Group (quality circles), Harvester Restaurants (autonomous work groups), the former Scott's Hotels (whatever-it-takes training), Hilton Hotels (team briefing). Brymer (1991) suggests that empowerment can affect guest satisfaction, employee satisfaction and bottom line profits. A natural development to teamworking initiatives is the formation of self-managed teams to solve problems and drive continuous improvement (CI). Atkinson (1994b) argues that the foundation to CI is workplace improvement teams which probably started as quality circles and may have evolved into self-managed work teams. Their aim is continuously to seek improvements within their own remit and they are supported by corrective action teams. Actual hospitality examples of self-managed teams are scarce, but Newton (1992) reports the efforts of Harvester Restaurants who formed teams according to Belbin's typology and asked them to formulate unit strategies and personal objectives over a two-day brainstorming period. Operational teams are led by an elected leader, self-managing and accountable for team recruitment and selection. Performance contracts are reviewed at meetings held bi-monthly and are supported by reward and recognition systems. To date, there is little evidence that teamworking has been as widely espoused in hospitality as in manufacturing. Ingram *et al.* (1997) contend that much of the literature on the subject is inconclusive and anecdotal and they propose a descriptive model of effective teamworking as a basis for future research. The comparative success of quality assurance schemes such as the government-led Investors in People scheme (Ball, 1993) suggests that hospitality firms are seeking new approaches to people which can address problems such as internal conflict and staff turnover.

Thematic Interrelationships

Having reviewed some dimensions of business performance and performance measurement, process and quality improvement and teamworking, it seem clear there are links between the three themes. This part explores some of these interrelationships and illustrates them in a relationship.

An integrated process/people approach must specify balanced standards of performance and empower staff to perform more effectively by working together in teams. This will enable organizations to operate a quality assurance programme which is accompanied by improved customer satisfaction and performance improvement.

Patterns from the Generic Literature

Outside the hospitality industry there are many examples from around the world which indicate that teamworking has the power to improve the way that firms operate and their outputs. This section reviews literature evidence from other industries and the world of sport and considers the benefits of teamworking. Suggestions about appropriate structures and team development will be applied to the context of hospitality firms.

Evidence from Other Industries

There is a considerable body of evidence which demonstrates that teamworking strategies are being applied in a range of industries with apparent success. Teare *et al.* (1997) have documented case study evidence which demonstrates the increasing role of teamworking in the new process paradigm approach to attaining higher levels of service and responsiveness. They cite examples of the role of continuous improvement and self-directed teams in identifying problems and applying solutions themselves. Brown (1996) reports evidence which concludes that a quarter of UK employers recognize teamworking in their pay systems and that another 17 per cent are actively planning its introduction.

The Power of Teamworking

The literature suggests that teamworking has the potential to provide such benefits as improved and sustained organizational outputs (Harris and Harris, 1996) and to act as an effective agent of change, especially with the trend towards horizontal structures (Stewart and Kleiner, 1996). Teams can refocus product design processes on the customer (Valdez and Kleiner, 1996) and help develop competitive advantage (Twomey and Kleiner, 1996). A major benefit of teamworking is greater co-ordination of departments (Nurmi, 1996) and the synergy that creates. The advantages for the teams and team members include greater job satisfaction and camaraderie (Elloy and McCombs, 1996) as well as self esteem and self-actualization (Stainforth, 1996). Shonk and Shonk (1988) submit that business teams can learn from the factors that make sports teams successful. These characteristics of unitary behaviour and "team spirit" in sports teams include, according to Syer (1986), morale, cohesion, confluence and synergy. Morale is an emotive term which refers to the contentment of the team, military unit or the organization as a whole. Cohesion is used by behaviourists who believe that an individual acts only according to the threat of a promise or reward and cohesive forces include commitment to success or task motivation, difficulty of withdrawing (due to inertia or fear of letting down the team) or social needs (Festinger *et al.*, 1950). It may be argued that cohesion is the result rather than the cause of improved performance. This is often demonstrated in football teams who, as a result of above average performance, derive what Syer describes as confluence or "peak experiences of intense concentration and awareness when it seems impossible to do wrong". This leads to a synergy, or a sense of additional energy, strength or creative ability which is available when teams work harmoniously together for each other and themselves.

Teamworking Structures

In order to succeed, teams need structures which enable them to develop and flourish. Elloy and McCombs (1996) describe a programme of greater employee participation in a US manufacturing plant based on the open systems concept. The process involved completely re-structuring the plant to form self-governing teams which were responsible for their own cost control, absenteeism, safety training, discipline and employee selection and in which leadership emerged naturally. Strachan (1996) reports on the formation of environmental action teams by such firms as Kodak, BT and Apple Computers and contends that traditional management structures may impose certain constraints on the way the team operates. He contends that "organic" cultures supported by participative styles of management best allow teamwork to flourish.

Building Teams

Practical advice about building teams is plentiful in the literature. McDonald and Keys (1996), for example, identify seven major errors in teambuilding programmes from real life episodes. They stress the mutual nature of teams, which they describe as "learning and sharing systems for organization". The point that is most often stressed is the need for upper management support, without which failure is likely. An example of an empowerment effort that "came undone" is recorded by Rothstein *et al.* (1995), who report the case of a sportswear manufacturer who attempted to establish self-managed work teams but, in the absence of wholehearted management support, the scheme fell at the first hurdle. If the teamworking ethic is to permeate down an organization, it must first be fully espoused at the top and the commitment of middle management secured. This was the case at the First National Bank of Chicago in the mid 1980s, where there was a development from a staid culture to one which showed more risk-taking and innovation through team management (Harris and Harris, 1996). While it is important that top management set the scene and focus the goals, they must allow the teams the space to develop themselves because, as Fred Wilson (1996) suggests, "great teams build themselves". An important contributory factor to teams' success is a suitable leadership style which enables synergy to take place. Nurmi (1996) contends that synergistic teams can be "fertilized" by management, but after that, management has little to say in igniting the process. Another role of the leader is to manage the team processes effectively towards the goals and in a mature and supportive atmosphere. Esquivel and Kleiner (1996) stress the importance of conflict management in which the focus is on the issues and not individuals and in which teams develop "a sense of family". Team members must feel that they can contribute "safely" in an ambience of trust and confidence.

The Framing of the Regulations in Hospitality Industry

The basic provisions of the Regulations, before considering the many derogations and flexibilities state that:

- The working week should not be longer than 48 hours.
- Workers are entitled to a break of at least 20 minutes after six hours of work (the work break provision).
- Workers should have 11 hours between periods of work (the daily rest provision).
- Workers should not work more than six days in a week (weekly rest).

- No more than eight hours should be worked on a night shift.
- Everyone is entitled to four weeks paid annual leave.

Upon the election of the New Labour Government, which immediately opted in to the Social Chapter of the Maastricht Treaty, stringent commitment to the principles of labour market regulation would be expected. The Blair administration also has a strong rhetoric of work-life balance, citizenship and equality of opportunity (*DTI Newman*) leading to what Edwards described as the promise of a "potentially radical set of reforms" (quoted in *Gilman and Arrowsmith*). The reality is different. Indeed Tony Blair's government have allowed all the derogations contained within the original WTD and have even interpreted certain areas of the legislation contrary to the WTD. For example:

- Workers who organize their own working time are not subject to the maximum working week.
- The maximum week is subject to a minimum 17 week averaging period and the weekly rest provision to a two week averaging period.
- Employees can sign "opt-outs" from the 48 hour maximum.
- Exemptions from daily and weekly rest are allowed where a worker changes a shift.
- Numerous "operational" reasons for non compliance exist, for example a "surge in activity" where "continuity of service" is required or where "unusual or unforeseen circumstances" make the assertion of rights problematic or impractical.

Employers thus have plenty of scope for "flexible" interpretation. One caveat to this myriad of operational derogations is that where they are used employers are supposed to provide equivalent "compensatory rest" at a later time. The dilution is further evidenced by the fact that the WTR have needed to be amended to comply with judgements made by the European Court of Justice, for example removing the qualifying period for annual leave. The Regulations concerning night work also contravene the EU Directive by not taking overtime into account (*Hall et al.*). This gap in interpretation is also apparent within other pieces of legislation motivated by European law, such as the Part-time Workers' Regulations and Maternity and Parental Leave Regulations. The trade union movement's criticisms may stem from a well rehearsed polemical viewpoint and any government has an unenviable task in framing legislation that is pleasing to everyone. The fact remains, however, that the WTR's design appears to leave some room for management manoeuvre. This study attempts to further clarify *why* employers perceive the impact of the WTR as minimal and circumstances in which they may not abide by the legislation. Furthermore, the dynamics of the employment relationship within this are essential to understand. Are employees being ruthlessly exploited as the TUC suggest or do other reasons exist for any observed breaches of the Regulations or use of derogations? The literature presented above informs us that the WTR have had little impact and are viewed as unproblematic, but more investigation is needed on whether employees are complicit in this process and the existence of any employer strategies to accommodate the WTR other than exploitation and ignorance. In this instance the hospitality industry is investigated, which is itself generally under researched (*Hoque*). The sector is also not well represented in work assessing the impact of the WTR, thus the article addresses some key empirical needs. A brief overview of employment relations in the hospitality industry are presented to set the debate in the correct context.

Employment Relations in Hospitality Industry

The employment relationship in the hospitality industry is frequently characterised as poor with long and anti-social hours and unfavourable pay and conditions (*Rowley et al.,* ; *Lindsay and Mc Quaid*). The typical hospitality employee is likely to be young and part-time. This is particularly the case in the restaurant and pubs, bars and night clubs sub- sectors into which the case study companies fall, with 75 per cent and 65.7 per cent of the workforce under 30, respectively according to data gathered by the hospitality sector skills council (*People st*). The whole sector also has 46.1 per cent of its workforce working part-time as opposed to 25 per cent in all industries; the restaurants and licensed trade sub sectors reporting a part-time contingent of 50.1 per cent and 56.2 per cent respectively.

The style of management is traditionally associated with "hard" HRM with pressures to lower the price of labour during times of fluctuating demand, with the ultimate aim of maintaining control over costs. This is particularly evident in large multinational fast food restaurants, of which one case study company is an example, where pressures to miss breaks and to remain at work once the shift has ostensibly finished are strong during busy periods (*Royle*). The flexibility allowed by part time workers is especially good at adjusting costs to match demand. As a result of this, *Head and Lucas* believe informal, "arbitrary" employment practices are often used to "let go" of people when they are no longer required. According to the same authors, hospitality employers may in fact engage in "determined opportunism"; manipulating the law and exploiting loopholes; interpreting legal provisions in ways contrary to the spirit in which they were meant. Given the design of the WTR the opportunity for this to happen in this industry is manifest. This is especially the case in small employers of which there are many in hospitality, as they are unlikely to have codified procedures, although there is also evidence that in larger companies written policies are not always adhered to (*Head and Lucas*). "Unitarism" also predominates with mean Union density in the sector shown by WERS98 to be 2 per cent compared to 34 per cent in all other sectors; 88 per cent of hospitality workplaces have no union presence (*Lucas, ; Head and Lucas*). It is also the case that there is a paucity of non-union forums in the industry with the WERS data showing only 11 per cent of workplaces having a consultative body compared to 23 per cent in other industries, although larger workplaces are more likely to have these than smaller ones (*Lucas*). The reasons for this poor union density range from deliberate employer strategy, particularly in the fast food sector; through the fact that the "typical" young part-time worker often cannot see the relevance of unions; to the power of the small employer, close to their staff, to resist union entry strategies (*Royle, ; Head and Lucas*). This individual management style can also manifest itself as *paternalism*; commitment is fostered to the firm via praise and recognition where it is warranted but communication is very much one way (*Royle, ; Head and Lucas*). A sense of collectivism is sometimes fostered within the firm with a commitment to each-other, reinforced by management such that trade unions are seen as extraneous and unnecessary. As a result, the cost centred strategies of hospitality managers are often left unopposed. The outcomes of the above are that hospitality is characterised by a high mean turnover rate of 42 per cent, twice that of other industries (*Lucas*) and also a higher discipline and dismissal rate than other industries (*Head and Lucas*). The sector is generally characterised by unbridled flexibility, a cost controlling and unitarist management style and capricious use of procedures and law. As a result it would be *expected* that breaches of the WTR would be attributable to unilateral management pressure or, at best, a paternalistic management style.

Teaching Order or Chaos in HRM with Refernce to Hospitality Industry

The teaching of human resource management within hospitality and tourism programmes has, traditionally, focused on equipping students with what were perceived as the necessary tools for effective management within the industry. The approach has been, generally, prescriptive and focused primarily on dimensions of HRM relating to the appropriate management of subordinate staff and the world of certainty which circumscribes the management—staff relationship in the hospitality industry—labour relations, employment practices, recruitment, selection and related personnel themes. Classroom practice reflects an approach within which certainty has primacy. Rather than developing approaches to the subject which are critical and questioning of industry practice, the emphasis has been on attempting to equip students for work within "the reality of the industry", able to cope with personnel and wider staffing issues on the ground as and when they occur rather than preparing them to question the origins of these issues. Emphasising the perceived "uniqueness" of the sector does not help in this respect because the potential for learning from other sectors, especially within the service economy, can only assist students in understanding and, hopefully, rectifying some of the undesirable human resource practices which are commonplace within tourism/hospitality. Textbooks, likewise, have generally mirrored this certainty. Boella's (1992) five editions of what has probably been the most utilised text in the UK represents a good example of this approach—there is a hospitality industry out there and people employed in it who need to be managed—this is how to do that job. There is little compromise or debate in order to reflect diverse industry or human situations which may exist in different hotels. Likewise, Magurn's (1977 and subsequent editions) *A Manual of Staff Management in the Hotel and Catering Industry* provides practitioners and students with specific guidance on recruitment, retention, staff welfare, staff discipline and staff relations with no compromise or variation in response to diversity of any kind within the industry. This prescriptive and, arguably, simplified approach is a tradition which has been maintained, in somewhat modified form, by Roberts (1995). There is, probably, an important role which prescription plays in preparing students for managerial responsibility within the hospitality industry. Managers have to operate within clear legal and corporate parameters and must be clear as to why the boundaries of their operational discretion lies in relating to both customers and staff. The problem lies in the frequent absence of anything else alongside prescription.

Therefore, as a consequence of this prescriptive approach to HRM teaching, students will graduate with, perhaps, some of the tools necessary to work with staff in the hospitality and tourism industry and certainly a knowledge of the legal framework within which human resource management operates. However, they may also graduate in blissful ignorance of the wider context in which HRM for the hospitality/tourism industry operates, a context which includes understanding some of the reasons why the hospitality/tourism industry faces problems and challenges of the kind that it does. They may not understand the implications which structural diversity within the industry imposes on the management of people within the sector. They may not recognise that the human resource issues faced within the hospitality and tourism industries of different countries are not necessarily those which they face at home and which were presented, in class, as universals. They may not recognise the relationship between what they are studying in the hospitality context and the wider theoretical context and underpinning within which that body of knowledge lies—psychology, sociology, economics etc. Carmouche and Kelly (1995) argue the case for theoretical underpinning very effectively and cogently but also raise problems in the form of addressing these areas without sufficient depth of understanding. Students may not understand the social origins of much that we take for granted within the hospitality and tourism industries—Carmouche and Kelly rightly point to the class structural origins of aspects of hospitality traditions and practice and the social origins of work in the industry are also discussed by Baum (1995). Likewise, a sociological perspective on consumer groupings and consumer behaviour is important from a marketing point of view but also as a means of explaining aspects of the host-guest interaction (Baum, 1996c).

There are good sources which attempt to place the management of people within the tourism and hospitality industry in a wider socio-economic context. Riley's (1991) contribution was one of the first (and remains probably the best) to explain some of the key issues relating to work in the hospitality industry in the context of wider labour market factors and forces. Wood's seminal analysis (1992 and 1997) of work in the hospitality industry adopts a sociological approach and interprets research and developments in the context of wider sociological theory. These inputs tend to be used (if at all) as "wrap-up" material to be employed in the Honours year of a UK programme or at Senior level in the US, following initial focus on the prescriptive. This is, perhaps, too little, too late.

The curriculum issue, here, is one, in part, of timing in addition to the wider concern as to whether the broader issues are addressed, within programmes, at all. Giving students "the real beef" at the end of the meal has clear attractions but certainly undermines their capacity to digest the earlier courses with full understanding. It also threatens the level and extent of potential learning within the context of their work placements or internship. It seems to these authors that hospitality students require a real and in-depth *understanding* of the industry and HRM issues within it from a theoretical and conceptual point of view before they are given operational and prescriptive models of how to operate within that environment. Failure to adopt this approach will mean that further generations of hospitality managers will emerge into the industry to perpetuate the simplistic and generalised HRM solutions adopted by their predecessors. Start with theory and context (in other words, an educational as opposed to a training approach) and, like a good aperitif, this will enable students to digest the more instructional and functional approaches to HRM which they receive later and which, together, will enable them to become effective and thinking managers in the hospitality industry.

Therefore, this study argues for a stronger pedagogical basis to the learning experience with which students are confronted in the human resource management area of the hospitality/tourism curriculum. While it is recognised that many programmes seek to ensure vocational application and do so in response to perceived "industry demand", such responsiveness is, perhaps, short-sighted and limited in that it does little more than encourage the perpetuation of existing human resource management practice and makes little or no contribution to change. Human resource management teaching needs to be approached from an educational perspective which is designed to equip students with the necessary critical factors to contribute to change in this area, to respond to the wide range of concerns, some structural and some within the instrumental control of tourism/hospitality managers, which Wood (1992 and 1997) among others addresses. The starting point needs to be one of engendering understanding of why certain situations exist within the sector (low pay, high labour turnover, poor perceptions of work in the area) in the wider historical, social and economic context of tourism and hospitality. Whether graduates, on entering the industry, decide to accept the environment in which they are operating or to become agents for change, they will do so on the basis of understanding rather than as uncritical perpetuators of the status quo.

An Assessment of the Human Resource Demands of the Hospitality Industries

This section is based on the work of Spivack (1997). Her study, using Delphi methodologies, sought to identify and measure gaps between the skills and wider human resource requirements of the tourism and hospitality industries, and the provision made by education and training providers in support of the sector. In addition, the study looks to the future and attempts to identify the educational and training priorities for tourism and hospitality in response to changes within the sectoral and wider socio-economic and political environment. The approach of the study was:

> To develop a qualitative methodology, through a consensus model approach, for determining gaps between the output of education and training delivery systems and the current and future needs of employers. Inherent in the premise is a falsifiable theory: there is no relationship

between education and training system outputs and the delivery of quality service (Spivack, 1997, p. 7).

This study brings together two areas of applied policy development which impact significantly on the development of a wider and cogent policy framework for human resource development within tourism and hospitality: first, that of quality service attainment as central to a successful tourism and hospitality sector, and, second, that there is a role which public education and training can play in achieving such quality. Spivack's study consisted of two components, employing similar methodologies but working with distinct groups in order to verify the approach and to test outcomes in different contexts. The first global survey was based on a sample drawn from international tourism interests, from both the public and private sector, and representing a wide range of sub-sectoral interests and geographical regions. The second component involved a localized study, employing a similar approach and located in a region of Spain. Modified Delphi methods were used for both components, recognizing both the benefits that this approach brings to a qualitative study but also its clear limitations (Witt and Moutinho, 1989). Its advantages include the potential breadth of the study, its internal anonymity the manner in which it permits reflection time for participants and the ability of the approach to tackle complex issues in a balanced manner.

Problems relate to the sampling process—the rationale for Delphi is that it draws on expert contributors, but there can be difficulties in defining and identifying appropriate expertise; in maintaining response levels over a number of survey rounds; and in the time commitment demanded of participants. The global study commenced with 100 participants, drawn on a controlled formula basis from both sectoral and geographical populations to ensure minimum representation within each category. The criteria used for inclusion of participants required that panellists exhibit some or all of the following:

- hold upper-level management positions within their field;
- serve in leadership positions in professional associations related to their field;
- demonstrate familiarity with many different career levels within their sector;
- demonstrate leadership and decision-making skills;
- articulate trends impacting their industry;
- possess familiarity with tourism education and training in their world region.

Selection of the sample was based on access to various databases and directories of international tourism. While there must be clear limitations to this process, the final sample met representation criteria in terms of both sectoral and geographical considerations. Communication was by mail and fax. The response rate to the two rounds of the study showed expected levels of drop-out so that the first round was completed by 66 per cent of the 100-member sample and the second round by 44, representing a 44 per cent participation rate from the original sample. The local study, based on the Castilla-La Mancha region of Spain, employed the same approach but saw some significant modifications to suit local conditions. Participation criteria were modified to reflect the different level of responsibility of tourism sector leaders at a regional level and, as a result, included rather more members with direct line management responsibility for enterprises or tourism agencies. Geographical considerations related to representation of the five provinces within the region, while the sectors were modified to reflect the structure of the local industry. The sample was 160 and the three rounds of the survey were conducted: first, by face-to-face personal interview; second, using a telephone survey based on a questionnaire resulting from analysis of the first-round outcomes; and, finally, through panel workshops in each of the five provinces, requiring panellists to prioritize the outcome issues relevant to their specific area and to develop regional action plans. Participation in the three rounds was as follows:

- Round 1: 160.
- Round 2: 140, representing a 13 per cent drop-off.
- Round 3: 39, representing a 76 per cent drop-off from the original sample.

The outcomes of the two studies identified a number of key gaps with respect to the human resource requirements, as articulated by the respondents (both public and private sector) and the skills and knowledge of those recruited into the tourism sector, whether from specialist vocational programmes or through the general education process. The main area of deficiency related to what Baum (1990) describes as soft competences within the sector, those relating to communication (with customers, colleagues and in various languages other than the mother tongue), information (technology-derived, but also analysis and interpretation) and service (marketing-related, understanding customer needs), all of which are attributes which are generic to the sector and, indeed, to services in general. By contrast, technical ability deficiencies were identified as far less significant within both surveys—there is growing recognition that the diminishing technical demands of the sector (as identified above) can readily be met within the workplace by larger employers, provided soft competences and attitude dimensions are in place. However, the skills requirements of SMEs remains an issue and it is noteworthy that the local study gave a rather less clear-cut endorsement of this assessment than did the global survey representing larger organizations and interests. In policy terms, this central finding affirms previous research at a more localized level and within the context of specific sub-sectors and suggests the need for review of public education and training provision for the tourism and hospitality sector in terms of curriculum and, indeed, wider focus and purpose. The global study also gives an indication of future education and training priorities for tourism and hospitality. Spivack (1997) reports a number of what she calls "skills development issues" derived from anticipated changes within the tourism and hospitality sector, and which the panel consensus process prioritized as central to education and training needs in the future. These were, in rank order:

- will need to develop more skills in human resource management, particularly in knowing how to build an enthusiastic workforce.
- continued internationalization of business, all levels of management will need more training, especially in interpersonal and multicultural skills.
- awareness and conservation techniques will become an essential part of tourism education at all levels.
- expansion of franchises among transnational firms will accelerate the need for international-level quality of service and skill standards.
- health issues, such as AIDS, that relate to the delivery of tourist products and services will become an essential part of tourism education at all levels.
- will need to learn more high-level management skills such as forecasting and strategic planning.

The local study did not generate significantly different responses from those presented above, with the main emphasis on the growing importance of environmental awareness, business acumen and the enhanced role of enterprises in the education and training of the workforce.

On the basis of this assessment, the study also considered and prioritized key training issues for the future. At an education and training level (Spivack, 1997), these were:

- of tourism and hospitality management will need to strengthen their curriculum content that deals with business administration skills.

- will need more training to direct a growing contract-based, part-time and possibly job-sharing workforce.
- continued technological change, alternative methods of training and education (such as distance learning, multimedia interactive training, etc.) will markedly replace traditional education.
- the future, industry will itself assume increasing responsibility for in-house training of employees at all levels, and rely less on formal education.
- with formal education in tourism and hospitality management studies generally perform better than colleagues who lack such education.
- will increasingly encourage and pay for continuing education for their employees to ensure employee commitment and retention.
- employee exchange programmes at all levels of employment will become commonplace.

With respect to wider personnel issues, a number of priorities were also identified (Spivack, 1997):

- will favour hiring employees who have a combination of on-the-job training and formal education.
- standards, rather than other criteria, will increasingly determine employee compensation and benefits.
- that have been traditionally been under-represented at management levels in the tourism workforce, such as women, will have a greater role in the future.
- family lifestyles will require companies to incorporate practices such as work-at-home employees (the virtual office) that lead to a more flexible workforce.
- will be required to adjust their expectations regarding promotion time-frames, entry-level positions and pay.
- downsizing will slow the advancement of employees within their own organizations.
- increase the quality of service and better compete in the marketplace, employee incentives, for example, stock options, will become standard for companies.

Spivack's study points to a future which is, in part, already here in that some of the indicators and priorities are already recognized by some sectors of the tourism and hospitality industry, and responses are clearly emerging in the light of such recognition. British Airways' planned reorganization of its personnel base, with a shedding of low-skills employees and the recruitment of a flexible, technology- and language-literate workforce in its place, is one example of this recognition. However, the situation is far from even; while some businesses are in a transition stage and moving towards the future painted by this research, others, especially SMEs are locked in the past in their human resource policies and practices, unable or unwilling to face up to the consequences of the issues addressed earlier in this article. If the human resource environment predicted by Spivack's study is taken to be a reasonable prognosis for the future, there are significant implications for both tourism enterprises and the wider communities within which they exist. What is implied is the need for a significant mind-shift by those providing leadership within the tourism sector, both public and private, but it also points clearly to the need for changes, at a policy and practice level, within the environment controlled by the wider public sector, both tourism-related and that within the provenience of education, training, employment or other labour market authorities.

Understanding Customers and Service Improvement in Hospitality Industry

The concept of mass customization has emerged in part, from a decade of debate centred on the mass production of inexpensive, commodity-like products or services (the assembly line approach) on the one hand and premium-priced, individually-tailored and highly differentiated offerings on the other. Hart' observes that much of the power of mass customization, like total quality management before it, lies in its visionary and strategic implications. Its application should enable companies to produce affordable, high-quality goods and services, but with shorter cycle times and lower costs. The key dimensions of his diagnostic framework for assessing the potential for mass customization are: customer sensitivity, process amenability, competitive environment and organizational readiness. Taylor and Lyon discuss the application of mass customization to food service operations and its likely adoption in a rapidly maturing marketplace. A compatible step is for management to create an appropriate form of internal customer orientation and Stauss notes that a deliberate and sustained effort is needed to create a climate that promotes a customer's viewpoint of work activities, processes and non-standardized support services. Customer orientation also implies a readiness to measure, and where necessary improve, the quality of service and support in keeping with customer expectations. Lee and Hing assess the usefulness and application of the SERVQUAL technique in measuring service quality in the fine dining sector. They demonstrate how easily and inexpensively the technique can be used to identify the strengths and weaknesses of individual restaurants' service dimensions. A periodic audit of customer service deliverables might also be usefully conducted and Congram and Epelman recommend the use of the structured analysis and design technique (SADT). This enables service providers to review the processes in which they participate, identify, implement and review improvements in service delivery and rethink aspects of the service package. The interpersonal aspects of service delivery are potentially the most difficult to audit and improve. A useful starting point is to undertake a programme of job analysis for service staff to identify the best fit between tasks, behaviours and personal attributes. Papadopoulou *et al.* identify the dimensions of a higher customer contact food and beverage operative's job as perceived by managers, supervisors and operatives and examine within-source and between source-differences in perceptions. Their study confirms the versatility of job analysis as an organizational and diagnostic tool. Among other uses, it depicts the dimensions of a job, the related personal qualities and experience and the training implications. In most cases, it is also helpful to profile ideal combinations of age and experience for different service roles, especially as the industry relies heavily on younger workers. Corporate level concern about service quality issues has stimulated interest in employee empowerment. In theory, empowered employees will be more committed to ensuring that service encounters satisfy customers as they have the necessary discretion and autonomy to "delight the customer". Lashley explores the implications of empowering employees and provides a framework for understanding managerial motives in selecting different forms of empowerment and their consequences for achieving improvements in customer service quality. To support empowerment and other customer-led initiatives, training and development is needed. Clements and Josiam outline a step-by-step procedure to evaluate both the costs and the benefits of any training proposal. Their approach utilizes a financial analysis model for identifying the dollar value of both performance outcomes and training costs. While interpersonal skills development and support is needed for service staff, supervisors and managers need to make appropriate decisions and Gore examines some of the theoretical models of decision making derived from the field of psychology and considers the related implications for training in decision making.

Market-driven Approach to Business Development and Service Improvement in the Hospitality Industry

The purpose of this article is to review hospitality research concerning the broad theme of business development and service improvement. This theme is divided into five sub-themes: market sensitivity and competitiveness; segmentation, branding and service customization; service quality and customer retention; product design and internal marketing. Journal articles from 1990 to June of 1997 were used in this study. Abstracts of most of the articles can be found on the WHATT CD. The objective of the study is to provide practitioners with suggestions and ideas for business improvement. Millions of dollars of research are referenced in this article. The results of the research are not proprietary, but available for all to use. For practitioners, the article will explain the management implications of the research. For academics, the article provides an overview of current research by area and presents suggestions for future research.

Theme 1: Market Sensitivity and Competitiveness

The research in the area of market sensitivity and competitiveness tended to be on yield management and positioning. The yield management research was grouped into two general issues, pricing systems to increase yield and the choice of market segments that would create the highest yield. The positioning articles discussed the use of perceptual maps as a strategic tool. The methodology used in the positioning articles could be applied to most hospitality companies, giving good information for strategic planning.

Yield management: The yield management articles are broken up into conventional yield management articles and methods for choosing the market segments that will create the highest yield. Griffin (1995) provided an overview of yield management and identified a number of critical success factors for yield management systems. Among these are several environmental factors that relate to booking patterns, price sensitivity of market segments, and the distribution channel's tolerance for differential pricing. Jeffrey and Hubbard (1994) developed a model of occupancy performance that can be easily applied by hotel managers and others with access to hotel occupancy data. The model looked at two fundamental aspects of a hotel's occupancy performance: the proportionality component, which includes the effects of regular and periodic demand fluctuations, and the competitive components, which include local and unique forces. Bull (1994) investigated the contribution a hotel's location makes to the market value of the hotel's rooms. This methodology makes it possible to put implicit price-location contours on an area map. The study also has implications for area growth that may affect the contribution of a property's location to its room rate. Weatherford (1995) cited the importance of incorporating a guest's length of stay into the room allocation decisions. He claimed proper use of the length of stay dimension can increase revenue by up to 3 per cent. One of the problems with most yield management systems is that they only look at room revenue. Quain

(1992) introduced profit analysis by segment (PABS). PABS takes into account room and non-room revenue to determine the value of different market segments. As yield management matures in the hotel industry, more robust models will be developed that take into account total guest expenditures and the long-term value of the guest. In developing yield management systems it is important that customer retention be included in the model. Maximizing revenue today has little value if it drives off tomorrow's customers.

Positioning/perceptual maps: Dev *et al.* (1995) cited the need for managers to monitor the implications of their marketing strategies. The authors stated that managers need to examine the attributes that consumers use to differentiate one hotel brand from another and illustrated how managers can do this by using multidimensional scaling to build perceptual maps. Kim (1996) used perceptual maps to show how customers perceive food and beverage at competing hotels. Kim also developed ideal points to show how a hotel can change its attributes to gain a better position *vis-à-vis* its competitors. The methodology used in the study could be used to position different product or product groups of a hotel or restaurant. Shaw (1992) investigated price from a strategic positioning viewpoint. She explained how price has both a strategic component and a tactical component. Shaw stated a positioning approach focuses first on price levels, then on actual price decisions for a specific product. Shaw's approach to pricing could help a brand achieve a desired position, which then could be validated through one of the perceptual mapping techniques.

Theme 2: Segmentation, Branding, and Service Customization

It is no secret that different customer segments want different product attributes. Commissioned sales people want hotel rooms with a free telephone, while upscale business travellers want expedited check-in. Thus, one of the first decisions for a company is to decide what segments it wants to target. This will determine the company's marketing mix. As segments grow and decline, a company must constantly review its segmentation strategy, looking for viable segments that are compatible with the company's objectives and products. After a company chooses a target market, the company must position itself in the marketplace *vis-à-vis* the other companies that are going after the target market. Two ways of accomplishing this positioning are through branding and service customization. This section looks at research on segmentation, branding, and service customization.

Segmentation: The segmentation research identifies product attributes that create value for market segments. This information is useful to companies targeting these segments or companies who may have a marketing mix that is valuable to these segments. It is always advisable to replicate segmentation studies using data from customers. Owing to time and regional differences, the wants of customer segments can vary. The segmentation research also presents a variety of research techniques that can be used to give greater insight into what the segments desire and the importance they put on different product attributes. Shaw *et al.* (1991) investigated product attributes of hotel convention services that create satisfaction among meeting planners. The authors went beyond just looking at the mean ratings of the attributes. They developed a multivariate approach to analysing the data, which could be applied to similar survey data to provide rich information. Several studies looked at specific segments. For example, Wight (1996) researched ecotourism and divided it into two market segments: general consumers interested in ecotourism and experienced ecotourism travellers. Her findings are useful for resorts that are interested in catering to this market. Callan (1996) compared UK leisure travellers with business travellers on their importance ratings of hotel attributes. Makens (1992) investigated catering to the family market at resorts. The article provides some case studies of resorts that have children's programmes. For more studies that looked at specific segments. Conjoint analysis gives insight to the importance that customers place on different product attributes. Several studies provided examples of how conjoint analysis can be used in segmentation studies. Hu and Hiemstra (1996) used hybrid conjoint analysis to measure meeting planners' preferences in hotel selection. Becker-Suttle *et al.* (1994) used conjoint analysis to explore restaurant benefits sought by seniors and non-seniors. The use of neural networks, a type of artificial intelligence, is becoming a popular segmentation technique. It is often used in data mining tools to discover relationships between customers, identifying customer segments that might not be apparent to the marketer. Mazanec (1992) illustrated the usefulness of neural networks by segmenting tourists.

Branding: Customers develop brand images, or a set of beliefs, about where each brand stands on different product attributes. One of the trends in the hospitality industry is to use brands that have a positive brand image, rather than a company's own products which may have little brand image. For example, many hotels and catering companies in the USA are using kiosks to sell Starbucks Coffee, which has a strong brand image. ARAMARK, a contract food service company, franchises Burger King and Pizza Hut outlets even though they have the ability to produce products that have a similar quality. Hotels are contracting out their food service to local providers and chains that have a strong image. Thus, brand management is an area that is emerging as an important marketing area.

The research on branding was scarce, indicating a need for future research in this area. Hallam and Baum (1996) surveyed hotel managers in North America and the UK to gain perceptions of why hotels may contract out portions or all of their food and beverage operations. One of the major reasons cited in the study was that a branded or well-known operator could help attract more accommodation guests. Thus, managers saw a branded restaurant as an amenity that was valued by the lodging guests. Connell (1992) looked at the benefits and problems of branding in the hotel industry. He used the rebranding of Forte after the acquisition of Crest as a case study.

Customization: Effective guest history systems now make it possible to customize guest service. Unpublished research by Bowen and Shoemaker found that customized services were one the most important attributes to luxury hotel customers. Ritz-Carlton used guest history very effectively to produce customized services (Partlow 1993). Dev and Ellis (1991) presented a guest history management model and explained how it could be used to customize service for repeat guests. Customization of services can create a competitive advantage by increasing guest loyalty.

Theme 3: Service Quality and Customer Retention

What is service quality?: A distinction can be made between two types of quality: product features that enhance customer satisfaction and freedom from deficiencies that increase customer satisfaction. The first type of quality, product features, adds to the cost of the product. Customers must be willing to pay for either the added costs of additional product features or these features must make them more loyal. For example, lettuce and tomato is found only on McDonald's more expensive hamburgers. Hotel rooms on concierge floors have more features than standard rooms and command a higher price. La Quinta Inns offers free local telephone calls to encourage loyalty among salespeople. The expectations of guests are formed by company image, word of mouth, the company's promotional efforts, and price. A guest paying $35 for a room at a Motel 6 or Formula 1 will have different expectations from a guest paying $250 for a room at a Four Seasons Hotel. The person staying at the budget hotel may be perfectly satisfied. The room features meet their expectations. The first type of quality, product features, relates to guest expectations. People staying in a budget hotel may perceive it as the best quality motel for less than $40. They are not comparing it to a Four Seasons Hotel. Both the guests of a Motel 6 or Formula 1 and a Four Seasons Hotel will expect the room to be free from deficiencies. For example, guests at the Four Seasons and those at the budget hotel are both likely to get upset if they return in the evening to rooms that have not been made up. There is another way to view quality. A distinction can be made between technical and functional quality. Technical quality refers to what the customer is left with after the customer-employee interactions have been completed. For example, technical quality relates to the guest room in the hotel, the meal in the restaurant, and the car from the rental agency. Functional quality is the process of delivering the service or product (Grönroos, 1982). While the service is being delivered, customers go through many interactions with the firm's employees. A guest makes a reservation, is greeted by the door attendant, is escorted to the front desk by a bellperson, checks in with the desk clerk, and is escorted to the room. The experience of checking into a hotel is an example of functional quality. Excellent functional quality may make up for a room that is not quite up to expectations. If functional quality is unpleasant, a high-quality room might not overcome the guests' previous dissatisfaction.

Models of quality management: For a good introduction to service quality see a series of articles by Johns (1992a, 1992b, 1993). In these articles he presented a comprehensive overview of quality management in the hospitality industry. Partlow (1993) provided a comprehensive overview of how Ritz-Carlton won the Malcolm Baldrige Award. In the article, Partlow presented an overview of Ritz's quality management program. Later, Partlow (1996) focused on the human resource practices that support TQM. Heymann (1992) provided a ten-point model for quality management.

Measuring service quality: A service quality audit can identify problems when a firm is first developing a quality management programme or it can be used to audit an existing programme. Luchars and Hinkin (1996) developed a service quality audit that can be used to identify errors and determine their frequency, assign costs of fixing (or not fixing) the errors, and identify steps to prevent them. They provided a case study of a New York hotel to illustrate their service-quality audit. SERVQUAL developed by Parasuraman *et al.* is one of the most popular instruments for measuring service quality. Knutson *et al.*(1991) adapted SERVQUAL into a specific instrument for hotels. They tested the reliability of their instrument, LODGSERV, and found it to be a reliable instrument. Later Stevens *et al.* (1995) developed DINESERV for measuring service quality in restaurants. Barsky (1992) discussed a theoretical model of customer satisfaction and then tested the model using a survey instrument. Using his survey instrument, he was able to support his hypothesis that intent to return will be positively related to customer satisfaction.

Customer retention: One desired outcome of service quality is customer retention. The following research investigated customer retention. Dube *et al.* (1994) used conjoint analysis to show the overall utility of seven service-quality attributes that all bear significantly on customers' intent to return. The authors' methodology provides managers with information that will help justify (or not justify) the costs of improving quality. Toh *et al.* (1991) researched the effectiveness of frequent-guest programmes in hotels. They found many of the programmes were not effective in creating repeat customers. The authors provide insights on how the programmes could be improved. Buttle and Bok (1996) provided an overview of Fishbein's theory of reasoned action. They found two predictor constructs: attitude towards the act, and subjective norm jointly explain about 65 per cent of the intention to stay in a hotel on the next trip.

Theme 4: Product Fesign

A company must build a service delivery system that provides product attributes desired by its target market. The articles on service design were on both the macro and micro level. Some articles looked at the overall design of a hospitality operation, while other articles looked at specific issues. This section will first review the macro articles and then discuss the micro articles.

Comprehensive design models: Pannell Kerr Forster Associates (1993) concluded that hotel design factors can be summarized into three areas: market factors including customer requirements, competitive influences and trends; impact of new technology enabling new services or increased levels of comfort to be available and leading to improvements in construction techniques and choice of materials used; and statutory requirements affecting the design and construction of buildings and specific legislation relating to hotels. Verma and Thompson (1996) illustrated how discrete choice analysis can be used to design business concepts based on the importance that customers place on different product attributes. The researchers use delivery pizza as an example, but the technique could be applied to the development or design of any concept.

New product design: Several articles looked at the development of new products. Jones (1995) applied Scheuing and Johnson's model for new service development to flight catering. His research found that airlines lack many of the systematic procedures suggested by Scheuing and Johnson. Shoemaker (1996) looked at how customers develop a series of actions regarded as necessary or appropriate for a service transaction. Variations from the script can be a source of dissatisfaction. Thus, when developing new service delivery systems, companies must assist customers in developing a new script. Miner (1996) presented a customer focused approach to developing new products in a restaurant.

The six stage process includes product ideas, initial evaluation, consumer reaction, sensory testing, field testing, and product introduction.

Specific products: Another set of research looked at the design of special projects. Goldman (1993) discussed the importance of concept selection for independent restaurants. He discussed the different external factors that affect concept selection. Makens and Bowen (1996) discussed merchandise opportunities for restaurants. Design consideration for restaurants wanting to implement a merchandising programme include space to merchandise the products and storage space. Bowen and Morris (1995) looked at the design of a menu to increase product sales. They found that menu design in a sit-down service restaurant may not be as effective in selling products as previously thought. Monteson and Singer (1992) explained how spas can add value as an amenity in a destination hotel or resort. They gave advice on how to manage and market a spa properly, so it creates maximum value for the guests and adds to the bottom line of the hotel. Conner (1991) focused on how renovations could capture the original glitz and glamour of the hotel, while making the hotel operationally efficient. Conner provides specific examples from design renovations in New York City. Knapp (1991) provides a case study of the renovation of the Sheraton Palace in San Francisco.

Theme 5: Internal Marketing

The hospitality industry is unique in that employees are part of the product. When people think of marketing, they usually think of efforts directed externally towards the marketplace; but a hotel or restaurant's first marketing efforts should be directed internally to employees. Managers must make sure that employees know their products and believe that they are good value. The employees must be excited about the company they work for and the products they sell; otherwise, it will be impossible for the guests to become excited. External marketing brings customers into the hotel but does little good if the employees do not perform to the guest's expectations. The sub-themes identified in the research relating internal marketing include culture, service orientation, empowerment and listening.

Culture: An internal marketing programme flows out of a service culture. A service marketing programme is doomed to failure if its organizational culture does not support serving the customer. It is difficult to establish an effective culture in a permanent organization and even harder to establish a culture in a temporary organization. Meudell and Gadd (1994) looked at the establishment of a culture in short-life organizations. The authors used an organizational beliefs questionnaire to investigate the National Garden Festival Wales' organizational culture. This article built on earlier work by the authors on short-life organizations.

Service orientation: If management expects employees' attitudes to be positive towards the customer, management must have a positive attitude towards the customer and the employees. Too often organizations hire trainers to come in for one day to get their customer-contact employees excited about providing quality customer service. The effect of these sessions is usually short-lived because the organizations do little to support the customer-contact employees. A company must develop policies and an organizational structure to support its service orientation. Barsky (1996) described how to build a system to deliver world-class service. In the article he provided numerous examples from hospitality firms, including a sample of a guest survey. Barsky also provided examples of how to map the customer cycle. At the heart of this process is a step that redesigns exiting processes based on both customer and employee input. The second part of this step is to develop employee programmes that support the new processes. Shimko (1994) explained how existing decision-making polices, coupled with the manner in which organizations reward conforming behaviour, may result in polices that prevent employees from providing optimal customer service. King and Garey (1997) looked at how the organizational context in which a service encounter takes place affects employee interactions with customers, and resulting guest satisfaction. They found that stress-related factors including a bureaucratic climate were negatively related to guest satisfaction ratings. Dienhart *et al.*(1991) and Dienhart *et al.* (1992) investigated factors that might influence restaurant employees' degree of service orientation. The authors developed a questionnaire that was administered to supervisory and non-supervisory employees. The results of the research suggest that increasing employee's job involvement, job satisfaction, and job security could assist in improving their overall service orientation.

Listening: Perhaps one of the most important research areas of internal marketing is the management of listening. Employees have the potential for collecting information directly from the guests. Through proper training and information collection systems employees can provide more information than market research costing tens of thousands of dollars. However, for these systems to work, employees must trust the organization. Good communication between employees and managers not only provides good customer information, but it also supports a service culture by identifying management problems and solutions to those problems. Several researchers investigated the area of listening and communication. Brownell (1994) focused on the importance of managers creating an environment that fosters good communication between employees and management. She stated, "The vision of strong listening environments may foster practices and attitudes that become the most important tools managers bring with them into the twenty-first century". Sparks (1994) found that customers evaluate the quality of the service, in part, on the manner in which information is communicated by employees. Thus, part of customer satisfaction is dependent on the ability of employees to listen to customers and communicate with them.

Empowerment: Empowerment has been associated with a number of benefits including increased employee and customer satisfaction. The increased customer satisfaction comes through better complaint resolution, ability to customize products, and more responsive service. One problem in the implementation of empowerment can be lack of management support. Most of the research on empowerment dealt with the process of empowering employees. Brymer (1991) presented a framework for implementing employee empowerment and also provided some guides which will help measure the results of empowerment. Lashley (1995) provided an overview of the benefits of empowerment and illustrated how different hospitality companies have implemented empowerment. Lashley (1997) later provided frameworks for employee empowerment and called for research to investigate the tradeoffs between employee empowerment and improved organizational performance. Sparrowe (1994) proposed that investments in psychological empowerment among hospitality employees seem worthwhile, as satisfaction with promotion opportunities should rise and intent to leave should decline. Thus, empowerment can not only lead to guest satisfaction, it can also result in employee satisfaction.

Thematic interrelationships: Through market analysis, perceptual maps are developed providing insights into attractive market segments. Much of the research in the area of market segmentation focused on the importance different market segments place on product attributes. The target market determines the design of the product. Quality management ensures that the product is being delivered at a level which will create repeat business. Quality measurement validates that the quality management system is working. The quality measurement also monitors changes in wants and expectations of the target market. Changes in market expectations or wants can be met through product redesign. Thus, the link between quality measurement and product design indicates an ongoing process of shaping the product to meet the needs of the target market. Since employees are part of the product, they need to be included in the design of service delivery systems. Employees that deliver good service also contribute to the quality of the organization and will be included in the quality management process. Finally, quality impacts on brand image. Customer retention is one of the objectives of most businesses. The brand image, service customization, and internal marketing all affect customer retention. At the heart of this model is the target market or customer. When a company chooses a market segment that can create value for the firm, then the firm must deliver a product that creates value to the market segment. The literature reviewed in this article will help hospitality managers gain insight into the process of choosing the right target markets and delivering value to their target markets.

Methodology of Measuring Quality in Hospitality Industry

Development of the HOLSERV Scale

The definition of service quality adopted in this study, is "the degree of discrepancy between customers' normative expectations for the service and their perceptions of the service performance" (Parasuraman *et al.*, 1988, p. 17). Thus the study pursues hotel guests' perceptions of the quality they receive, compared to their expectations in a one-column format. Modification to suit the hospitality setting resulted in changes to some existing items, the inclusion of new items and deletion of items. In addition, a new item, "Guests feel safe and secure in their stay" was included in the questionnaire, as security is regarded as an important issue in a hotel stay. In all, eight items were either modified or added to the original SERVQUAL scale, and three items were deleted, leaving a total of 27 items in final scale. The items in the questionnaire were measured on a seven-point scale ranging from "completely failed to meet my expectations" to "far exceeded my expectations", consistent with the earlier work of Parasuraman *et al.* (1991). In addition, a separate overall service quality measure that used a single rating ten-point scale (1 = very poor, and 10 = excellent) was included to enable identification of the best predictor of overall service quality.

The Sample

A total of 1,000 questionnaires and covering letters were distributed to guests of five hotels in Australia, ranging in standard from three to five stars. The recruitment process for this study took place for a duration of four months, from July to October 1998. A sample size of 155 participants was collected, representing a response rate of 15.5 per cent which compares favourably to other hospitality studies (Barsky and Huxley, 1992; Danaher and Haddrell, 1996). The participants of this study are predominantly business travellers, as 72 per cent of the respondents described the purpose of their visit as being a business trip. Thirty-two per cent of the respondents were female, and most of the respondents were between 41 and 50 years of age. Forty per cent of the respondents in this study were staying for one night, 43 per cent for two to three nights, and 17 per cent for more than three nights. Finally, 28 per cent of the respondents were new customers who have not stayed at the hotel before, while 71 per cent are repeat travellers.

Staffing and Hospitality Service Delivery

Managing employees, especially customer contact employees, in hospitality organizations calls for different staffing strategies than in manufacturing. In hospitality services, the customer contact employee is in the service factory, producing the service experience for or with the guest. In most cases, this production process requires involvement from the guest as an input and/or a co-producing role. This means that the employee has to have the necessary knowledge, skills and abilities to perform the task and also be interactively skilled. In providing a service to the guest, the employee has to get informational input from the customer (information about the guest room preference, how to prepare a steak, etc.). Thus, the employee has to not only know how to produce the service product but also how to listen to the customer to find out what specific service product is desired. Also, the employees need the problem solving skills to identify and fix customer problems in real time. When production and consumption occur simultaneously, the burden of responsibility that falls on the guest contact employee is very much different than it is for the product producer.

In regard to the additional complexity and ambiguity created by customer interaction, there are several issues. These are recruiting, selecting, training, and rewarding employees for the complex roles they play in customer interactions. Thus, the service writers seek to identify and train the attitudes and values that their people need to be successful in a service encounter. While a machine doesn't care if the riveter has bad attitude, the restaurant patron or hotel guest does. Having satisfied employees is especially important for hospitality organizations (Berry, 1981; Loveman, 1998)

Recruiting and Selecting

The research on this issue suggests that the quality of service can be enhanced if the employer selects people that have appropriate personal characteristics (Albrecht and Zemke, 1985; Bowen *et al.*, 1989). Because some of these characteristics are not amenable to training, some hospitality companies use some form of personality selection devices to hire the kind of people that can provide the service experience (Hogan *et al.*, 1984). The importance of personality in the selection process is supported by McCallum and Harrison (1985), who state service encounters are first and foremost social encounters, understanding the social dynamics involved becomes a uniquely important issue to hospitality organizations:

Selecting people for customer service roles is similar to casting people for roles in a movie. First, both require artful performances aligned with the audience expectations. Creating an interpersonal experience that customers remember as satisfactory, pleasant, or dazzling is like an actor's mission of having audiences so caught up in the play or movie that they start believing the performer is the person portrayed. Second, both require a casting choice based on personality (Bell and Anderson, 1992, p. 52).

The above discussion has stressed the importance of personality in the selection of customer contact employees. Hospitality organizations must use tactics that will attract employees with a service attitude and personalities that will fit with their organization. Berry (1999, p. 83) states excellent service businesses realize the quality of the employee's performance is integral to the quality of the customer's experience. Thus these companies don't just recruit employees, they compete for talent.

Internal Marketing: A Systematic Approach to Training

"Everything a service organization does for its customers is first perceived by its employees" (Groonroos, 2000, p. 331). If employees do not understand the wants of the customers and how the service offering can fulfill these wants, they will not be effective in their interaction with the customers. The customer contact employee can only do their job if they are supported by back of the house employees. Thus, the organization must learn to engage everyone in the service mission. Internal marketing includes both the customer contact employee and the many others who support that customer contact person. As one author writes, "If you're not serving a customer, you'd better be serving someone who is or we don't need you" (Albrecht and Zemke, 1985, p. 96). What this means is that the hospitality managers spend considerable effort communicating the service mission and vision to all employees so that those in the "back of the house" or "off stage" know how important their role is in supporting those in the "front of the house" or "on stage". This concept of internal marketing has been described as a philosophy for managing the organization's human resources based on a marketing philosophy (George and Gronroos, 1991).

Groonroos (2000) claims training is a basic component of an internal marketing program. Employees must understand the service culture of the organization, the company's products and the company's promotions. The information from this training will help them serve the customer. At

Disney all employees take a course called "Traditions," in which they learn about the company, its founder and its values and beliefs. Disney trains ticket takers for four days because it wants them to be more than ticket takers; Disney wants them to be cast members. Disney also knows tickets takers will be asked many questions. They must know the answer to these questions or know how to quickly find the answer (Pope, 1979 (also in Sasser *et al.*, 1991)).

Role Conflict/Role Ambiguity

The hospitality employee is more likely to experience role conflict and role ambiguity than would a manufacturing counterpart. This is due to the intangibility of the service experience and the customer interaction requirement of simultaneous production with consumption. Because the customer contact employee is responsible for producing or co-producing the service experience in a way that meets that unique customer's expectations, there is great opportunity for role ambiguity in the service encounter (Jackson and Schuler, 1992). The employee is frequently faced with potential conflicts between the role expected by the customer and the role expected by the organization or even other employees (Zeithaml *et al.*, 1988). For example, dealers in a casino may be asked to speed up the number of hands they deal per hour, however players may expect the dealers to engage them in conversations about local tourist attractions, slowing down their play. Role conflict can also be caused by company policies that conflict with customer expectations. For example, if hotel customers normally expect to be able to cash a check and the hotel has a no check-cashing policy this can create conflict (Zeithaml *et al.*, 1988). As Broderick (1998) notes, role theory helps service organizations understand how to manage the employee-customer relationship.

In an effort to clarify the role ambiguity in service experiences, some writers have emphasized the importance of a service culture or service climate. Gronroos (1990, p. 7), for example, stresses the importance of a service climate or culture to fill in any gaps or the difference between what the employee can be trained to do and what that employee will have to do to satisfy the customer. Customers and their behaviour cannot be standardized and totally predetermined. The situations vary and therefore a distinct service-oriented culture is needed that tells employees how to respond to new, unforeseen ad even awkward situations. Cahill (1995) refers to the importance of organizational memory. Cahill states that organizational memory is most useful when the organizations learn from and build on the memory. Thus, the memory is constantly updated and helps the organization manage environmental uncertainty. He proposes that a strong culture is one that can withstand environmental shocks and help the organization learn.

Communication between managers and employees (Readon and Enis, 1990) and good socialization and training programs (Grove and Fisk, 1993) are ways hospitality organizations can reduce role conflict. Zeithaml *et al.* (1988) suggest providing clear and unambiguous communication regarding goals, strategies, and objectives for the organization, and job instruction and procedures will reduce role ambiguity. This communication should be part of the organization's internal marketing system.

Managing the Guest as Partial Employee

Customers are involved in the production of many hospitality products. For years writers have recognized the unique managerial problems of having the customer inside the boundary of the organization (Bernard, 1938). More recent writers have been focused on customer co-production and offer ideas on how to effectively utilize this "partial" employee. For example, Bettencourt (1997) states that customers may help the organization in three ways. They can be effective marketers, they can co-produce the product, and they can provide information to the organization. Bowen and Shoemaker (1998) suggest that customers should even get involved in the hiring process. Allowing customers to be involved in the hiring process is one way of reducing role conflict.

Successful hospitality firms look beyond traditional employment definitions of the firm and include customers as potential partners (Bettencourt, 1997; Lengnick-Hall; 1966). In other words, if customers contribute time, effort or other resources to the service production process, they should be considered a part of the organization (Zeithaml and Bitner, 2000, p. 322). Further, if customers are considered part of the organization's production resources, they should be managed the same as other parts of the service delivery system.

Bowen (1986) argues the customer should be managed as a quasi or partial employee. Bowen suggests using the same general motivation strategy for customers that are proposed for any employee. Hospitality firms must ensure that the guest has the appropriate knowledge, skills, and abilities to perform whatever role he or she has to play to obtain the quality service experience sought. If we are going to have the customer involved in service delivery, Bowers *et al.* (1990) suggest that organizations have to train customers like employees. Also, just as employees are rewarded for their efforts, customers should also be rewarded. Schneider and Bowen (1995) identify several reasons why customers might find it to their benefit to co-produce. First, they may get lower prices by helping to produce their own service experience such as bussing tables at a fast food restaurant. Second, they may save waiting time by self-registering at a kiosk in a hotel. Third, they may have greater choice by serving themselves at a buffet. Fourth, they may be able to achieve greater customization of the service experience to allow higher satisfaction of the service's quality and value. For example, customers can select their deserved seats from an airplane diagram during a booking process on the Internet.

Kelly *et al.* (1990, p. 318), discussing the problems of managing customers as partial employees, offer a number of methods to socialize the customer to perform their co production roles properly. These include offering customers formal socialization/training programs, printing and distributing instructional literature such as resort maps, establishing good signage, providing behaviour reinforcement, and allowing observation of other customers performing the roles correctly. Customers involved in co-production of the service must be managed to make sure they successfully co-produce the service.

Distinguishing characteristics of services related to staffing:

- In hospitality organizations personality is one of the major selection criteria for customer contact employees. In manufacturing firms, personality is less important as a selection criterion for employees.
- Unlike manufacturing, in hospitality organizations the customers and employees interface. This creates the need for service employees to be given skills and knowledge enabling them to become part-time marketers.
- In hospitality organizations the customer is involved in the service delivery system. Staffing functions apply to customers; they need to be recruited, selected, trained, rewarded, and fired.

A Conceptual Quality Assurance Framework in Hospitality Delivery

The quality assurance framework depicted and integrates the input, process and output elements of a hotel's operational system and takes an open system perspective where service quality and operational efficiencies work together rather than against each other. The framework stresses customer orientation as its guiding principle, and merges statistical and affordable computer technologies in delivery of high quality service to customers. The framework divides the operations system of a hotel into two subsystems: manufacturing and service subsystems. While having different characteristics, the two systems are highly interdependent. The overall effectiveness and efficiency of the entire operation is very much dependent on the synergies of the two subsystems and their abilities to contribute to the goals of the entire system. The nature, features and objectives of these two subsystems are discussed next.

The Manufacturing Subsystem

This subsystem represents the back-stage operations and activities of a hotel which, typically, are not directly observable by customers. It resembles the production operations system of a manufacturing organization and shares several of its characteristics. For instance, like a manufacturing operations system, the subsystem is responsible for the efficient performance of all operational tasks, which among others, include demand forecast, material acquisition and handling, staff scheduling, work-load determination and production planning. As in the case of a production operations system, this subsystem is also process driven and quality control charts such as the x bar, sigma and R charts are used to monitor various processes and to determine whether they are in or out of control. The overall objective of the quality assurance efforts is to ensure internal quality and adherence to process standards. To achieve these objectives, the subsystem relies on a user-friendly information system and related technologies in the forms of hardware, software, networks and databases.

It should, however, be noted that while many of the backstage activities are not directly observable by customers, any problems in their performance may have direct influence on customer satisfaction. For instance, understaffing due to poor work scheduling may translate into delays in cleaning the rooms and having them ready for customer check-in at promised times. This may be a cause of irritation for customers who are unaware of the "behind the scenes" problems and could result in dissatisfaction.

The Service Subsystem

This subsystem encompasses the "front-stage activities" in a hotel. Because these activities involve direct encounter with the service provider, customers are extremely concerned with the performance of the service subsystem. Each service encounter is as important as any other, and each and every one of them has to be managed well since customer satisfaction with these encounters ultimately affects their perception of service quality. The service subsystem is outcome driven and customer focused. Not only perceived quality but also consistency of service are of utmost significance. Customers expect the same level of service from all the staff all the time. Any inconsistencies in the chain of services provided by the luggage handlers, bill captain, receptionist, the cleaning staff, the hotel-shuttle driver, restaurant staff, etc. may not only irritate the customers but also magnify any negative perceptions they may have. This chain is easily broken at its weakest point: one bad experience may destroy the image of the entire hotel.

Functional rather than technical quality is of utmost concern in the service subsystem. For example, whether a clerk at the front desk is using the latest computer hardware and software are of little concern to the customer. What is important to the customer is the accuracy and efficiency of the reservation system. Hence, human, as opposed to technological approaches, are more critical in the service subsystem.

Factors Contributing to the Success of Quality Assurance Systems and Necessary Steps

To ensure successful implementation of a quality assurance system as outlined in the preceding section certain steps are in order.

First, while many informed observers of the hospitality industry have advocated divergent perspectives on service quality and quality assurance, they all agree that the success of a quality assurance system depends on an organizational culture that fosters and facilitates service quality (Clark, 1984; Glover *et al.*, 1984; Pickworth, 1987). For example, the Stouffer Hotel chain, which has a successful quality assurance programme, prides itself on its organizational culture motivated by the broad vision "We intend to be the place to stay, the place to work and the place to invest" (Bohan and Horney, 1991). Without a doubt, top management's commitment to service quality and quality assurance is vital to the success of any quality assurance programme (Comen, 1989) as demonstrated by the experience of the Roadway Inns (*Lodging Hospitality*, 1982).

Second, an audit of entire operations is needed to determine whether various organizational strategies are in harmony or not. In carrying out this audit, the assistance of external experts should be sought.

Third, given the tremendous importance of service provider-customer interaction in the hospitality industry, hiring the right people, and then training and rewarding them for quality performance are crucial (Breen, 1985; Hesser, 1988; Horak, 1991; Selwitz, 1992). To guide the selection of the right people, job descriptions should be examined critically and, wherever necessary, be modified with a view to promote customer orientation. Training of employees should not be geared only at skills-training. Through role-playing and sensitivity training techniques, employees also must be taught how to handle delicate encounters and how to deal with the frustrations and stresses of their jobs. It is likewise important to get the employees involved in quality assurance efforts by soliciting their concerns, opinions and suggestions. For instance, via the "Bright Idea Programme", the management of the Captain Cook Hotel not only encourages employees to provide suggestions but also seeks their input in setting the standards for various tasks performed at the hotel (*Lodging Hospitality*, 1987). Employee involvement is vital in identifying problems as seen by employees and motivating them towards solutions.

Fourth, an audit of back-stage (i.e. the manufacturing subsystem) operations should be undertaken. A multifaceted analysis should aim at establishing performance standards for tasks related to the back-stage operations. In setting the standards, besides employees, industry experts should be used. The standards should be clear, realistic and firm. In addition, the standards should be consistent with the overall organizational culture.

Fifth, technologies used should be examined critically to determine whether they are state-of-the-art and/or how much new investment is needed to update them. This is imperative at a time when the automation wave revolutionizing various aspects of hotel operations including reservations systems, environmental control systems and security systems all of which are critical for operational efficiency and customer orientation.

Sixth, current channels and flow of information and feedback mechanisms should be scrutinized carefully. This may reveal areas where modifications are needed and enable the management to make the necessary operational and strategic adjustments.

Seventh, the relationship between the organization and its main suppliers should be analysed thoroughly. Establishment of just-in-time (JIT) and total quality management (TQM) programmes with suppliers may indeed enhance both operational and strategic efficiency and effectiveness.

Eighth, the feasibility of incorporating quantitative tools such as waiting line models, demand forecasting models, scheduling techniques, quality control procedures and inventory models into existing operations should be investigated.

Ninth, to assess current levels of customer satisfaction with service quality and to ascertain their expectations, customer surveys and focus group interviews should be conducted. Such surveys should be complemented by direct observations of customers while they interact with the service providers.

As a closing note it should be reiterated that the success of a quality assurance programme depends on commitment to customers, commitment to excellence, team work and, above all top management enthusiasm. This means top executives should take the lead to create an organizational culture which is conducive to the success of a quality assurance programme and must champion efforts in that direction.

Segmentation, Branding, and Service Customization in Hospitality Industry

It is no secret that different customer segments want different product attributes. Commissioned sales people want hotel rooms with a free telephone, while upscale business travellers want expedited check-in. Thus, one of the first decisions for a company is to decide what segments it wants to target. This will determine the company's marketing mix. As segments grow and decline, a company must constantly review its segmentation strategy, looking for viable segments that are compatible with the company's objectives and products. After a company chooses a target market, the company must position itself in the marketplace *vis-à-vis* the other companies that are going after the target market. Two ways of accomplishing this positioning are through branding and service customization. This section looks at research on segmentation, branding, and service customization.

Segmentation

The segmentation research identifies product attributes that create value for market segments. This information is useful to companies targeting these segments or companies who may have a marketing mix that is valuable to these segments. It is always advisable to replicate segmentation studies using data from customers. Owing to time and regional differences, the wants of customer segments can vary. The segmentation research also presents a variety of research techniques that can be used to give greater insight into what the segments desire and the importance they put on different product attributes. Shaw *et al.* (1991) investigated product attributes of hotel convention services that create satisfaction among meeting planners. The authors went beyond just looking at the mean ratings of the attributes. They developed a multivariate approach to analysing the data, which could be applied to similar survey data to provide rich information. Several studies looked at specific segments. For example, Wight (1996) researched ecotourism and divided it into two market segments: general consumers interested in ecotourism and experienced ecotourism travellers. Her findings are useful for resorts that are interested in catering to this market. Callan (1996) compared UK leisure travellers with business travellers on their importance ratings of hotel attributes. Makens (1992) investigated catering to the family market at resorts. The article provides some case studies of resorts that have children's programmes.

For more studies that looked at specific segments. Conjoint analysis gives insight to the importance that customers place on different product attributes. Several studies provided examples of how conjoint analysis can be used in segmentation studies. Hu and Hiemstra (1996) used hybrid conjoint analysis to measure meeting planners' preferences in hotel selection. Becker-Suttle *et al.* (1994) used conjoint analysis to explore restaurant benefits sought by seniors and non-seniors. The use of neural networks, a type of artificial intelligence, is becoming a popular segmentation technique. It is often used in data mining tools to discover relationships between customers, identifying customer segments that might not be apparent to the marketer. Mazanec (1992) illustrated the usefulness of neural networks by segmenting tourists.

Customization

Effective guest history systems now make it possible to customize guest service. Unpublished research by Bowen and Shoemaker found that customized services were one the most important attributes to luxury hotel customers. Ritz-Carlton used guest history very effectively to produce customized services (Partlow 1993). Dev and Ellis (1991) presented a guest history management model and explained how it could be used to customize service for repeat guests. Customization of services can create a competitive advantage by increasing guest loyalty.

Branding

Customers develop brand images, or a set of beliefs, about where each brand stands on different product attributes. One of the trends in the hospitality industry is to use brands that have a positive brand image, rather than a company's own products which may have little brand image. For example, many hotels and catering companies in the USA are using kiosks to sell Starbucks Coffee, which has a strong brand image. ARAMARK, a contract food service company, franchises Burger King and Pizza Hut outlets even though they have the ability to produce products that have a similar quality. Hotels are contracting out their food service to local providers and chains that have a strong image. Thus, brand management is an area that is emerging as an important marketing area. The research on branding was scarce, indicating a need for future research in this area. Hallam and Baum (1996) surveyed hotel managers in North America and the UK to gain perceptions of why hotels may contract out portions or all of their food and beverage operations. One of the major reasons cited in the study was that a branded or well-known operator could help attract more accommodation guests. Thus, managers saw a branded restaurant as an amenity that was valued by the lodging guests. Connell (1992) looked at the benefits and problems of branding in the hotel industry. He used the rebranding of Forte after the acquisition of Crest as a case study.

Analysing Service Quality in the Hospitality Industry

In today's changing global environment, many businesses are facing intensifying competition and rapid deregulation, and in order to achieve competitive advantage and efficiency, businesses have to seek profitable ways to differentiate themselves. One strategy that has been related to success is the delivery of high service quality, especially during times of intensive competition both domestically and internationally (Rao and Kelkar, 1997). This concept has been the subject of many conceptual and empirical studies, and it is generally accepted that quality has positive implications for an organization's performance and competitive position. However, despite the vast amount of research done in the area of service quality, quality related issues have received little research attention within the hospitality context (Harrington and Akehurst, 1996).

Further, authors of studies conducted on quality in the service industries have also expressed concern regarding the quality dimensions in hotels and, in particular, with methods used to measure customer perceptions of hotel service quality (Johnston *et al.*, 1990). As service quality is becoming a major part of business practice, it is important to be able to measure and research its effectiveness.

The purpose of this paper is to examine the different dimensions of service quality and determine which dimensions best predict overall service quality in the hospitality industry by applying a modified version of SERVQUAL (Parasuraman *et al.*, 1988). This kind of information has practical implications for managers of hotels as they can direct their resources to improving weak service dimensions and to refining their marketing efforts so that customer expectations are met by the service delivered.

Early Research on Quality

From the review of literature on quality, it has been found that early research efforts concentrated on defining and measuring the quality of tangible goods and products, while the seemingly more difficult services sector was ignored. Gronroos (1990) has noted that product quality was traditionally linked to the technical specifications of goods, with most definitions of quality arising from the manufacturing sector where quality control has received extensive attention and research. Conversely, Crosby (1979) defined quality of goods as "conformance to requirements"; Juran (1980) defined it as "fitness for use"; while Garvin (1983) measured quality by counting the incidence of "internal" failures (those observed before a product left the factory) and "external" failures (those incurred in the field after a unit had been installed). These product-based definitions of quality may be appropriate to the goods-producing sector, however, knowledge about the quality of goods is insufficient to understand service quality (Parasuraman *et al*., 1985).

Service Quality in the Hospitality Industry

Services are generally described in terms of four unique attributes, namely:

- Intangibility;
- Heterogeneity;
- Inseparability; and
- Perishability

(Bateson, 1977; Lovelock, 1981; Gronroos, 1990; Zeithaml and Bitner, 1996). In the hospitality industry, other attributes, such as imprecise standards and fluctuating demand have been identified and further complicate the task of defining, delivering and measuring service quality. For example, while firms in the hospitality industry have established policies, rules and procedures to govern the standardization of their product, many aspects of service quality do not lend themselves to standards. Quality aspects such as "friendliness", "helpfulness" and "politeness" are likely to be interpreted differently by various guests and are assessed subjectively. Moreover, demand for service in the hospitality industry is generally clustered around peak periods of the day or year, such as check-out time or holiday season (Sasser *et al.*, 1978) and these peaks create an environment which make it difficult to provide consistent service quality.

Measuring Service Quality

One of the most widely used instruments to measure service quality is the SERVQUAL scale developed by Parasuraman *et al.* in 1985, and then refined in 1988 and 1991. The model on which SERVQUAL is based proposes that customers evaluate the quality of a service on five distinct dimensions:

- Reliability;
- Responsiveness;

- Assurance;
- Empathy; and
- Tangibles

and that service quality is the difference between a customer's expectations and perceptions of the quality of a service. In order to operationalise this model, the authors developed 22 items that were designed to capture, in two separate columns, customers' perceptions and expectations of a service on those dimensions, making a total of 44 questions in all. Despite SERVQUAL's wide usage by academics and practicing managers in various industries, across different countries, a number of studies have questioned the conceptual and operational base of the model (Babakus and Boller, 1992; Carman, 1990; Teas, 1994). More specifically, these studies have failed to confirm the five dimension structure across different industries. For example, a study conducted in the hospitality industry reported five dimensions of service quality, and these differed from those in SERVQUAL (Saleh and Ryan, 1991). These findings suggest that further customization of the scale for the hospitality industry is necessary. To address concern about the soundness of using a perceptions minus expectations score, researchers have combined the expectations and perceptions scores into a single measure. They subsequently found the reliability and validity of this single measure superior to the score based on the difference method (Babakus and Boller, 1992; Brown *et al.*, 1993). In 1991, Parasuraman *et al.* published their own one-column scale format which cuts the questionnaire size in half and reduces the time required for completion (Bouman and Van der Wiele, 1992), thus minimising the likelihood of response error.

Aims of the Study

The specific aims of the study are to:

- test the reliability and validity of a customised SERVQUAL scale;
- establish the number of dimensions of service quality in the hospitality industry; and
- determine which dimension is the best predictor of overall service quality.

In order to distinguish between the revised SERVQUAL (Parasuraman *et al.*, 1991) and the version customised for this study, the latter will now be referred to as HOLSERV.

Service Innovation and Customer Choices in the Hospitality Industry

Customers, in a number of industries, are constantly bombarded with run-of-the-mill product and service offerings. As a result, customers both desire and more often demand innovative alternatives. In response, many service-oriented firms are striving to integrate novel features into their product-service offerings. Even product-oriented firms have noted the benefits of adding service innovation to their business strategies. For example, during recent years, IBM, a predominantly product-oriented firm, generated over half of its total revenue from services. Yet, only 15 percent of IBM's research and development budget was being allocated to services (Fitzgerald, 2005). Realizing this discrepancy, IBM recently realigned its strategy and business plan emphasizing service-based innovations. The new strategy was a resounding success. With one of IBM's innovative service programs adding over $300 million to last year's total revenue (Fitzgerald, 2005). The benefits of service innovation are apparent. What is not as clear is how managers should decide on which innovations to implement. In some cases, innovative service offerings are necessary just to maintain a firm's current market share. This phenomenon suggests "... that some innovations may merely raise the cost of doing business without a significant economic benefit, other than to preserve current business and without providing a competitive edge..." (*Reid and Sandler*). However, other innovations may enhance service differentiation and induce financial gains. Thus, it is important for managers to implement innovations which are not only desired by customers but also are economically beneficial to the firm (*Reid and Sandler*).

Hospitality firms, such as hotels, are an ideal example of a market which could benefit from the implementation of service innovation. First, from a customer's perspective, the hospitality market is perpetually inundated by many similar, often easily substitutable service offerings. This can cause difficulties for hotel managers as they attempt to differentiate an individual hotel from its competitors (*Reid and Sandler*). One solution to this challenge may be to offer new and innovative features to customers. Secondly, the hospitality industry is rapidly changing due to accelerations in information technology (*Olsen and Connolly*). Managers will need to make proactive changes which focus even more intensely on customer preferences, quality, and technological interfaces in order to stay competitive in such a dynamic environment (*Karmarkar*). Thirdly, travelers today do not exhibit, as in past decades, a truly brand loyal behaviour. Travelers instead are choosing to patronize hotels that offer the best value proposition under existing budgetary constraints. (*Olsen and Connolly*). In order to add value to the guests' experience, hotel managers and marketers must meet the challenge of determining which services are preferred by hotel guests (*Olsen and Connolly*). Once a manager understands customers' preferences, the challenge then becomes prioritizing those preferences which add the greatest value to the hotel's existing service offering.

The purpose of this study is to explore customer tradeoffs for service innovation. The paper will examine the addition of innovative offerings and its relation to the hotel's core service concept. The service concept encompasses both the "how", in other words, the operations content, and the "what", the marketing content, of service design as well as the integration of the two (*Goldstein et al.*). In other words, we will examine the innovative service preferences of hotel guests, while also exploring how these preferences align with the strategic intent of the firm. Aligning customer preferences with operational strategy is important because operational constraints make it impossible to implement all options of innovative service offerings. Instead, hotel managers need to develop an understanding of market preferences prior to the addition of new services. This type of knowledge will enable managers to select innovative offerings that are most beneficial to the firm and that will truly have an impact on customer's choices.

The importance of studying innovation's role in services seems obvious. Yet, analysis in service innovation research is lacking in comparison to product innovation research (*Chesbrough*). Research which examines the opportunities and risks specific to service innovation as well as the choice sets for system design is needed to further the knowledge in service innovation research (*Chesbrough*). In this paper, we provide insight into service innovation by exploring the hotel preferences of both business and leisure travelers. We specifically aim to: Understand the trade-offs made for business and leisure travelers when choosing a hotel, in terms of innovative hotel market drivers or attributes. Explore the influence the addition of innovative services has on the design of the core service concept. Examine the impact of innovative service preferences on operational strategy formulation. We believe that achieving these objectives will be beneficial to academics and practitioners when considering the impact service innovation has on a given firm's core concept. The structure of the paper is organized in the following manner: first, we give a general overview of the previous research regarding the service concept and innovation value. Next we discuss the current hotel innovations that pertain to our study. We then describe our research methods and the application of discrete choice modeling. In addition, we discuss the tradeoffs made by business and leisure travelers when selecting a hotel. We conclude by providing insights into service concept development as well as operational strategy formulation.

Background

The Service Concept

The wide array of research related to service innovation has primarily focused on the definition of the "service concept" (Goldstein *et al.*, 2002). *Edvardsson and Olsson* defined the service concept as a "prototype for service, covering the needs of the customer and the design of the service". Previous research has discussed the critical role of the service concept in service design and development (*Edvardsson and Olsson*). Furthermore, Goldstein *et al.* (2002) propose that the service concept is the missing key element in service design research. They suggest that the service concept integrates the "how" and "what" of service design while keeping both the customers' needs and strategic intent of the firm in mind. In other words, the service concept gives a detailed description of what the customer needs and how the organization will deliver the service. The conceptual background of the "service concept" in operations management literature is similar to "marketing concept". The marketing concept is the key to achieving organizational goals and involves "... determining the needs and wants of target markets and delivering the desired (customer) satisfactions more effectively than competitors..." (*Agarwal et al.*). Firms that are considered to be market-oriented are presumed to have the capability of understanding their customers better than their competitors. Innovation plays an important role in the marketing concept because it gives the service firm the ability to stay ahead of its competitors through new market offerings. The association between innovation and the market-orientation of a firm was determined to be both positive and significant (*Agarwal et al.*). In other words, a more market-oriented firm is more likely to consider innovation, which ultimately leads to superior firm performance (*Agarwal et al.,* ; *Han et al.*). The relationship found between innovation and market orientation emphasizes the importance of identifying customers' needs. By understanding customer tradeoffs, service firms will have a better market orientation with a resulting improvement in firm performance.

Innovative Value Strategy

Managers when reexamining their existing service offering also need to decide which innovations will create value. For example, managers must ask themselves, which innovations not only deliver additional value to their customers but also are economically viable to the firm. Customer value can be defined as, "the customer's perception of what they want to have happen in a specific-use situation, with the help of a product and service offering in order to accomplish a desired purpose or goal". (*Stahl et al.*). The hospitality industry has an abundance of options which to choose from, when determining which products and services will add value for their customers. For example, a hotel operator can offer various combinations of traditional value drivers such as price, location, and typical hotel amenities, such as pool or work-out facilities. On the other hand, new and innovative value drivers could be offered which include features such as online reservations, in-room high-speed internet access, customization of room décor, and flexible check in/out policies. Before introducing a new service innovation, hotel managers need to assess the value that it will bring to their customers. A good understanding of value can be gained through empirical research methods, such as customer surveys. Survey research relies heavily on a customer's perception of the functionality, performance, and worth of a supplier's offerings (*Anderson and Narus*). By acquiring the vital information of why guests choose to stay at particular hotels, hotel managers are better able to understand the attributes which drive guest's purchasing decisions. Furthermore, understanding the guest's needs and desires is invaluable when determining methods for improving company image. A lack of customer preference understanding leads to problems in both product and service design (*Schall*). Research shows that the most successful companies are the ones which are fully aware of customer preferences and develop their services in line with targeted market needs (*Karmarkar*). As a competing service firm, it is essential to not only consider the types of innovative attributes to offer but also which operational strategy must be implemented to achieve the firm's goals. *Kim and Mauborgne* coined the term "value innovative logic" which differs from a more conventional approach. The conventional objective is to maximize the value of industrial bound offerings while the value innovative goal is to aid the innovative aspect of the service offering (*Kim and Mauborgne*). Our research focuses on the value innovation logic for product and service offerings. Therefore, rather than taking a more traditional approach in determining which product and services to offer, an innovative logic approach presents options, "... in terms of the total solution customers seek, even if that takes the company beyond its industry's traditional offerings" (*Kim and Mauborgne*).

Innovations in Hospitality Firms

Hotel Type

The emergence of "boutique" hotels during recent years is an excellent example of an innovative offering in an otherwise standardized industry. The boutique hotel typically features a contemporary or minimalist décor while also offering many additional lifestyle amenities. Hotel guests tend to perceive boutique hotels as a stylish location for which they are willing to pay premium room rates for (*Binkley*). Recently, the boutique hotel trend has crossed over into the mid-priced hotel market (*Chittium*). Rather than focusing exclusively on the functionality of the hotel product offering, mid-price hotels are beginning to consider the aesthetic appearance of the building's structure and décor (*Chittium*). Hotels' guest rooms as well as lobbies are being redesigned in order to stand out amongst the basic hotel offerings. For example, Choice Hotels are planning a new chain of hotels, tentatively named the Diplomat that will feature flat-screen TVs and stylish shelving in its guest-rooms (*Chittium*). Another higher-priced hotel chain has adopted amenities that are typically associated with boutique hotels while pricing its rooms to be competitive with the mid-priced market. These innovative changes are expected to boost their occupancy rates beyond their rivals (*Binkley*). Amenities being offered will include platform beds with no box springs, wire storage racks rather than dressers, plasma television screens, and complimentary wireless DSL access (*Binkley*). The trendy boutique hotel is an innovation to the traditional hotel experience and an attractive option to consider when designing a hotel service concept, especially when it crosses the traditional industry boundaries into co-branded fashion and jewelry concepts (e.g. the Bulgari-Marriott alliance).

Use of Information Technology

Another example of innovation in hotel services is the use of information technology. One study determined which of the recent technological innovations were most beneficial, least beneficial, and had future benefits for hotels (*Reid and Sandler*). The technological innovations that were found to be most beneficial included: a wake up system, electronic door locks, in-room pay-per-view, video cassette players, multiple phone lines, video library, personal computers, voice mail, computer modem connections, video check out, electronic in-room safes, and a software library (*Reid and Sandler*). However, it may be impractical for a specific hotel or chain to adopt all available technological amenities due to a lack of operational capabilities or limited resources. Instead, hotels must determine which technological innovations will most benefit their organization.

Aside from customer preferences for technology, the addition of new technological features to a hotel's service concept has distinct phases of adoption (*Namasivayam et al.*). The technology adoption process includes:

- customer signaling, such as internet booking and in-room modems;
- enabling management, such as management email;
- enabling employees, such as voice mail;

- customer service revenue add-ons, such as ATM and interactive TVs;
- customer service value add-ons, such as internet access and in-room fax machines; and
- wireless technology, such as curbside check-in, voice recognition, and smart cards (Namasivayam *et al.*, 2000).

With the intricacies of implementing technological advances to the service concept, hotel managers need to also take into consideration the adoption process of implementing technology on top of understanding the operational capabilities of the hotel.

Customization of Service

Customizing the service experience for hotel guests is another means of service innovation. Some examples of service customization include: allowing guests to have flexible check in/out times, personalizing room décor, or having child care options available. Customized options adapt the hotel's service offering to each individual guest's preferences. However, customization is not easy to implement due to the operational capabilities of the firm. For example, a flexible check in/out policy could lead to labor scheduling problems. Adding such a policy successfully requires the alignment of hotel's marketing and operational activities. *Skinner* provides a product-oriented example of the importance of balancing marketing and operational activities. He suggests that while it may seem profitable to add more products/features to the product mix, it may be too difficult operationally to implement (*Skinner*). This dilemma is equally applicable to a service setting, in which adding more services may not operationally be possible.

As we discussed earlier, service innovation is a crucial aspect of a firm's ability to differentiate itself from its competitors and can contribute more to a firm's revenues. Yet, service innovation research is lacking in comparison to product innovation. In this paper, we address this discrepancy by presenting an analysis of hotel travelers' preferences for innovative service offerings and the role innovation plays in service development. The next section describes our research methodology in exploring the innovative choice drivers for business and leisure hotel travelers.

Appendix

TOWARDS ORGANIZING THE DINING ROOM BETTER TO ACCEPT GUESTS

The key person in the dining room is the individual who greets the guests. This person may be called the maitre d'hotel, the director of service, or the host or hostess. The host must be staffed by a competent individual. In many instances he is the first human contact the guest will have with the restaurant. Therefore, the host represents the restaurant to the patrons. Guests often decide to patronize a restaurant based upon the greeting and attention they receive from the host. The mood for the evening is set by his actions. Ben Franklin said, "The taste of the roast is determined by the handshake of the host."

In addition to greeting the guests, the host is responsible for the operation of the dining room; he is the one who must insure that the guests have an enjoyable dining experience; and must solve any problems that may arise. Give customers "the free gifts they cherish most: recognition, recommendation, and reassurance," said the late Michael Hurst of the 15th Street Fisheries. The job of the host has evolved from the classical restaurant. In this type of restaurant, the job titles were as follows: directeur du restaurant; maitre d'hotel; deuxieme maitre d'hotel; and a maitre d'hotel de carre. This type of staffing had a host for each area of the restaurant. The directeur du restaurant had complete charge of the restaurant, including the kitchen and dining room staff.

He was also responsible for long-term planning, food and beverage cost controls, and service. The maitre d'hotel was the host of all the dining rooms in the hotel. He was responsible for what occurred in all the different restaurants in the hotel, and he was in charge of the dishwashers, cleanup crew, and linen service. If the hotel was large, there may have been a second or deuxieme maitre d'hotel, who was responsible for one dining room. The maitre d'hotel de carre had the responsibility of a section of the dining room similar to the captain of today. Because of the high labor cost involved in employing a large number of individuals in a restaurant, many operations have consolidated these jobs into the position of host. However, there are larger restaurants that still have a director of food and beverage and also a host. The early job titles to the responsibilities of restaurant personnel today.

Knowing the Authority of the Host Better

The authority and respect of the host has deteriorated over the years. As service became more and more lax in America, the job of the host was considered an entry-level position. Restaurant owners paid the host minimum wage because the owners felt that a host did not directly produce money like a service person. Consequently, the person who was given the host position was poorly trained if trained at all. This position changed from one of prestige, power, and respect, to a job that restaurant owners felt anyone could do. Instead of having experienced wait people striving to become the host, they avoided it, because it did not pay as much money as their tipped position. Guest service and the industry suffered tremendously. Today, the pendulum has begun to swing back to the experienced and respected host. Restaurant owners are realizing the importance of having a well-trained host.

A well-informed and personable individual holding the job of host will make the restaurant a success. Restaurant owners are now compensating their hosts at a higher pay rate than minimum wage. As the laws regarding tip reporting and taxes become more stringent on restaurant owners, more and more are instituting a fixed service charge. From this fixed service charge, the host is being paid a much higher wage than minimum. Restaurants that still have a voluntary tipping policy may make the service staff contribute part of their tips to the host. Restaurant owners are, once again, realizing the importance of having a competent, personable host to greet their guests.

Knowing About Better Host Selection

Selecting a person for the host's job is important and challenging for the manager or owner of the restaurant. This is because a major portion of the job is dependent upon the host to observe a situation or problem, weigh the positive versus the negative aspects, and make a decision—all in a few seconds. Because the ability to think quickly and react to situations positively is a necessary qualification, the manager must try to select an individual who is personable and can work well under stress. The selection process should be structured in such a manner as to determine the personality of the applicants and how they handle stressful situations.

The criteria for selecting a host. In addition, the manager should look for some specific qualifications that have been identified with excellent hosts. These qualifications are discussed in the next section. To determine the personality of his applicants, the late Michael Hurst would ask, "What is the funniest thing that ever happened to you?"

Major Criteria for Making Host Selection

Individual selected to be a host must:

- be personable
- work well under stress
- be able to think quickly
- be able to make decisions

Importance of the Qualifications of the Host

It is significant to mention that the qualifications for a host fall into two general categories: physical and behavioural. The first relates to the appearance of the individual. The second refers to the manner in which the person interacts with people. In most instances, the host is the first person guests see when they walk into a restaurant, therefore the physical appearance of the host must be exemplary. A host at his restaurant. This host makes a positive physical appearance. As with the service staff, cleanliness is essential. Any uniform must be neat and clean, as these are a symbol of professionalism. The host should be proud of wearing the uniform. The behavioural qualification is the ability to deal with people. The host must be able to meet the needs of the restaurant's guests and employees. Sometimes this is not easy.

Many guests are not pleasant, because they may be having a bad day or are not used to waiting for a table, or for a myriad of reasons that the host has little, if any, control over. Employees provide another challenge. They will complain about the amount of tips that the guests have left and about their stations, for example. The host must have the ability to satisfy all the employee and guest complaints, whether legitimate or not. Who's in Control Here? George Goldoff, the author of the foreword to this book, tells about an incident that occurred when he was the manager at the Rainbow Room in New York City and the extreme measures he took to solve the problem. In this case, he was able to take control of the situation. Four guests came into the Rainbow Room. When they were brought to their table, they told him that they did not like the table assigned to them. He explained to them that all of the other unoccupied tables were reserved for that night. When he left the table, the four of them moved to the table they wanted. He went to the group, told them that they would have to move back to the original table. They refused. He had his staff go to the table and physically remove it from the dining room. He then went to the table and informed the guests that he did not have a table for them. This is a technique that would only be used as a last resort.

Focus on Useful Behavioural Tips

For the host to do the job effectively, other behavioural traits are needed. The book The Professional Host lists some of them: attentiveness, courteousness, dependability, economy, efficiency, honesty, loyalty, knowledge, preparedness, quietness, sensitivity, skill, tact, productivity, and persuasiveness. Even though it would appear that every person has the common sense to know and use these traits, many do not. The following information will give examples of the importance of the specific traits.

Courteousness: The host must treat the guests as though they were guests in his home. Words such as "please" and "thank you" are thought by many to be magic. Guests appreciate hearing these magic words, and the host is encouraged to use them whenever appropriate. Greeting and addressing the guests by name throughout the dining experience, the host should return to the table to show his genuine concern for their satisfaction. By using the magic words "please," "thank you," "excuse me," and especially the guest's name, the host will not only impress the guest by his courtesy but will provide a positive model for the service staff to follow. Courteousness also includes assisting guests with little things that show concern. These little things are not something that will make a person jump up and down and say, "Wow, did you see what the host did!" Instead, they are displays of courteousness that will make the guests feel that the restaurant really cares about them and is happy to receive their business. Examples of courteousness are: assisting guests removing or putting on coats; pulling out chairs for guests as they are shown to their table; and checking back with guests to determine if the table and temperature of the room are pleasing. Pulling the shades down so the sun will not shine in guests' eyes is another example. The difference between a great restaurant and a good restaurant is taking care of the details—and courteousness is a detail. Sweet or Sour? On a hot August night, we climbed up the stairs and entered The Sardine Factory restaurant in Monterey, California. The host—we later discovered his name was Marty—welcomed us and asked if we had a reservation.

Dependability: Dependability is a trait that is valued highly by restaurant owners. It is a sign of maturity. Basically, it means that the employees will be responsible for their own actions. It also includes the fact that the employees will accomplish the goals that have been set, either by management or by the employees themselves on their own. This trait is important in all positions, but is extremely critical for any person who will hold the job of host. Offer to take pictures of guests together when you see them taking pictures.

Attentiveness: The host must be ubiquitous. He must know what is occurring in the dining room at all times and must appear to have eyes in the back of his head. The host must know the status of all tables at all times; whether table three has been served the main course; if table five needs more wine. An absentminded person or daydreamer does not belong in the position of host. This job requires a person who will be consistently alert to the guests' needs.

Efficiency: Efficiency means finding the quickest and easiest way to do a task without jeopardizing guest satisfaction. The ability to organize reservations in a systematic manner is an example of efficiency. By having an efficient reservation system, the host can take reservations correctly. This will allow him to spend more time in the dining room or working the floor instead of trying to straighten out a mess caused by an inefficient reservation system. An organized host has more time to spend with the guests.

Economy: Economy means keeping costs at a minimum. This will be the host's responsibility. The dining room is an area where costs can rapidly get out of control because of improper scheduling, improper use of linen, and food waste. If the host schedules too many service people, the labor cost will be a drain on the restaurant. If staff are allowed to use extra equipment—like extra side towels—when they are not needed, money is lost. Common sense is important in keeping waste to a minimum. An example of economy is to save and reuse individual packaged jellies if they have not been opened.

Honesty: A person who deals with the public, especially in the host's job, will have to make many decisions that will test his honesty. For example, a guest approaches the host and asks for a table. The host has all the tables reserved and informs the guest of this. The guest produces a $50 bill and asks, "Are you sure?" The host and the guest both know that the patron is buying the table. What should the host do? Other opportunities will arise to deceive the customer as well as the employees. In all instances, if the host is dishonest and allows the staff to be dishonest, word will spread that the establishment is dishonest. This will result in negative word of mouth from both guests and employees, and the business will suffer. Danny Meyer of the Union Square Cafe says, "It's less appropriate to 'grease the palm' of a maitre d' to get a better table on your way in. Maitre d's who 'sell' good tables for tips are not providing good service for other guests."

Knowledge: As with the service staff, the host has to know all facets of the operation of the restaurant. In fact, he must know more about the operation than the service staff, because the guests perceive the host as the key figure in the restaurant. The host should know everything, including the preparation and service of food and beverage. In addition, the host has to be aware of the physical layout of the restaurant, how to deal with credit card charges, and the accounting procedures of the restaurant. With today's ever-changing technology, knowledge of computers and computer systems is critical. Knowledge of community events and area attractions is an important aspect of the host's concern. If a guest asks a question and the host does not know the answer, he will have to find out the answer and return to the guest with it. Sweet or Sour? A couple invited two friends to dinner and a play on Saturday evening. A reservation was made at one of the couple's favourite restaurants; in addition, that restaurant was to provide the catering for the theater where the party of four were to attend the play. While driving to the restaurant, the host turned to the invited couple and said, "Well, we won't be late for the play, but we will be a little early, because our tickets are for next Saturday. We called and tried to exchange the tickets and get us seats for tonight; but as the theater only seats 200 people, they are sold out." When they arrived at the restaurant, the host-owner greeted them warmly and inquired whether they were going to the play or were there for a leisurely dinner. The guest explained the problem. The owner asked for the tickets and said "Let us see what we can do." By the time the salad arrived, the owner was back at the table to inform the group that he had secured tickets for that evening's performance.

Loyalty: Loyalty is another highly rated trait for a host. It can be defined as being, or giving the impression to the public of being, totally supportive of the ideas and philosophies of the restaurant. An example of not being loyal is downgrading the establishment to the guests with such comments as, "Management has no idea how to run this place."

Preparedness: Nothing is more frustrating for guests than to have to wait for a reservation, food, or drinks. The host has to be ready to accept guests into the dining room at its stated opening time. If a guest is promised a 3:00 P.M. reservation, then the table should be ready for them at 3:00 P.M. Preparedness is the act of planning and organizing all equipment and supplies so that the guest will not have to wait for service. Procrastinators do not belong in the hospitality industry. The host should have a plan for each situation and consider alternative plans in case of a problem.

Sensitivity: Restaurants are where many special occasions are celebrated, such as engagements, wedding anniversaries, births, and job promotions. Unfortunately, it is also the place where many marriages and relationships are ended. People often choose a restaurant in which to tell their spouse or lover that the relationship is finished, because they think that the hurt party will not make a scene in so public a place. The host has to be sensitive to the needs of the guests and observe their actions to determine how much attention they want. Sensitivity is a two-part trait: first, to observe what is occurring between the guests or to the guests, then act appropriately; if the guests have just become engaged, congratulations should be offered. A dessert or drink may be offered, compliments of the restaurant. If the couple obviously is having a fight, then staying away from the table is best. Going to the table to ask how the food is would not be appropriate, but would show a lack of sensitivity. Provide immediate service recovery by immediately resolving a guest service failure before it becomes a problem.

Quietness: A good host is always available when needed. However, the host has to be aware of the proper time to talk to guests and when to leave them alone. When talking to the guests, it is done in a courteous manner, not in a loud or boisterous one. The host must act with dignity, and do the job quietly.

Skill: A skillful host knows how to "work the floor." He knows how to obtain the most efficient or effective use of the tables in the shortest period of time. The skillful host knows how to keep the guests happy and how to motivate them to return. Skill also involves making salads tableside, carving meats and poultry, and pouring wine.

Productivity: Productivity is defined as the ability to get the maximum amount of tasks accomplished in the shortest period of time. There are times when the host must take reservations, greet guests, take their orders, and return to their table to see if the meal is to their satisfaction. In addition, the host must monitor the service staff's performance, seeing that the sidework is being done and that the dining room is operating to its maximum potential.

Tact: The ability to say the right phrase at the right time without offending the guest would be a definition of tact. Saying to a guest, "Where have you been, we haven't seen you in a long time: can be interpreted by many guests as tactless. A more tactful way of saying this would be, "It's nice to have you visit us, we're glad to see you here again." This says the same thing, but it will not offend the guest. Tact is also involved when inquiring about the guests or their families. The host has to be aware of what is happening in the community. Reading the local newspapers will give the host information needed to avoid embarrassment and appearing tactless. For example, in last week's newspaper, the host read that John Smith had been cut from the professional baseball team. When Mr. and Mrs. Smith come to the restaurant, the host would not ask them, "How is your son's baseball career going?"

Persuasiveness: This is another important behavioural trait, especially when dealing with guests who have problems. Persuasiveness could be used to convince the guest to take a different table, or to take a different time, because the restaurant is booked solid. Convincing the guest to change his or her mind about something requires persuasiveness.

It would be a wonderfully simplistic business if restaurants were only about food. The reality is that it is about people, the ones that keep you in business, and the ones that work for you. It is no longer just a meal out; people are paying for an experience. Everyone has heard the expression "you never get a second chance to make a first impression." This cannot be more stressed about the host or, now more popularly titled, "reservationists" in your restaurant. The initial telephone greeting, including the tone of voice, inflection and verbiage tells the guest what kind of experience is ahead of them. Finding the right person to "read" a guest through the phone is invaluable. You want every guest to hang up and think that was the nicest person they ever spoke to. They should "feel" a smile through the phone.

As for the host that actually greets your guests upon arrival, there are many skills required that need constant maintenance. Smiles, now more than ever, are paramount. It tells the guest we are happy to see them, whether they have a reservation, or not. Conveying to the guest that you have anticipated their arrival, and are anxious to accommodate them sets the pace for their entire experience in your restaurant. Displaying the appropriate sense of urgency, reading body language, comfortably using their name tells them they can relax; they are in the hands of hospitality professionals. Upon departure, the ideal host has anticipated the guest's departure, asked them by name how their experience was, and invites them back soon. The host then genuinely thanks them and says goodnight. In the end, they felt cared for.

The entire experience started and ended with the host. The food was someplace in the middle. Denise Volpicello General Manager East Hampton Point (Restaurant) East Hampton, New York (EastHamptonPoint.com) The East Hampton Point restaurant is on the eastern end of Long Island located on the water. This is a 450 seat restaurant with 2 kitchens. It is a seasonal restaurant, open from April to Labor Day. After Labor Day, the restaurant does special events, mostly high end weddings for not less than 100 people. The food is progressive American, with an emphasis on local seafood and produce. They also own 3 other restaurants in East Hampton, NY which are open year round: Citta Nuova; Wei Fun; and the 1770 House. General Manager Volpicello has had experience working for restaurants such as the Striped Bass in Philadelphia and Morton's Steak House in New York City. There are many more behavioural traits that the reader will be able to identify; however, an individual has to exhibit some, if not all, of the traits reviewed here in order to be an excellent host.

Five Ps of Management w.r.t. the Host's Responsibilities

For any restaurant to run efficiently, the host must be prepared. The key to having a successful restaurant or banquet are the five Ps of management: Prior Planning Prevents Poor Performance. This phrase and the meaning of it are important for all restaurant employees. However, this philosophy is especially critical in the host's job. The five Ps of management mean that if all tasks are planned in advance, problems will be kept to a minimum.

Realizing the Fact that Prior Planning Prevents Poor Performance

Therefore, a plan is needed before each meal period. This plan may be in the form of a checklist. Each restaurant may design one that fits the needs for that particular unit. By completing it, the host ensures that the restaurant is prepared to accept guests. The following are some examples of what items may be on the checklist and why they are important. The list should include checking both the men's and women's rooms for all paper products and for cleanliness. If the host does not do this, it will have to be attended to during a busy time, taking valuable time away from the guests. Another important area to check is the physical cleanliness of the dining room. Are the floors free of crumbs or lint? If the floor is dirty, it will have to be cleaned or vacuumed before the guests arrive.

All light fixtures are inspected for burned out bulbs or cobwebs. The host may think, "It's not our job," but the host is responsible for the operation of the dining room. The guests want to feel that they are eating in a clean and safe restaurant. Burned out light bulbs, dirty floors, and cobwebs send a message to the guest that the restaurant does not care about cleanliness. A sample checklist for the host, to be done daily.

Focus on Host's Daily Checklist for Opening the Dining Room

- Inspection of the service staff for proper grooming guidelines
- Men's restroom and women's restroom:

  - Clean
  - Paper products
- Physical cleanliness of the dining room:
  - Floor free of crumbs and lint
  - Light fixtures clean and no burned-out bulbs
- Printers have enough paper to complete meal period
- Menus are clean and chef's creations have been added
- Reservations have been blocked
- Computer system has been programmed with the chef's creations
- Host is neat and clean, ready to accept guests

For restaurants with a computer system, printers have to be checked to see whether there is enough paper to last though the meal period. With some computer systems, if the paper runs out, the computer will not work. All prices and new items should be put into the memory of the computer before staff take their first orders. The host may assign an employee to complete any task not completed. The first responsibility of the host is to prepare the dining room to accept guests. The host must have the dining room ready to accept guests when it is scheduled to open its doors. As has been said before, the difference between a good and a great restaurant is attention to detail. A good host will anticipate and avoid problems. A great host will use the five Ps of management to have an excellent restaurant.

Towards Better Organization of the Dining Room

Knowledge of the menu, pricing, ingredients, and all facts essential to the smooth and profitable operation of a restaurant is as essential to the host as it is to the service staff. In addition, the host has to supervise the service staff. The host is responsible for making the service excellent. Successful restaurants constantly evaluate service throughout an employee's career. The host is responsible for the training and performance of the service staff. In addition, the host has to schedule employees and assign stations and sidework to make the dining room operate at maximum efficiency.

Factors that Affect Scheduling

Have you ever been to a restaurant where you are served slowly because there are too many guests and not enough staff? Sometimes there is an obvious shortage of service staff to serve the guests. For example, a restaurant has 120 seats filled and only two service people to tend to the guests. The person responsible for scheduling has not scheduled enough service staff to meet the demand. The host must schedule the correct amount of staff to meet the demands of business, while not overstaffing the restaurant. Overstaffing causes a loss of money and, at times, even results in poor service. In order to schedule effectively, the host must take certain factors into consideration and then schedule the employees correctly.

The first step begins with forecasting. Planning for anticipated business based upon previous history of the restaurant is called forecasting. Reservations and events that are planned for the community that will affect the business must be taken into account. A formal written forecast on a weekly basis is the most important aspect in scheduling. There are many factors that affect correct scheduling. The first has to do with the qualifications of the individual waitpeople. The next has to do with the type of menu and style of service that the restaurant offers. The third involves events occurring in the community in which the restaurant is located. If the restaurant is located in a hotel, expected occupancy rates of the hotel will play a major part in scheduling.

Another factor is based upon the history from previous years' business. The final factor would be the number of reservations for the meal period. Scheduling is one area where the five Ps of management are extremely important. The first consideration is qualifications of the individual waitpeople. For example, one service person may be able to work best waiting on a lot of small parties; another may work better with large parties. Knowing this information allows the host to compensate for the strengths and inadequacies of the staff. Next, the host has to consider the type of menu and the style of service offered by the restaurant. If the restaurant uses American service, the number of guests that can be served efficiently by one service person is anywhere from 12 to 24. Individual restaurants determine how many guests a service person is required to serve. This depends on the menu, the meal period, and the atmosphere of the restaurant. The host can use this standard in forecasting and scheduling. The third factor that affects scheduling are events occurring in the community that will positively or negatively affect the restaurant's business. For example, if there is a parents' weekend at the local college, and the restaurant serves breakfast, then it should be staffed to accommodate extra guests. If there is a youth sporting event scheduled in the community, and the restaurant appeals to that market, it will be busier than usual.

The host, the service staff, and the cooks want to avoid surprises. No one likes to be swamped with business when they are not prepared to handle it. Manage your restaurant from the front door, not from the kitchen. In other words, be visible so that you can observe what is occurring in your restaurant and the guests can see that you are in control of the operation. The next factor is particularly for restaurants located in a lodging establishment. Almost all hotels send out a forecast of the prospective occupancy rate; this is the anticipated number of guests staying in the establishment on a certain night. If the rate is expected to be 100 percent, then the restaurant will be very busy for breakfast. It is amazing that when a hotel has 100 percent occupancy, the restaurant is not staffed properly for breakfast: the meal that will be eaten most often by the hotel's guests. Effective staffing in this category also means scheduling employees to work at the correct time. Having employees come in from 8:00 A.M. to 4:00 P.M. would be a mistake if the hotel's clientele are business people.

They want to be out of the restaurant by 8:00 A.M. It is easy to obtain advance occupancy figures, thereby reducing the probability of an insufficiently staffed restaurant. A word of caution: The restaurant manager has to determine if the high occupancy rate is the result of a large convention. If so, the manager must determine what banquet meals have been planned for the convention. For example, at the American Culinary Federation National Convention, breakfast, morning break, luncheon, afternoon break, and dinner are included in the convention. At this convention, the vast majority of attendees would be eating all their meals at banquets, not in the a la carte restaurant. The next factor is determined by the history of the restaurant. Every restaurant needs a book at the host stand—some call it a logbook—for the purpose of recording the history of that day's business. Included should be the number of meals that were served for each meal period, the weather, and special events that were occurring in the community, such as conventions.

The guest history also includes how much money was generated per hour and per meal period. This information may be computerized. This will assist the host in forecasting the staffing for the same day of the week next year. In addition, it is recommended to have an area where the day shift host can leave messages for the night shift host concerning important items, such as, "Jane called in, and she will be 20 minutes late tonight." Finally, the manager reviews the number of reservations normally taken on a particular day. If the restaurant is booked up far in advance, all the reservations will be factored into the scheduling. By no means is this a complete listing of the factors that the host must consider when staffing the restaurant; however, these items will help the host in this regard.

This planning allows the host to staff the restaurant properly for all types of business, including the least busy nights. For example, the night before Thanksgiving is traditionally not busy in a hotel dining room. However, the dining room must be open. Using the previous history, plus the expected occupancy rates, the host can schedule a skeleton crew. On the other hand, one of the biggest business days at a restaurant like Churchill Downs in Louisville, Kentucky, is Thanksgiving. At the racetrack, the restaurant must be staffed to accommodate the large group of guests. Taking into account all necessary factors, the host can develop a schedule to satisfy the demands. Based upon the factors that were discussed previously, the host can determine how many service people are needed for a certain time period. This time period is usually a week. It is beneficial to the host and employees to have the work schedule completed and posted in advance. This lets all employees know when they are scheduled to work.

The restaurant industry has a reputation for not treating its service staff decently. Many times, restaurant owners engage in day-to-day scheduling. When service persons ask for their schedules, they are told to call at 10:00 A.M. the next day. Then they are told to work or not to work. This type of scheduling negatively affects morale. Posting the schedule on the same day every week for the same period of time will alleviate the problem. The busiest days in the restaurant business are the times when everyone else is enjoying themselves—weekends and holidays. Employees should be told when hired that they will have to work weekends and holidays. The host should strive to give his employees two days off in succession. The authors have designed a system to improve scheduling that resulted in improved morale. First, the schedule was made every Wednesday and posted every Thursday. As an example, the schedule went from Friday, April 1, to Sunday, April 10. The employees would know a week in advance who had to work the following weekend. The next week's schedule went from Friday, April 8, to Sunday, April 17. Using this method, the host plans for seven days but always schedules for ten. An example of the two-week schedule.

This method improves morale, and it will allow the employees to plan in advance if there is a special event they wish to attend. For instance, Justina knows on Wednesday, April 6, that she has the weekend of the 16th and 17th off. In addition, if the employees wanted a special day or weekend off, they were allowed to switch with other employees as long as the host was told. However, it was made clear to the employees who were scheduled to work that they were responsible for covering the shift. If their replacement did not show up, then the originally scheduled employee would pay the consequences. This system made the host's job easy. The staff was motivated because they knew exactly when they had to work and knew that they could take a day off if some special event occurred. Of course, if employees knew far enough in advance before the schedule was to be made up that they needed a day off, they would inform the host and they would be accommodated. Regardless of how the stations are arranged in the restaurant (team or individual), stations and sidework responsibilities have to be posted. Sidework should be with the station.

An example of how stations and sidework can be planned. Notice that the sidework corresponds to the station assignment. The host must be flexible and on occasion must combine stations or service staff from different stations when it would benefit the guests. For example, a party of 12 went to a restaurant on New Year's Day. The host assigned two service people to take care of the table even though it was on one station. The group was served more quickly than if one person had served them.

The host is usually responsible for making sure the proper meal period menus are clean and ready to distribute to the guests. In some establishments, the host has to write or print out the daily specials to insert into the menu and/or write them on the blackboard. When putting the specials into the menus, the host also checks the condition of the menus. Dirty, torn, or smudged menus should be discarded. If the restaurant serves three meals a day, the host checks that the menu is correct for that meal period. Have you ever received a menu that was for lunch when the other guests in your party had a dinner menu? Guest checks are sometimes given out to the service staff by the host or cashier; at other times, computer systems print them automatically. All service staff are responsible for the checks they receive.

Staff Inspection and Daily Meeting

Before each meal period, the host has to conduct a staff inspection and hold a daily meeting. It is at this time that the host inspects the employees regarding the grooming and cleanliness policies set by the restaurant. If a member of the staff does not meet the grooming standards that have been set, the host cannot allow that individual to work. Allowing a service person to work who has not met the restaurant's standards will make it difficult to enforce the rules to the other staff members. Once the service staff realize that the grooming and cleanliness policies will be enforced, they will comply. The daily meeting usually consists of a short information session that the host conducts before each meal period. Information is shared with the staff, such as the description and price of the day's chef creations. Any new wines or beverages that the restaurant is featuring will be explained. The soup or vegetable of the day and items that the restaurant is temporarily out of are also communicated by the host. Any special requests from the reservations, such as a birthday cake for the Smith reservation at 8:00 P.M., and any new promotions are also explained.

This informational session should not last long. There will be regularly scheduled meetings for the purpose of tasting food and wine, reviewing policies in depth, and soliciting new ideas from the staff. This meeting is only informational in nature so that the dining room runs smoothly for that particular meal period. In sum, the host's job historically evolved in the classical restaurant. In classical restaurants, each area of the restaurant had a host. Today the host may also serve as an owner, food and beverage director, or manager of the restaurant—all depending upon the size of the restaurant. The host must be attentive, courteous, dependable, honest, loyal to the establishment, tactful, knowledgeable, sensitive to guests' needs and moods, and persuasive.

The host should have a knowledge of where stations are located in the restaurant and the sidework that has to be completed by staff. On occasion, the host must combine stations or service staff from different stations when it would benefit the guests. Stations and sidework should be posted by the host so that service people know their duties and responsibilities. This will create a accountability for the duties to be performed by staff. The five Ps of management are Prior Planning Prevents Poor Performance. To have the dining room run smoothly, the host should have a plan. With a plan, when change occurs, the host will be able to make adjustments as necessary to insure a favourable dining experience for the guests.

Glossary

à la carte. A menu giving a selection of individually priced dishes. The customer can order one or more dishes.

A/R. Accounts Receivable - direct bill accounts of companies or individuals who buy hotel services.

ABA. American Bus Association; comprised of bus companies, operators and owners

ADS. Alternate Distribution System, such as Expedia and Travelocity

Attendance Building. Marketing and promotional programs designed to increase attendance at conventions, trade shows, meetings, and events.

Attraction. Any visitor service or product which tourists would enjoy visiting or using. An attraction may not be an "attractor" but can still be an attraction. To be considered an attraction, a product must be: A. Findable (clearly located on maps and street addresses, and directions provided). If tourists can't find the facility, it is not a tourist attraction. B. Hours of operation clearly denoted in any and all promotional materials (if a tourist arrives only to find the attraction closed, it is not an attraction). Examples of attractions include everything from a theme park that attracts over a million visitors a year, to a produce stand by the side of the road. General all-inclusive term travel industry marketers use to refer to products that have visitor appeal, like museums, historic sites, performing arts institutions, preservation districts, theme parks, entertainment and national sites.

Attractor. A significant tourist attraction, which compels visitation. The primary "must sees" in an area. The top reasons a tourist would choose to visit this area.

AVHRM. Association of Vacation Home Rental Managers.

Bed Tax (Transient Occupancy Tax of TOT). City or county tax added to the price of a hotel room.

Benchmarking. The process of comparing performance and processes within an industry to assess relative position against either a set industry standard or against those who are "best in class" (Synergy, 2000).

Best Practice(s). A term used to designate highest quality, excellence, or superior practices in a particular field by a tourism operator.

Blocked rooms. Hotel rooms held without a deposit.

Blocked. (1) Hotel rooms held without deposit. (2) Hotel rooms, airline tickets or other travel services held for a specific client.

Booking. Term used to refer to a completed sale by a destination, convention center, facility, hotel or supplier (i.e. convention, meeting, trade show or group business booking).

Brigade. French term used to describe all the staff working on the floor of the restaurant or the kitchen.

Business Travel. Travel for commercial, governmental or educational purposes with leisure as a secondary motivation.

Business Travel. Travel for commercial, governmental or educational purposes with leisure as a secondary motivation.

Buyer. A member of the travel trade who reserves room blocks from accommodations or coordinates the development of a travel product.

BYO. Bring Your Own. A restaurant which allows patrons to bring their own alcohol.

Carrier. Any provider of mass transportation, usually used in reference to an airline.

Chambers of Commerce. Typically, a Chamber of Commerce will specialize in local economic development that can include tourism promotion.

Charter Group. Group travel in which a previously organized group travels together, usually on a custom itinerary.

Commissions. A percent of the total product cost paid to travel agents and other travel product distributors for selling the product to the consumer.

Consumer Show. A product showcase for the general public. Differs from a "Trade Show" as a trade show generally targets industry professionals. Consumer Shows target the consumer. Often there is a charge to get into the show.

Convention and Visitors Bureau. These organizations are local tourism marketing organizations specializing in developing conventions, meetings, conferences and visitations to a city, county or region.

Conventions and Trade Shows. Major segment of travel industry business. Trade shows differ from conventions in that they have exhibit space that provides product exhibition and sales opportunities for suppliers, as well as information gathering and buying opportunities for customers.

Conversion Study. Research study to analyze whether advertising respondents actually were converted to travelers as a result of advertising and follow-up material.

Co-op Advertising. Advertising funded by two or more destinations and /or suppliers.

Cooperative Marketing. Marketing programs involving two or more participating companies, institutions or organizations.

Cooperative Partner. An independent firm or organization which works with a tourism office by providing cash or in-kind contributions to expand the marketing impact of the tourism officeÕs program.

Country of Residence. Consists of the country where she/he has lived for most of the past year (12 months), or for a shorter period if she/ he intends to return within 12 months to live there.

Cover. Each diner at a restaurant.

CRS. Central Reservation System

CTRLA. Car and Truck Rental and Leasing Association.

Cultural tourism. Travel for the purpose of learning about cultures or aspects of cultures (NEAP, 2000).

CVB. Convention and Visitors Bureau.

Day visitors. Visitors who arrive and leave the same day for leisure, recreation and holidays, visiting friends and relatives, & business and professional.

Destination Marketing Organization (DMO). A company or other entity involved in the business of increasing tourism to a destination or improving its public image. Local tourism marketing organizations, such as convention and visitors bureaus or chambers of commerce.

Destination Marketing. Marketing a city, state, country, area or region to consumers and trade.

Destination. **A hotel, resort, attraction, city, region, or state.**

Discounted Fare. Negotiated air fare for convention, trade show, meeting, group and corporate travel.

Discover America. Theme used by the Travel Industry Association and its marketing partners to market travel within the United States.

Ecotourism. "Responsible travel to natural areas that conserves the environment and improves the welfare of local people," according to The International Ecotourism Society.

Fam Tours. Organized trips for travel agents, tour operators, tour wholesalers or other members of the travel trade for the purpose of educating and "familiarizing" them with tourism destinations. By seeing the destinations where they are sending travelers, the travel trade is better prepared to answer customer questions and promote travel to the location. Also called "fams" or "familiarization tours."

Familiarization Trip. A complimentary or reduced-rate travel program for travel agents, airline or rail employees or other travel buyers, designed to acquaint participants with specific destinations or suppliers and to stimulate the sale of travel. Familiarization tours, also called fam tours, are sometimes offered to journalists as research trips for the purpose of cultivating media coverage of specific travel products.

Feeder Airport/City. An outlying city which feeds travelers to hubs or gateway cities.

FIT (Free Independent Travel). Individual travel in which a tour operator has previously arranged blocks of rooms at various destinations in advance for use by individual travelers. These travelers travel independently, not in a group, usually by rental car or public transportation.

Foreign Independent Travel or Foreign Individual Travel (FIT). An international pre-paid unescorted tour that includes several travel elements such as accommodations, rental cars and sightseeing. A FIT operator specialises in preparing FITs documents at the request of retail travel agents. FITs usually receive travel vouchers to present to on-site services as verification of pre-payment.

Frequency. The number of times an advertisement appears during a given campaign.

Fulfillment. Servicing consumers and trade who request information as a result of advertising or promotional programs. Service often includes an 800 number, sales staff and distribution of materials.

Function. Term used to for specialty catering such as weddings, meetings, birthdays, dances and product launches etc.

Gateway or Gateway City. A major airport, seaport, rail or bus center through which tourists and travelers enter from outside the region.

GDS. Global Distribution System, such as Sabre and Worldspan

GIT (Groups Independent Travel). Group travel in which individuals purchase a group package in which they will travel with others along a pre-set itinerary.

Gourmet. French term, originally and still used to describe a person who is a critic of food and beverage. Also used to describe establishments that provide sophisticated food and beverage.

Gross lettings. This refers to all room lettings, i.e. both paid & complimentary listings are included

Group Rate. Negotiated hotel rate for convention, trade show, meeting, tour or incentive group.

Group Tour and Group Leader - Group Tour. A travel agent type company which plans motor coach trips. Group Leader: A small, informal group, such as a church group, scout troop, or social group. Usually one person plans the activities for the group. Some travel shows target these planners such as GLAMER.

Head in Beds. Industry slang referring to the primary marketing objective of accommodations and most destinations. increasing the number of overnight stays.

Hospitality Industry. Another term for the travel industry.

Hospitality. A general term used in travel & tourism describing the "hospitality industry"; Refers to the general greeting, welcoming, food service, etc

Hotel Package. A package offered by a hotel, sometimes consisting of no more than a room and breakfast; sometimes, especially at resort hotels, consisting of (ground) transportation, rooms, meals, sports facilities and other components.

Hub and Spoke. Air carriers use of selected cities as "hubs" or connected points for service on their systems to regional destinations.

Hub. An airport or city which serves as a central connecting point for aircraft, trains or buses from outlying feeder airports or cities.

Icon. A facility or landmark which is visually synonymous with a destination.

IDS. Internet Distribution System

Incentive Tour. A trip offered as a prize, usually by a company to stimulate employee sales or productivity.

Incentive Travel. Travel offered as a reward for top performance and the business that develops, markets and operates these programs.

Inclusive Tour. A tour program that includes a variety of feature for a single rate (airfare, accommodations, sightseeing, performances, etc.)

Inclusive Tour. A tour program that includes a variety of feature for a single rate (airfare, accommodations, sightseeing, performances, etc.)

Inquiry. A request for more information about an attraction or destination.

International Marketing. Marketing a destination, product or service to consumers and the trade outside the of the United States.

IPU. Interface Processing Unit

Itinerary. A travel schedule provided by a travel agent for his/her customer. A proposed or preliminary itinerary may be rather vague or specific. A final itinerary however provides all details (flight numbers, departure times, reservation confirmation numbers) and describes planned activities.

Joint venture. A form of strategic alliance or co-operative arrangement where ownership is shared and a separate enterprise formed. This may strengthen existing businesses through shared expertise, capital, removal of competition and creation of economies of scale. International tourism joint ventures between foreign organizations and local partners facilitate introduction of foreign products into local markets.

Jungle tourism. Jungle tours have become a major component of green tourism in tropical destinations. A jungle is a subclimax tropical forest consisting of a tangled growth of lianas, trees and scrub which may form an almost impenetrable barrier to the tourist. Jungle tours are a relatively recent phenomenon of Western international tourism.

Key-informant Survey. This involves interviewing people who are likely to have some insight into a problem: operating managers; sales staff; managers; suppliers; and consultants.

Keying. A social convention by which social 'reality' is transformed and seen as something else, such as the presentation of a fight as mere horseplay. In tourism, a peculiar, inverted variety of keying is frequently employed: the 'as if' situation in which participants are induced to playfully make believe that presented settings, activities or events are 'real', when as tourists they may be well aware that such occurences are contrived.

Leisure Tourist. Leisure tourists, in contrast with business travellers, travel for pleasure and thus are not under any obligations to frequent specific destinations or facilities. They tend to be price and fashion conscious, concentrate their touristic activities to specific (vacation) times, and are influenced by marketing and publicity. Leisure tourism is heavily influenced by living standards, discretionary income levels and vacation entitlements.

Leisure Travel. Travel for recreational, educational, sightseeing, relaxing and other experiential purposes.

Length of Stay. This refers to the period of time which people spend in a destination. Many definitions require that visitors to a destination stay at least 24 hours or overnight, and less than one year, to be considered a tourist. Destination areas often look for means to extend tourists' length of stay in order to increase positive economic impacts.

Limited Bar. Restricted service of alcoholic beverages at a function. For example, $1000 limit for beer, wine and soft drinks, or unlimited beer wine and soft drinks for four hours. In both cases spirits would incur additional costs.

maître*d'*. Full term is 'maître d' hôtel'. Literally 'master of the hotel'. In English we sometimes call this position the headwaiter, but the French term is frequently used.

Market Share. The percentage of business within a market category.

Market Volume. The total number of travelers within a market category.

Maximum Room Nights. This is calculated based on the total room inventory for all gazetted hotels.

Mise en place. Literally this means to 'put in place' and generally refers to pre-service preparation, including setting the tables and stocking up the stations. Also used in the kitchen, where it refers to the pre-preparation before cooking takes place.

Mission (Sales). A promotional and sales trip coordinated by a state travel office, conventional and visitors bureau or key industry member to increase product awareness, sales and to enhance image. Target audiences may include tour operators, wholesales, incentive travel planners, travel agents, meeting planners, convention and trade show managers and media. Missions often cover several international or domestic destinations and include private and public sector participants. Mission components can include receptions, entertainment representatives of the destination, presentations and pre- scheduled sales and media calls.

Motorcoach. Deluxe equipment used by most tour operators in group tour programs. Amenities include reclining seats, bathrooms, air conditioning, good lighting and refreshment availability.

Nature Tourism. Travel to unspoiled places to experience and enjoy nature.

Net Rate. The rate provided to wholesalers and tour operators that can be marked up to sell to the customer.

No Show. A customer with a reservation at a restaurant, hotel, etc. who fails to show up and does not cancel.

NTA. National Tour Association, comprised of domestic tour operators.

Occupancies. A percentage indicating the number of bed nights sold (compared to number available) in a hotel, resort, motel or destination.

Occupancy Rate. A tourism business occupancy rate refers to the number of airline seats or the units of hotel room space sold. This demand is usually measured as a percentage of available seats or space occupied for a given period of time. It is calculated by dividing the number of occupied rooms/seats by the total number available for sale during the same period.

Open Bar. unrestricted service of alcoholic beverages at a function. plated food presentation of food on plates by kitchen staff.

Outbound. Outbound tourism is defined as tourism involving residents of a country travelling to another country. Outbound tour operators offer package tours abroad. They either operate the tours themselves, or they commission the services of an inbound operator to handle local arrangements at the destination. The country from which the tourists originate is known as the generating market or country.

Package Tour. A saleable travel product offering an inclusive price with several travel elements that would otherwise be purchased separately. Usually has a predetermined price, length of time and features but can also offer options for separate purchase.

Package. A fixed price salable travel product that makes it easy for a traveler to buy and enjoy a destination or several destinations. Packages offer a mix of elements like transportation, accommodations, restaurants, entertainment, cultural activities, sightseeing and car rental.

Paid Lettings. This refers to room lettings that are paid for by hotel guests

Peaks and Valleys. The high and low end of the travel season. Travel industry marketers plan programs to build consistent year-round business and event out the "peaks and valleys."

Person Trip Visit. Every time a person travels more than 100 miles (round-trip) in a day or stays overnight away from their primary domicile, whether for business or leisure purposes, they make one "person trip visit."

Pow Wow. The largest international travel marketplace held in the United States, sponsored by the Travel Industry Association of America.

Press Trips. Organized trips for travel writers and broadcasters for the purpose of assisting them in developing stories about tourism destinations. Often, journalists travel independently, though with the assistance of a state's office of tourism of a DMO.

Press/Publicity Release. A news article or feature story written by the subject of the story for delivery and potential placement in the media.

Property. A hotel, motel, inn, lodge or other accommodation facility.

Quality. In tourism, the product is often intangible and quality is not apparent until after it is consumed. Quality has been defined as zero defects or defections, but still may be defined by the customer. The International Organization for Standardisation defines quality as 'the totality of features and characteristics of a product or service that bear on its ability to satisfy stated or implied needs'. Others believe that quality is a combination of outcome and processes, including internal and external conditions, and is obtained when the expectations and needs of customers are met.

Rack Card. The typical tourism brochure sized 4" x 9" and used primarily in tourism racks. Also known as a "teaser."

Rack Rate. The official cost posted by a hotel, attraction or rental car, but not used by tour operators. The rate accommodations quote to the public. Group rates, convention, trade show, meeting and incentive travel rates are negotiated by the hotel and program organizers.

Reach. The percentage of people within a specific target audience reached by an advertising campaign.

Receptive Operator. Specialists in handling arrangements for incoming visitors at a destination including airport transfers, local sightseeing, restaurants, accommodations, etc. Receptive operators can be a travel agent or tour operator.

Repeat Business. Business that continues to return, thereby generating increased profits.

Reservation Systems (Automation Vendors). Computerized systems leased to travel agencies offering airline, hotel, car rental and selected tour availability and bookings. Systems are affiliated with major carriers, including American (Sabre), United (Apollo), Eastern (System One), TWA (PARS), and Delta (DATAS II) and feature flight schedules of the sponsoring and other carriers, plus additional travel products.

Resident. A person living in a given country, whether he is a national or not.

Retail Agent. A travel agent.

Retail Agent. A travel agent. **Retailer.** Another term for travel agents who sell travel products directly to consumers.

Retailer. Another term for travel agents who sell travel products directly to consumers.

Room Block. Several rooms held for a group.

Room. Double: No guarantee of two beds; Double Double: Two double beds (or two queens or kings); Twin: Two twin beds (or two doubles or queens)

Sales Mission. Where suppliers from one DMO travel together to another state of country for the purpose of collectively promoting travel to their area. Sales missions may include educational seminars for travel agents and tour operators.

Sales Seminar. An educational session in which travel agents, tour operators, tour wholesales or other members of the travel trade congregate to receive briefings about tourism destinations.

Shells. A marketing and sales promotional piece that depicts a destination, accommodation or attraction on the cover and provides space for copy to be added at a later date. Usually shells fit a #10 envelope.

Site Inspection. An assessment tour of a destination or facility by a meeting planner, convention or trade show manager, site selection committee, tour operator, wholesaler or incentive travel manager to see if it meets their needs and requirements prior to selecting a specific site for an event. After site selection, a site inspection may be utilized to make arrangements.

Spouse Program. Special activities planned for those who accompany an attendee to a convention, trade show or meeting. Note that programs today are not simply for women, but rather for men and women, spouses and friends. Programs must be creatively designed to interest intelligent and curious audiences.

Station. The preparation, or worktable allocated to dining room staff. It also serves as limited storage for crockery, cutlery and table linen in the restaurant or dining room.

Supplier. Those businesses that provide industry products like accommodations, transportation, car rentals, restaurants and attractions.

Sustainable tourism. This is, according to the World Tourism Organization, "envisaged as leading to management of all resources in such a way that economic, social and aesthetic needs can be fulfilled with maintaining cultural integrity, essential ecological processes, biological diversity, and life support systems."

Table d'hôte menu. Set menu of two or more courses and maybe one or more choices within each course. The price is pre-set for this style of meal.

Target Audience/Market. A specific demographic, sociographic target at which marketing communications are directed.

Target Rating Points. TRPÕs are a statistical measurement which allows one to evaluate the relative impact of differing advertising campaigns.

Tariff. Rate of fare quoted and published by a travel industry supplier (i.e. hotels, tour operators, etc.) Usually an annual tariff is produced in booklet form for use in sales calls at trade shows.

TIA. Travel Industry Association of America.

TIA. Travel Industry Association of America.

TOT. Transient Occupancy Tax.

Tour Operator. Develops, markets and operates group travel programs that provide a complete travel experience for one price and includes transportation (airline, rail, motorcoach, and/or ship), accommodations, sightseeing, selected meals and an escort. Tour operators market directly to the consumer, through travel agents and are beginning to be listed on computerized reservation systems.

Tour Wholesaler. An individual or company that sells tour packages and tour product to travel agents. Tour wholesalers usually receive a 20% discount from accommodations, transportation companies and attractions and pass on a 10 to 15% discount to the retail agent.

Tourism Receipts. Tourism Receipts (TR) measures the total revenue received by Singapore from tourism activity. It includes all payments and prepayments for goods and services made by visitors, transit passengers, air & sea crew and foreign students (staying for one year or less) during their stay in Singapore. Visitors' payments to our national carriers (SIA & Silk Air) for international transport are also included.

Tourism. Leisure travel.

Tourism. The business of providing and marketing services and facilities for pleasure travellers. Thus, the concept or tourism is of direct concern to governments, carriers, and the lodging, restaurant and entertainment industries and of indirect concern to virtually every industry and business in the world.

Tourist. Temporary visitor staying at least twenty-four hours in the country visited for a purpose classified as either holiday (recreation, leisure, sport and visit to family, friends or relatives), business, official mission, convention, or health reasons.

Tourist/Visitor/Traveler. Any person who travels either for leisure or business purposes more than 100 miles (round-trip) in a day or who stays overnight away from his/her primary domicile.

Tourist/Visitor/Traveler. Any person who travels either for leisure or business purposes more than 100 miles (round-trip) in a day or who stays overnight away from his/her primary domicile.

Trade Show. A product showcase for a specific industry. Generally it is not open to the public. Differs from a "Consumer Show" in that a trade show targets the professional industry, while a consumer show targets consumers.

Transient Occupancy Tax. TOT or bed tax is a locally set tax on the cost of commercial accommodations and campgrounds.

Travel Agent. (1) An individual who arranges travel for individuals or groups. Travel agents may be generalists or specialists (cruises, adventure travel, conventions and meetings.) The agents receive a 10 to 15% commission from accommodations, transportation companies and attractions for coordinating the booking of travel. They typically coordinate travel for their customers at the same or lower cost than if the customer booked the travel on his/her own. (2) The individual who sells travel services, issues tickets and provides other travel services to the travel services to the traveller sat the retail level.

Travel Product. Refers to any product or service that is bought by or sold to consumers of trade including accommodations, attractions, events, restaurants, transportation, etc.

Travel Seasons. Travel industry business cycles including: *Peak:* Primary travel season *Off Peak:* Period when business is slowest *Shoulder:* Period between peak and off peak periods when business is stronger, but has room for growth.

Travel Trade. The collective term for tour operators, wholesalers and travel agents.

Travel. Leisure and other travel including travel for business, medical care, education, etc. All tourism is travel, but not all travel is tourism.

Traveler. (1) Definitions very, but in general a traveler is someone who leaves their own economic trade area, (usually going a distance of a minimum of fifty to one hundred miles) and stays overnight. (2) Someone who leaves his or her own economic trade area, (usually going a distance of a minimum of fifty to one hundred miles) and stays overnight.

Underdevelopment. Within development theory, the concept of underdevelopment suggests that wealthy capitalist countries have held back the development of so-called Third World countries. Tourism in Third World destinations is controlled for the economic benefit of foreign owners, reinforces dependency, lacks involvement of local decision makers, leads to negative sociocultural impacts, and results in the promotion of staged attractions to capture an international tourism market.

Urban recreation. The concept of urban recreation covers recreational activity that takes place in an urban environment in contrast to a rural setting. Participants in such activities are either urban residents themselves, day visitors from rural areas, or tourists. The major activities are shopping, visits to heritage sites, museums, movie theatres, operas, sport and music events, and indoor sports activities.

VFR. Visiting friends and relatives

Visitor Arrivals. Includes all who go through immigration clearance regardless of length of stay. This excludes the following: (a) All Malaysian citizens arriving by land, (b) Returning Singapore citizens residing abroad, (c) Non-resident air and sea crew (except for sea crew flying in to join ship), (d) All visitors arriving and leaving Singapore on the same ship/vessel and stayed in Singapore for less than 24 hours are not required to complete Disembarkation / Embarkation (D/E) cards, if passenger manifest is submitted, (e) All organized tour groups leaving Singapore for Johor Bahru, Batam and Bintan, returning on the same day are not required to complete Disembarkation / Embarkation (D/E) cards, if passenger manifest is submitted, (f) Air transit passengers

Visitor Expenditure. Includes expenditure incurred during a visitor's stay in Singapore, or prepayment by non-package tour visitors (this took effect from 1995). This excludes: (a) international air and sea fare. It is made up of the following components: (a) Shopping, (b) Accommodation, (c) Entertainment, (d) Sightseeing, (e) Food & beverage (f) Local transportation, (g) Medical/dental treatment, (h) Miscellaneous

Visitor. Any person visiting a country other than that in which he has his usual place of residence for any reason other than following an occupation remunerated from within the country visited.

Visitors Center. Travel information center located at a destination to make it easier for visitors to plan their stay; often operated by a convention and visitors bureau, chamber of commerce or tourism promotion organization.

Vouchers. Forms or coupons provided to a traveler who purchases a tour that indicate that certain tour components have been prepaid. Vouchers are then exchanged for tour components like accommodations, meals, sightseeing, theater tickets, etc. during the actual trip.

World Tourism Organization (WTO). The World Tourism Organization, a UN-related institution based in Madrid that collects data on tourism and lobbies on behalf of the industry.

World Travel and Tourism Council (WTTC). The WTTC is made up of chief executives from all sectors of the tourism industry, including accommodation, catering, cruises, entertainment, recreation, transportation and travel-related services. Its central goal is to work with governments to realise the full economic impact of tourism. Its millennium vision is to make tourism a strategic economic and employment priority, to move towards open and competitive markets, to pursue sustainable development, and to eliminate barriers to growth.

Xenophobia. Xenophobia is an irrational fear or contempt of strangers or foreigners. This ancient cultural and political phenomenon is also present in contemporary tourism, mainly manifesting itself in the hostile attitudes of residents towards tourists. Xenophobia should be considered in domestic and international tourism in terms of economic, social and cultural distance, which is accentuated by the type and the number of tourists and the rate of tourism development.

Yield Management. The concept of maximising the revenue by raising or lowering prices in respect to demand is known as yield management. The necessary conditions for a successful application of yield management include a fairly fixed capacity, high fixed costs, low variable costs, fluctuations in demand and similarity of inventory capacity. Yield management was popularised with the deregulation of the US airline industry and it is extensively used by this and other tourism sectors.

Bibliography

Alexander, N., McKenna, A. (1999), "Rural tourism in the heart of England", *International Contemporary Hospitality Management*, Vol. 10 No.5, pp. 203-7.

Allen, R.E. (1994), "Hospitality group: underpromising and overdelivering", *Nation's Restaurant News*, Vol. 28 No.13, pp. 110-2.

Amoah, V., Baum, T. (1997), "Tourism education: policy versus practice", *International Journal of Contemporary Hospitality Management*, Vol. 9 No.1, pp. 5-12.

Ananth, M., DeMicco, F.J., Moreo, P.J., Howey, R.M. (1992), "Marketplace lodging needs of mature travellers", *The Cornell Hotel and Restaurant Quarterly*, Vol. 33 No.4, pp. 12-24.

Anderson, G.K. (1991), "The education and training of general managers in Scotland", *International Journal of Contemporary Hospitality Management*, Vol. 3 No.2, pp. 26-9 .

Barron, P, Maxwell, G (1993), "Hospitality management students' image of the hospitality industry", *International Journal of Hospitality Management*, Vol. 5 No.5, pp. v-viii.

Barton, L., Eichelberger, J. (1994), "Sexual harassment: assessing the need for corporate policies in the workplace", *Executive Development*, Vol. 7 No.1, pp. 24-8.

Baum, T., Mudambi, R. (1996), "Attracting hotel investment: insights from principal-agent theory", *Hospitality Research Journal*, Vol. 20 pp. 15-30.

Bennett, R., Krebs, G. (1993), "Chambers of Commerce in Britain and Germany: the Challenges of the Single Market", in Bennett, R.J., Krebs, G., Zimmermann, H. (Eds),*Chambers of Commerce in Britain and Germany and the Single European Market*, Anglo-German Foundation, London, pp. 1-38.

Bosco, J. (1992), "Taiwan factions, Guanxi, patronage, and the state in local politics", *Ethnology*, Vol. 31 No.2, pp. 157-83.

Bosselman, R.H. (1996), "Current perceptions of hospitality accreditation", *FIU Hospitality Review*, Vol. 14 No.2, pp. 77.

Brander-Brown, J., McDonnell, B. (1995), "The balanced score-card: short-term guest or long-term resident?", *International Journal of Contemporary Hospitality Management*.

Breiter, D. (1993), "Student achievement of experiential learning objectives", Vol. 11 No.2, pp. 41-8.

Brymer, R.A. (1991), "Employee empowerment: a guest driven leadership strategy", *The Cornell Hotel and Restaurant Quarterly*, Vol. 32 No.1, pp. 58-68.

Buhalis, D. (1993), "RICIRMS as a strategic tool for small and medium tourism enterprises", *Tourism Management*, pp. 366-78.

Cai, L., Ninemeier, J.D. (1993), "Food service styles in Chinese hotels: tradition and tourism pressures merge", Vol. 11 No.2, pp. 33-40.

Callan, R.J. (1994), "Statutory hotel registration and grading: a review", *International Journal of Contemporary Hospitality Management*, Vol. 6 No.3, pp. 11-17.

Callan, R.J. (1994), "Development of a framework for the determination of attributes used for hotel selection-indications from focus group and in-depth interview", Vol. 18 No.2, pp. 53-64.

Cameron-Jones, M., O'Hara, P. (1990), "Placement as part of higher education", *Higher Education*, Vol. 19 pp. 341-9.

Carman, J.M. (1990), "Consumer perceptions of service quality: an assessment of the SERVQUAL dimensions", *Journal of Retailing*, Vol. 66 No.1, pp. 33-55.

Carmouche, R., Kelly, N. (1995), *Behavioural Studies in Hospitality Management*, Chapman and Hall, London.

Carper, J (1993), "The painful truth: operations is no longer King", *Hotels*, Vol. 50.

Carson, D., Cromie, S., McGowan, P., Hill, J. (1995), *Marketing and Entrepreneurship in SMEs: An Innovative Approach*, Prentice-Hall, London.

Cassee, E.H. (1983), "Introduction", in Cassee, E. H., Reuland, R. (Eds), *The Management of Hospitality*, Pergamon, Oxford, pp. xiii-xxii.

Charles, K.R. (2000), "Future HRD needs of the Caribbean tourism industry", in Jayawardena, C. (Eds), *Tourism and Hospitality Education and Training in the Caribbean*.

Charles, K.R., Marshall, L.H. (1992), "Motivational preferences of Caribbean hotel workers: an exploratory study", *International Journal of Contemporary Hospitality Management*, Vol. 4 No.3, pp. 25-9.

Chesser, J.W., Ellis, E.T (1995), "Hospitality administration program administrators view core areas of knowledge", Vol. 13 No.2.

Chesworth, N., Pine-Coffin, S. (1998), *The EMU Fact Book: Everything You Need to Know Sbout the Euro*, Kogan, London.

Cho, W., Sumichrast, R.T., Olsen, M.D. (1996), "Expert-system technology for hotels: concierge application", *Cornell Hotel and Restaurant Administration Quarterly*, Vol. 37 No.1, pp. 54-60.

Choi, J.G., Woods, R.H., Murrmann, S.K. (2000), "International labor markets and the migration of labor forces as an alternative solution for labor shortages in the hospitality industry", *International Journal of Contemporary Hospitality Management*, Vol. 12 No.1, pp. 61-7.

Chon, K.S., Huo, Y.H. (1993), "Environment for future conference centers: perceptions of managers", Vol. 11 No.1, pp. 25-30.

Chow, I.H.S., Ng, I. (2004), "The characteristics of Chinese personal ties (Guanxi): evidence from Hong Kong", *Organization Studies*, Vol. 25 No.7, pp. 1075-93.

Choy, D. (1995), "The quality of tourism employment", *Tourism Management*, Vol. 16 No.2, pp. 129-37.

Christensen, J. (1993), "The diversity dynamic: implications for organizations in 2995", Vol. 17 No.1, pp. 69-86.

Christensen, J. (1993), "The diversity dynamic: implications for organizations in 2005", *Hospitality Research Journal*, Vol. 17 No.1, pp. 69-86.

Christou, E. (2000), "Revisiting competencies for hospitality management: contemporary views of the stakeholders", *Journal of Tourism and Hospitality Education*, Vol. 14 No.1, pp. 25-32.

Cichy, R.F., Aoki, T., Patton, M.E., Sciarini, M.P. (1992), "The five foundations of leadership in Japan's lodging industry", Vol. 10 No.2, pp. 65-78.

Cichy, R.F., Schmidgall, R.S. (1996), "Leadership qualities of financial executivies in the US lodging industry", *Cornell Hotel and Restaurant Administration Quarterly*, Vol. 37 No.2, pp. 56-62.

Cichy, R.F., Sciarini, M.P., Cook, C.L., Patton, M. (1991), "Leadership in the lodging and non-commercial food service industries", Vol. 9 No.1, pp. 1-10.

Clark, M (1993), "Communications and social skills: perceptions of hospitality managers", *Employee Relations*, Vol. 15 No.2, pp. 51-60.

Clark, M. (1991), "Training for tradition at Opryland Hotel", *Cornell Hotel & Restaurant Administration Quarterly*, Vol. 31 No.4, pp. 46-51.

Clarke, J.J., Arbel, A. (1993), "Producing global managers: the need for a new academic paradigm", *Cornell Hotel and Restaurant Administration Quarterly*, pp. 83-9.

Clements, C.J., Josiam, B.M. (1995), "Training: quantifying the financial benefits", *International Journal of Contemporary Hospitality Management*, Vol. 7 No.1.

Clifton, W.J., Johnson, K. (1994), "A structural analysis of the European hotel sector: a simple case of déjà-vu?", *International Journal of Contemporary Hospitality Management*, Vol. 6 No.4, pp. vii-viii.

Close, A., Teare, R. (1990), "Effective management development", *International Journal of Contemporary Hospitality Management*, Vol. 2 No.4, pp. i-ii.

Coates, D.S. (1971), *Industrial Catering Management*, Business Books, London.

Conaway, R.N., Fernandez, T.L. (2000), "Ethical preferences among business leaders: implications for business schools", Business Communication Quarterly, Vol. 63 No.1, pp. 23-8.

Confederation of Australian Industry (1990), *Flexibility of Working Time in Australia*, Melbourne.

Conlin, M.V, Baum, T (1996), "Macro aspects of productivity planning for the hospitality industry", in Johns, N (Eds), *Productivity Management in Hospitality and Tourism: Developing a Model for the Service Sector*, Cassell, New York, NY, pp. 55-67.

Connell, J. (1992), "Branding hotel portfolios", *International Journal of Contemporary Hospitality Management*, Vol. 4 No.1, pp. 26-32.

Cook, S. (1995), *Practical Benchmarking: A Manager's Guide to Creating a Competitive Advantage*, Kogan Page, London.

Cooper, C., Westlake, J. (1989), "Tourism teaching into the 1990s", *Tourism Management*, Vol. 10 No.1, pp. 69-72.

Cooper, C., Westlake, J. (1998), "Stakeholders and tourism education", *Industry and Higher Education*.

Corsun, D.L, Young, C.A., Enz, C.A. (1996), "Should NYC's restaurateurs lighten up? Effects of the city's smoke-free-air act", *Cornell Hotel and Restaurant Administration Quarterly*, Vol. 37 No.2, pp. 25-33.

Costa, J., Teare, R. (1994), "Environmental scanning and the Portuguese hotel sector", *International Journal of Contemporary Hospitality Management*, Vol. 6 No.5, pp. iv-vii.

Cracknell, H.L., Kaufmann R.J., Nobis, G. (1983), *Practical Professional Catering* , Macmillan, Basingstoke, pp. 22.

Craft, A. (1992), Quality Assurance in Higher Education: Proceedings of an International Conference, Hong Kong, 1991, Falmer Press, London.

Crosby, L.A., Stephens, N. (1987), "Effects of relationship marketing on satisfaction, retention, and prices in the life insurance industry", *Journal of Marketing Research*, Vol. 24 No.4, pp. 404-11.

Curland, S, Stoney, C (1993), "Numeracy – a barrier to finance", IAHMS Conference, Manchester University.

Damiti, J.W., Schmidgall, R.S. (1994), "Bartering practices in the lodging industry", Vol. 17 No.3, pp. 101-10.

Damitio, J.W, Schmidgall, R.S. (1989), "A comparative analysis of lodging general managers' and hospitality accounting educators' views of the importance of accounting skills", *Hospitality Education and Research Journal*, Vol. 13 No.3, pp. 43-52.

Damitio, J.W., Schmidgall, R.S. (2001), "The value of professional certifications for hospitality financial experts", *Cornell Hotel & Restaurant Administration Quarterly*, Vol. 42 No.1, pp. 66-70.

Damitio, J.W., Schmidgall, R.S., Whitney, D.L. (1992), "Ethical orientation of hospitality educators", Vol. 16 No.1, pp. 75-92.

Dann, D.T. (1990), "The process of managerial work in the hospitality industry", University of Surrey, Guildford., PhD thesis.

Darkenwald, G.G, Merriam, S.B (1982), *Adult Education: Foundations of Practice*, Harper and Rowe, New York, NY.

Davidson, T.L. (1989), "Primary market research: its role in feasibility studies", Vol. 7 No.1, pp. 23-30.

Deery, M, Iverson, R (1995), "Enhancing productivity: intervention strategies for employee turnover", *Proceedings of IAHMS Spring Conference*, Norwich Hotel School, Norwich.

DeFranco, A.L., Weatherspoon, K.E. (1996), "Go green: an environmental checklist for the lodging industry", *Cornell Hotel and Restaurant Administration Quarterly*, Vol. 37 No.6, pp. 84-5.

deRoos, J.A., Rushmore, S. (1996), "Investment values of lodging property: proof of value for selected models", *Cornell Hotel and Restaurant Administration Quarterly*, Vol. 37 No.1, pp. 89-95.

Dev, C.S., Brown, J.R. (1991), "Franchising and other operating arrangements in the lodging industry: a strategic comparison", Vol. 14 No.2, pp. 22-42.

Dev, C.S., Ellis, B. (1991), "Guest Histories: an untapped service resource", *The Cornell Hotel and Restaurant Quarterly*, Vol. 32 No.2, pp. 29-37.

Diaz, P.E., Krauss, J.L. (1996), "A needs analysis of an expanding hospitality market - Asian students", *Hospitality Research Journal*, Vol. 20 No.1, pp. 15-26.

Diaz, P.E., Park, J. (1992), "The impact of isolation on hospitality employees' job satisfaction and job performance", Vol. 15 No.3, pp. 41-50.

Diaz, P.E., Umbreit, W.T. "Women leaders - a new, beginning", Vol. 18 No.3.

DiBlase, D. (25), "Worker sues Marriott for AIDS discrimination", *Business Insurance*.

Dickinson, A., Ineson, E.M. (1993), "The selection of quality operative staff in the hotel sector", *International Journal of Contemporary Hospitality Management*, Vol. 5 No.1, pp. 16-21.

Dienhart, J.R., Lefever, M.M. (1989), "Restaurant marquees: a help or hindrance?", Vol. 7 No.2, pp. 77-83.

Donaldson, T., Werhane, P.H., Cording, M. (2002), Ethical Issues in Business, 7th ed., Prentice Hall, New Jersey.

Donnellan, L. (1996), "Lessons in staff development", *Cornell Hotel and Restaurant Administration Quarterly*, Vol. 37 No.6, pp. 42-5.

Durocher, J.F., Niman, N.B. (1993), "Information technology: management effectiveness and guest services", Vol. 17 No.1, pp. 121-32.

Dwan, T. (1994), "'Excellence in hospitality': quality management for the hospitality industry", *Australian Journal of Hospitality Management*, Vol. 1 No.2, pp. 55-7.

Dwyer, F.R., Schurr, P.H., Oh, S. (1987), "Developing buyer-seller relationships", *Journal of Marketing*, Vol. 51 No.2, pp. 11-27.

Earnshaw, J., Davidson, M.J. (1994), "Remedying sexual harassment via industrial tribunal claims: an investigation of the legal and psychosocial process", *Personnel Review*, Vol. 23 No.8, pp. 3-16.

Echtner, C.M. (1995), "Tourism education in developing nations: a three pronged approach", *Tourism Recreation Research*, Vol. 20 No.2, pp. 32-41.

Eisenberg, T (1991), "On building self-confidence in mathematics", *Teaching Mathematics and its Applications*, Vol. 10 No.4, pp. 154-8.

Elfrink, J.A, Agbeh A., Krause, F. (1993), "A survey of student assessment in hospitality education: implications for the future", Vol. 17 No.1, pp. 259-272.

Elfrink, J.A., Anthony, K.F. (1995), "A survey of student assessment in hospitality education: implications for the future", *Hospitality Research Journal*, Vol. 18 No.3, pp. 143-53.

Enghagen, L.K. (1990), "Teaching ethics in hospitality and tourism education", *Hospitality Research Journal*, Vol. 14 No.2, pp. 467-74.

Entwistle, N., Ramsden, P. (1983), *Understanding Student Learning*, Croom Helm, London.

Evans, M., McDonagh, P. , Moutinho, L. (1991), "The development of the Portuguese hotel industry: contributory factors", *International Journal of Contemporary Hospitality Management*, Vol. 3 No.2, pp. 10-13.

Farrar, A.L., Murrmann, S.K., Vest, J.M. "Profiling managerial entrants to the hospitality industry", Vol. 18 No.1994, pp. 65-76.

Fenich, G.G. (1996), "The uses and abuses of multipliers: a current case", *Hospitality Research Journal*, Vol. 20 No.1, pp. 101-8.

Ferreira, R. (1998), "A comparison of the response rates, return times, return methods and costs for surveys faxed and mailed in clubs", *Journal of Hospitality & Tourism Research*, Vol. 21 No.3, pp. 81-91.

Ferreira, R. (1998), "The demographic effect on the performance level of private clubs", *Journal of Hospitality & Leisure Marketing*, Vol. 5 No.4, pp. 23-32.

Ford, L., Ford, R.C., LeBruto, S.M. (1995), "Is your hotel MISsing technology?", *FIU Hospitality Review*, Vol. 13 No.2, pp. 53-66.

Ford, R.C, Bach, S.A (1996), "Hospitality education for the year 2000 and beyond", in Kotas, R, Teare, R, Logie, J., Jayawardena, C, Bowen, J. (Eds), *The International Hospitality Business*, Cassell, London, pp. 145-51.

Ford, R.C., Heaton, C.P. (2000), *Managing the Guest Experience in Hospitality*, Delmar, Albany, NY.

Gamble, P.R. (1991), "An information technology strategy for the hospitality industry of the 1990s", *International Journal of Contemporary Hospitality Management*, Vol. 3 No.1, pp. 10-16.

Geddie, M.W., DeFranco, A.L., Geddie, M.F. (2002), "From Guanxi to customer relationship marketing: how the constructs of Guanxi can strengthen CRM in the hospitality industry", *Journal of Hospitality and Tourism Marketing*, Vol. 13 No.3, pp. 19-33.

Gee, D. (1994), "The Scottish Hotel School – The first fifty years", in Seaton, A.V., Jenkins, C.L., Wood, R.C., Dieke, P.U.C., Bennett, M.M., MacLellan, L.R., Smith, R. (Eds), *Tourism: The State of the Art*, John Wiley, Chichester, pp. xvi-xxiii.

George, R.T. (1991), "Voluntary termination in restaurants: an exploratory determination of causes", Vol. 9 No.1, pp. 59-66.

George, W.R., Gronroos, C. (1991), "Developing customer-conscious employees at every level: internal marketing", in Congram, C.A. (Eds), *The AMA Handbook of Marketing for the Service Industry*, AMACOM, New York, NY, pp. 85-100.

Ghiselli, R., Ismail, J. (1996), "Characterizing poor performance in for-profit and not-for-profit food service operations", *FIU Hospitality Review*, Vol. 14 No.2, pp. 53-64.

Ghiselli, R., Ismail, J.A. (1995), "Gauging employee theft and other unacceptable behaviours in food service operations", Vol. 13 No.2, pp. 15-24.

Gillin, L.M., Davie, R.S., Beissel, K.R. (1984), "Evaluating the career progress of Australian engineering graduates", *Journal of Cooperative Education*, Vol. 23 pp. 53-70.

Gittins, R (1994), "Wages, the unions and interest rates", *The Sydney Morning Herald*, pp. 25-6.

Go, F. (1994), "Emerging issues in tourism education", in Theobald, W. (Eds), *Global Tourism: The Next Decade*, Butterworth- Heinemann, London.

Goffman, E. (1959), *Presentation of Self in Everyday Life*, Anchor, Garden City, NY.

Goll, G. (1989), "Management by values: consistency as a predictor of success", Vol. 14 No.1, pp. 55-68.

Goymour, D. (1994), "A wealth of experience", *Caterer and Hotelkeeper*, pp. 36-7.

Grant, Y.N.J., Weaver, P.A. (1996), "The meeting selection process: a demographic profile of attendees clustered by criteria utilized in selecting meetings", *Hospitality Research Journal*, Vol. 20 No.1, pp. 57-72.

Green, R, MacDonald, D (1991), "The Australian flexibility paradox", *Journal of Industrial Relations*, Vol. 33 No.4, pp. 564-85.

Greenberg, J., Baron, R.A. (1997), *Behaviour in Organizations: Understanding and Managing the Human Side of Work*, Prentice-Hall International, Upper Saddle River, NJ.

Griffin, R.K. (1996), "Factors of successful lodging yield management systems", *Hospitality Research Journal*, Vol. 19 No.4, pp. 17-30.

Grundy, C. (1994), "What are the issues?", *HCIMA European Hospitality Management Issues*, Amsterdam.

Guerra, D., Peroni, G. (1991), *Occupations in the Hotel Tourist Sector within the European Community: A Comparative Analysis*, CEDEFOP, European Centre for the Development of Vocational Training, Berlin.

Guerrier, Y, Lockwood, A (1989), "Developing hotel managers – a reappraisal", *International Journal of Hospitality Management*, Vol. 8 No.2, pp. 82-9.

Guerrier, Y, Lockwood, A (1990), "Managers in hospitality: a review of current research", *Progress in Tourism, Recreation and Hospitality Research*, Vol. 2 pp. 151-67.

Guerrier, Y. (1987), "Hotel managers' careers and their impact on hotels in Britain", *International Journal of Hospitality Management*, Vol. 6 No.3, pp. 121-30.

Hales, C., Mercrate-Butcher, J. (1994), "'Internal marketing' and human resource management in hotel consortia", *International Journal of Hospitality Management*, Vol. 13 No.4, pp. 313-26.

Hamilton, A.J., Veglahn, P.A. (1992), "Sexual harassment: the hostile work environment", *The Cornell Hotel and Restaurant Administration Quarterly*, Vol. 33 No.2, pp. 88-92.

Harris, P.J. (1992), "Hospitality profit planning in the practical environment: integrating cost-volume-profit analysis with spreadsheet management", *International Journal of Contemporary Hospitality Management*, Vol. 4 No.4, pp. 24-32 .

Harris, V. (1997), *Report to the Quality Assurance Agency of a Pilot GSP Project in Hospitality Management*, Council for Hospitality Management Education, CHME.

Hasek, G. (1992), "Country lodging seeks perfection", *Hotel & Motel Management*, Vol. 207 No.5, pp. 1.

Hasek, G. (1995), "Choice unveils radical plans", *Hotel & Motel Management*, Vol. 210 No.7, pp. 1.

Hawkes, G. (1983), "Industrial catering", in Cassee, E., Reuland, R. (Eds),*The Management of Hospitality*, Pergamon Press, Oxford, pp. 165-87.

Hawkes, G. (1989), "An overview of the contract catering industry in the United Kingdom: a view from the industry", in Cooper, C.P. (Eds),*Progress in Tourism, Recreation and Hospitality Management*, Belhaven Press, London, pp. 212-21.

Hay, J (1990), "Managerial competencies or managerial characteristics", *Journal of Management Education and Development*, Vol. 21 No.5, pp. 305-15.

Haynes, A., Lackman, C., Guskey, A. (1999), "Comprehensive brand presentation: ensuring consistent brand image", *Journal of Product and Brand Management*, Vol. 8 No.4, pp. 286-300.

Heal, F. (1990), *Hospitality in Early Modern England*, Clarendon Press, Oxford.

Hegarty, J. (1992), "Towards establishing a new paradigm for tourism and hospitality development", *International Journal of Hospitality Management*, Vol. 11 No.4, pp. 309-17.

Heide, J.B., John, G. (1990), "Alliances in industrial purchasing: the determinants of joint action in buyer-supplier relationships", *Journal of Marketing Research*, Vol. 27 No.1, pp. 24-36.

Henley Centre (1996), *Hospitality into the 21st Century. A Vision for the Future*, Henley Centre.

Hesser, J.L. (1988), "Quality assurance: nuisance or necessity?", *Lodging Hospitality*, No.October, pp. 211-14, 233.

Heymann, K. (1992), "Quality management: a ten-point model", *Cornell Hotel and Restaurant Administration Quarterly*, Vol. 33 No.5, pp. 50-60.

Higher Education Funding Council – England (1998), *Review of Hospitality Management*, HEFCE, Bristol.

Higher Education Funding Council for England (1997), *Review of Hospitality Management*, HEFC.

Hing, N. (1997), "A review of hospitality research in the Asia Pacific: a thematic perspective", *International Journal of Contemporary Hospitality Management*, Vol. 9 No.1, pp. 5-12.

Hirst, M. "Creating a service-driven culture globally", *International Journal of Contemporary Hospitality Management*, Vol. 4 No.1, pp. i-iii.

Hobson, J. (1995), "The development of hospitality and tourism education in Australia", *Hospitality and Tourism Educator*, Vol. 7 No.4, pp. 25-9.

Hobson, J.S.P. (1994), "Feng shui: its impacts on the Asian hospitality industry", *International Journal of Contemporary Hospitality Management*, Vol. 6 No.6, pp. 21-6 .

Hobson, J.S.P. (1995), "The development of hospitality and tourism education", *Hospitality and Tourism Educator*, Vol. 7 No.4, pp. 25-9.

Hobson, P.J.S. (1995), "The development of hospitality and tourism education in Australia", *Hospitality & Tourism Educator*, Vol. 7 No.4, pp. 25-9.

Hoque, K. (2000), *Human Resource Management in the Hotel Industry: Strategy, Innovation and Performance*, Routledge, London.

Hotel and Catering International Management Association (1996), *The Hospitality Year Book*, HCIMA, London.

Hotel and Catering International Management Association (1998), *Hospitality Adding Value for Education Information Pack and Update*, HCIMA.

Howey, R.M., Savage, D.S. (1995), "Information processing: coordination and control in large hotels", *FIU Hospitality Review*, Vol. 13 No.1, pp. 51-62.

Hsu, C.H.C. (1996), "Evolution of the hospitality management education at Iowa State University", *Hospitality and Tourism Educator*, Vol. 8 No.2/3, pp. 60-3.

Hughes, H. (1993), "The structural theory of business demand: a comment", *International Journal of Hospitality Management*, Vol. 12 No.4, pp. 309-11.

Ingold, T., Worthington, T. (1994), "Prophylaxis, not diagnosis and cure ", *International Journal of Contemporary Hospitality Management*, Vol. 6 No.1/2, pp. 46-52.

Ingram, H. (1996), "Clusters and gaps in hospitality and tourism academic research", *International Journal of Contemporary Hospitality Management*, Vol. 8 No.7, pp. 91-5.

Iverson, K. (1996), "Exploring student interest in hospitality distance education", *Hospitality Research Journal*, Vol. 20 No.2, pp. 31-44.

Jameson, S (1998), "Employment and employee relations", in Thomas, R (Eds), *The Management of Small Tourism and Hospitality Firms*, Cassell, London, pp. 174-91.

Jameson, S.M., Holden, R. (2000), "'Graduateness' who cares? Graduate identity in small hospitality firms", *Education and Training*, Vol. 42 No.4/5, pp. 264-71.

Johanson, M. (1999), "An outlook on the past, present and future of travel education", *Journal of Hospitality and Tourism Education*, CHRIE, Washington DC, Vol. 11 No.4, pp. 5-8.

Johns, N. (1992), "Quality management in the hospitality industy: Part 1. Definition and specification", *International Journal of Contemporary Hospitality Management*, Vol. 4 No.3, pp. 14-20.

Johns, N. (1993), "Quality management in the hospitality industry: part 3: recent developments", *International Journal of Contemporary Hospitality Management*, Vol. 5 No.1, pp. 10-15.

Johns, N., Edwards, J. (1994), *Operations Management: A Resource-Based Approach for the Hospitality Industry*, Cassell, London, pp. ii-iv.

Johns, N., Ingram, H., Lee-Ross, D. (1994), *Operational Techniques: A Resource-Based Approach for the Hospitality Industry*, Cassell , London, pp. ii-iv.

Johns, N., Lee-Ross, D., Ingram, H. (1997), "A study of service quality in small hotels and guesthouses", *Progress in Tourism and Hospitality Research*, Vol. 3 No.4, pp. 351-63.

Johns, N., Wheeler, K.L. (1992), "Productivity angles on sous-vide", in Teare, R., Adams D., Messenger, S. (Eds), *Managing Projects in Hospitality Organizations*, Cassell, pp. 146-168.

Jones, P. (1995), "Developing new products and services in flight catering", *International Journal of Contemporary Hospitality Management*, Vol. 7 No.2, pp. 24-8.

Jones, P. (1996), "The hospitality industry", in Jones, P. (Eds), *Introduction to Hospitality Operations*, Cassell, London, pp. 1-20.

Jones, P. A. (1992), "The effective hospitality manager", *Hospitality*, No.134, pp. 16-7 .

Jones, P., Iannon, A. (1993), "Measuring guest satisfaction in UK-based international hotel chains: principles and practice", *International Journal of Contemporary Hospitality Management*, Vol. 5 No.5, pp. 27-31.

Kasavana, M.L. (1996), "Slot machines: methodologies and myths", *FIU Hospitality Review*, Vol. 14 No.2, pp. 37-44.

Kasavana, M.L. "Hospitality information systems: intuitive, object-oriented, and wireless technology", *FIU Hospitality Review*, Vol. 12 No.1, pp. 37-50.

Keiser, J. (1998), "Hospitality and tourism: a rhetorical analysis and conceptual framework for identifying industry meanings", *Journal of Hospitality and Tourism Research*, Vol. 22 No.2, pp. 115-28.

Kelley-Paterson, D., George, C. (2001), "Securing graduate commitment: an exploration of the comparative expectations of place students, graduate recruits and human resources managers within the hospitality, leisure and tourism industries", *Hospitality Management*, Vol. 20 pp. 311-23.

Kelley-Patterson, D., George, C. (2001), "Securing graduate commitment: an exploration of the comparative expectations of placement students, graduate recruits and human resource managers within the hospitality, leisure and tourism industries", *International Journal of Hospitality Management*, Vol. 20 No.4, pp. 311-23.

Kelliher, C., Blackman, D. (1991), "Human resource strategies for the 1990s", *International Journal of Contemporary Hospitality Management*, Vol. 3 No.2, pp. 4-9.

Kelly, I. (1994), "Caravan parks: the Cinderella subsector", *Australian Journal of Hospitality Management*, Vol. 1 No.2, pp. 37-46.

Kent, W.E., Cannon, D.F. (1996), "Teams: vehicle of choice for transporting the organizational future", *FIU Hospitality Review*, Vol. 14 No..2, pp. 65-76.

Kim, H. (1996), "Perceptual mapping of attributes and preferences: an empirical examination of hotel F&B products in Korea", *International Journal of Hospitality Management*, Vol. 15 No.4, pp. 373-91.

King, C. A. (1995), "What is hospitality?", *International Journal of Hospitality Management*, Vol. 14 No.3/4, pp. 219-34.

King, C.A., Garey, J.G. (1997), "Relational quality in service encounters", *International Journal of Hospitality Management*, Vol. 16 No.1, pp. 39-63.

Kivela, J (1996), "Marketing in the restaurant business", *Australian Journal of Hospitality Management*, Vol. 3 No.1, pp. 1-12.

Knutson, B.J., Stevens, P., Patton, M., Thompson, C. (1992), "Consumers' expectations for service quality in economy, mid-priced and luxury hotels", *Journal of Hospitality and Leisure Management*, Vol. 1 No.2, pp. 27-43.

Koss-Feder, L. (1994), "Howard Johnson keeps improving", *Hotel & Motel Management*, Vol. 209 No.21, pp. 3.

Kwansa, F.A., Farrar, A.L. (1992), "A conceptual framework for developing a hospitality educators' code of ethics", Vol. 15 No.3, pp. 27-40.

Lage, B.H.G., Milone, P.C. (1998), "Impactos sócio-econômicos do turismo", *Revista de Administração*, São Paulo, Vol. 33 No.4, pp. 30-44.

Larsen, S., Folgero, I.S. (1993), "Supportive and defensive communication", *International Journal of Contemporary Hospitality Management*, Vol. 5 No.3, pp. 22-5.

Larsen, S., Rapp, L. "Creating the service driven cruise line", *International Journal of Contemporary Hospitality Management*, Vol. 5 No.1, pp. iv-vi .

Lashley, C (1999), "Cutting across the grain: educating reflective practitioners for hospitality management", *The Hospitality Review*, Vol. 1 No.1, pp. 35-41.

Lashley, C. (1997), "Research issues for employee empowerment in hospitality organizations", *International Journal of Hospitality Management*, Vol. 15 No.4, pp. 333-46.

Lee-Ross, D. (1993), "Two styles of hotel manager, two styles of worker", *International Journal of Contemporary Hospitality Management*, Vol. 5 No.4, pp. 20-4.

Lewis, R.C. (1993), "Hospitality management education: here today, gone tomorrow", *Hospitality Research Journal*, Vol. 17 No.1, pp. 273-83.

Li, L., Bai, B., McCleary, K. (1996), "The giant awakens: Chinese outbound travel", *Australian Journal of Hospitality Management*, Vol. 3 No.2, pp. 59-68.

Litteljohn, D. (1993), "Western Europe", in Jones, P., Pizam, A. (Eds),*The International Hospitality Industry*, Pitman, London, pp. 3-24.

Luchars, J.Y., Hinkin, T.R. (1996), "The service quality audit", *The Cornell Hotel and Restaurant Quarterly*, Vol. 37 No.1, pp. 34-41.

Martin, W.B. (1986), "Defining what quality service is for you", *Cornell Hotel & Restaurant Administration Quarterly*, Vol. 26 No.4, pp. 32-8.

Mazanec, J. (1993), "'Exporting' Eurostyles to the USA", *International Journal of Contemporary Hospitality Management*, Vol. 5 No.4, pp. 3-9.

McKenna, M, Larmour, R (1984), "Women in hotel and catering in the UK", *International Journal of Hospitality Management*, Vol. 3 No.3, pp. 107-12.

Messenger, S.J., Arkins, T. (1994), "The Prudential experience of total quality management", *International Journal of Contemporary Hospitality Management*, Vol. 6 No.1/2, pp. 37-41.

Mills, S., Riehle, H. (1993), "Foodservice manager 2000", *Hospitality Research Journal*, Vol. 17 No.1, pp. 147-60.

Morrison, A. (1996), "Guesthouses and small hotels", in Jones, P. (Eds),*Introduction to Hospitality Operations*, Cassell,, London, pp. 73-85.

Morrison, A. (2002), "The small hospitality business: enduring or endangered?", *Journal of Hospitality and Tourism Management*, Vol. 9 No.1.

Morrison, A., Thomas, R. (1999), "The future of small firms in the hospitality industry", *International Journal of Contemporary Hospitality Management*, Vol. 11 No.4, pp. 148-54.

Morrison, P. (1994), "Degrees in hospitality management: quality or quantity?", *Australian Journal of Hospitality Management*, Vol. 1 No.1, pp. 38-9.

Mullins, L., Davies, I. (1991), "What makes for an effective hotel manager?", *International Journal of Contemporary Hospitality Management*, Vol. 3 No.1, pp. 22-5.

Mutch, A. (1998), "Using information technology", in Thomas, R. (Eds),*The Management of Small Tourism and Hospitality Firms*, Cassell, London,, pp. 92-206.

Nailon, P. (1982), "Theory in hospitality management", *International Journal of Hospitality Management*, Vol. 1 No.3, pp. 135-43.

Olsen, M., Tse, E., West, J. (1992), *Strategic Management in the Hospitality Industry*, Van Nostrand Reinhold, New York, NY.

Olsen, M.D. (1991), "Structural changes: the international hospitality industry and firm ", *International Journal of Contemporary Hospitality Management*, Vol. 3 No.4, pp. 21-24.

Ozer, B. (1996), "An investment analysis model for small hospitality operations", *International Journal of Contemporary Hospitality Management*, Vol. 8 No.5, pp. 20-24.

Parry, B., Collins, B. (1993), "Where is facilities management going?",

International Journal of Contemporary Hospitality Management, Vol. 5 No.2, pp. 36-40 .

Pavesic, D.V (1993), "Hospitality education 2005: curricular and programmatic trends", *Hospitality Research Journal*, Vol. 17 No.1, pp. 285-94.

Phillips, P.A. (1994), "Welsh hotel: cost-volume-profit analysis and uncertainty", *International Journal of Contemporary Hospitality Management*, Vol. 6 No.3, pp. 31-6 .

Purcell, K. (1993), "Equal opportunities in the hospitality industry: custom and credentials", *International Journal of Hospitality Management*, Vol. 12 No.2, pp. 127-40.

Williams, A. (2002), *Understanding the Hospitality Consumer*, Butterworth-Heinemann, Oxford.

Witt, C., Witt, S.F. (1989), "Why productivity in the hotel sector is low", *International Journal of Contemporary Hospitality Management*, Vol. 1 No.2, pp. 28-33.

Yasim, M., Zimmerer, T.W. (1995), "The role of benchmarking in achieving continuous service quality", *International Journal of Contemporary Hospitality Management*, Vol. 7 No.4, pp. 27-32.

Index

A

ABS, 64, 76
Accommodation, 13
Adam, 5
Additional cost, 2
Agarwal et al., 81
AIDS, 178
Anderson, 81
ANOVA, 65, 103
Apple Computers, 168
ASTD, 102
Atkinson, 166

B

Barsky, 152, 189
Bateson, 203
Baum, 173, 201
Bitner, 203
Boella, 173
Brownell, 152, 189
Brymer, 153, 166, 190
Burgess, 10, 11
Buttle, 6

C

Callan, 200
Campbell, 58
Catering, 4
CEN, 40
CHAE, 115
Charles Horton Cooley, 99
China, 83
CHTP, 115
CNAA, 84
Continuous improvement, 166
Cornell Quarterly, 24
Council for National Academic Awards, 84
Crowne Plaza, 161

D

Dann, 9
Danny Meyer, 219
Denise Volpicello, 222
Deva Bhumi, 27
DHR, 104
DNH, 8

E

Elloy, 168
Ervin Goffman, 8
Esquivel, 169
Experience Rules, 68

F

Farquhar, 164
Fisk, 195
Fitzgerald, 131, 205
France, 2

G

Germany, 2
Goss-Turner, 58
Griffin, 145
Grove, 195
Guerrier, 58

H

Harris, 169
HCIMA, 84
HCITB, 6
HCTC, 106
Heal, 12
Henri J.M. Nouwen, 1
Hepple, 10, 11
HFTP, 115
Hiemstra, 201
HITEC, 115
HND, 91
Holiday Inn, 161
HOLSERV, 191
Holy trinity, 14
Hoskins, 53
Hospitality, 4
  management, 4
  paradigms, 9
  research, 9
Hotel type, 157
HRM, 175
HTNG, 125, 126

J

Jackson, 194
Johnston, 7
Jones, 4, 12, 13

K

Khatri, 24
King, 10, 12, 13
Kleiner, 169
Knowles, 5
Knutson, 71
Kodak, 168

L

Lashley, 3, 166
Letty M. Russell, 90, 159
Ligouri, 12
Lockwood, 58
Lovelock, 203
Lyons, 21

M

Maharashtra, 26
Makens, 201
Management of Regional Tourism, 32
Mazanec, 201
McCombs, 168
McDonald, 7
McIntosh, 87
Measuring Service Quality, 203
Mehta, 45
Mennell, 2
MICROS system, 211
Mihalik, 160
MNL, 155
Mone, 58
Morehead, 74

N

Namasivayam, 19
National Tourism Administrations, 39
Newton, 166
Nicod, 8
NSW, 75, 76, 97
Nurmi, 168, 169

O

ONHTEC, 115
Operations management, 9

P

Patterns from the Generic Literature, 167
PCNs, 127
Pfeifer, 12, 13
Poffley, 160
POS, 214
Power of Teamworking, 168

Q

Queensland, 76
Quinn, 73

R

RCA, 62
Reichheld, 161, 165
Rimmer, 74
Roberts, 173

S

SADT, 154, 181
Schuler, 194
Scottish Islands, 25
Seacord, 161
SERVQUAL, 159
Shaw, 200
Shimko, 152, 189
Shonk, 168
SIC, 6, 14
Smith, 58
Spivack, 176, 179
SPSS, 116
Stainforth, 168

T

Team spirit, 168
Thematic Interrelationships, 167
Thompson, 7
Tideman, 13
Tomlin, 58
Tourism, 25
    and Hospitality, 25
Transportation Management, 96

U

Umbreit, 58
Uniqueness, 3
USA, 1, 3, 34

V

Vanna Bonta, 24
VAT, 140
Victoria, 76

W

White, 12
Whitelaw, 34
Wilson, 22
Wood, 3, 9, 12
World War II, 9
Worsfold, 6
WTO, 39, 40
WTTC, 60

Y

Yellow menace, 82
YHA, 34

Z

Zeithaml, 194, 203